PENGUIN P[...]

SELEC[...]

BY J[...]

JOHN KEATS (1795–1821). Famous poet and principal figure in the Romantic movement, he is best remembered for his beautifully descriptive odes and *Endymion*, a highly imaginative epic poem.

John Keats was born in Moorfields in 1795, son of the manager of a livery stables. His parents died when he was a child, but he had a close relationship with his two brothers and his sister Fanny. He was apprenticed to an apothecary-surgeon in 1810, and his first attempts at poetry apparently date from 1814. Keats cancelled his apprenticeship in 1815 and became a student at Guy's Hospital. A year later he abandoned medicine to write poetry full time, which is when he met Leigh Hunt, who published 'O Solitude' and the sonnet 'On First Looking into Chapman's Homer' in the *Examiner*. Keats then met Shelley and in 1817 he published his first volume of poems, which included 'I Stood Tiptoe Upon a Little Hill'. It met with little success and Lockhart viciously attacked Keats and his associates in *Blackwood's Magazine* as the 'Cockney School of Poetry'. *Endymion*, dedicated to the notorious poet and forger Chatterton, greatly admired by Keats, was published in 1818, when he also completed 'Isabella, or the Pot of Basil'. He toured the Lakes and Scotland, and the magnificent scenery had a profound effect on his poetry, particularly when writing *Hyperion*. Keats wrote to his brother George, 'I think I shall be among the English poets after my death', even though he was deeply wounded by the harsh and critical reviews of *Endymion*. He nursed his brother Tom, who had tuberculosis, which severely affected his own health. After his brother's death in December 1818 Keats moved to Hampstead, where he met and became engaged to Fanny Brawne, the great love of his life. He produced his finest poetry in the next year, including 'La Belle Dame Sans Merci', 'Ode to Psyche', 'Ode on a Grecian Urn', 'Ode on Melancholy' and *The Fall of Hyperion*. John Keats died of tuberculosis in Rome in 1821.

This classic collection encompasses his lifetime's achievement, containing the much-loved poems: *Endymion*, *Hyperion*, 'The Eve of St Agnes', 'Ode to a Nightingale' and 'To Autumn'.

PENGUIN POPULAR CLASSICS

SELECTED POEMS

JOHN KEATS

PENGUIN BOOKS

PENGUIN BOOKS

Published by the Penguin Group
Penguin Books Ltd, 80 Strand, London WC2R ORL, England
Penguin Putnam Inc., 375 Hudson Street, New York, New York 10014, USA
Penguin Books Australia Ltd, Ringwood, Victoria, Australia
Penguin Books Canada Ltd, 10 Alcorn Avenue, Toronto, Ontario, Canada M4V 3B2
Penguin Books India (P) Ltd, 11 Community Centre, Panchsheel Park,
New Delhi – 110 017, India
Penguin Books (NZ) Ltd, Cnr Rosedale and Airborne Roads, Albany, Auckland,
New Zealand
Penguin Books (South Africa) (Pty) Ltd, 24 Sturdee Avenue, Rosebank 2196, South Africa

Penguin Books Ltd, Registered Offices: 80 Strand, London WC2R ORL, England

www.penguin.com

Published in Penguin Popular Classics 1996
5

Printed in England by Cox & Wyman Ltd, Reading, Berkshire

CONTENTS

Sonnets—*Continued*

1818

1820

DEDICATION.

TO LEIGH HUNT, ESQ.

Glory and loveliness have passed away;
  For if we wander out in early morn,
  No wreathed incense do we see upborne
Into the east, to meet the smiling day:
No crowd of nymphs soft voic'd and young, and gay,
  In woven baskets bringing ears of corn,
  Roses, and pinks, and violets, to adorn
The shrine of Flora in her early May.
But there are left delights as high as these,
  And I shall ever bless my destiny,
That in a time, when under pleasant trees
  Pan is no longer sought, I feel a free,
A leafy luxury, seeing I could please
  With these poor offerings, a man like thee.

POEMS.

"Places of nestling green for Poets made."
STORY OF RIMINI

I STOOD tip-toe upon a little hill,
The air was cooling, and so very still,
That the sweet buds which with a modest pride
Pull droopingly, in slanting curve aside,
Their scantly leaved, and finely tapering stems,
Had not yet lost those starry diadems
Caught from the early sobbing of the morn.
The clouds were pure and white as flocks new shorn,
And fresh from the clear brook; sweetly they slept
On the blue fields of heaven, and then there crept
A little noiseless noise among the leaves,
Born of the very sigh that silence heaves:
For not the faintest motion could be seen
Of all the shades that slanted o'er the green.
There was wide wand'ring for the greediest eye,
To peer about upon variety;
Far round the horizon's crystal air to skim,
And trace the dwindled edgings of its brim;
To picture out the quaint, and curious bending
Of a fresh woodland alley, never ending;
Or by the bowery clefts, and leafy shelves,
Guess where the jaunty streams refresh themselves.
I gazed awhile, and felt as light, and free
As though the fanning wings of Mercury
Had played upon my heels: I was light-hearted,
And many pleasures to my vision started;
So I straightway began to pluck a posey
Of luxuries bright, milky, soft and rosy.
A bush of May flowers with the bees about them;
Ah, sure no tasteful nook would be without them;
And let a lush laburnum oversweep them,

3

And let long grass grow round the roots to keep them
Moist, cool and green; and shade the violets,
That they may bind the moss in leafy nets.

A filbert hedge with wildbriar overtwined,
And clumps of woodbine taking the soft wind
Upon their summer thrones; there too should be
The frequent chequer of a youngling tree,
That with a score of light green brethren shoots
From the quaint mossiness of aged roots:
Round which is heard a spring-head of clear waters
Babbling so wildly of its lovely daughters
The spreading blue bells: it may haply mourn
That such fair clusters should be rudely torn
From their fresh beds, and scattered thoughtlessly
By infant hands, left on the path to die.

Open afresh your round of starry folds,
Ye ardent marigolds!
Dry up the moisture from your golden lids,
For great Apollo bids
That in these days your praises should be sung
On many harps, which he has lately strung;
And when again your dewiness he kisses,
Tell him, I have you in my world of blisses:
So haply when I rove in some far vale,
His mighty voice may come upon the gale.

Here are sweet peas, on tip-toe for a flight:
With wings of gentle flush o'er delicate white,
And taper fingers catching at all things,
To bind them all about with tiny rings.

Linger awhile upon some bending planks
That lean against a streamlet's rushy banks,
And watch intently Nature's gentle doings:
They will be found softer than ring-dove's cooings.
How silent comes the water round that bend;
Not the minutest whisper does it send
To the o'erhanging sallows: blades of grass

Slowly across the chequer'd shadows pass.
Why, you might read two sonnets, ere they reach
To where the hurrying freshnesses aye preach
A natural sermon o'er their pebbly beds;
Where swarms of minnows show their little heads,
Staying their wavy bodies 'gainst the streams,
To taste the luxury of sunny beams
Temper'd with coolness. How they ever wrestle
With their own sweet delight, and ever nestle
Their silver bellies on the pebbly sand.
If you but scantily hold out the hand,
That very instant not one will remain;
But turn your eye, and they are there again.
The ripples seem right glad to reach those cresses,
And cool themselves among the em'rald tresses;
The while they cool themselves, they freshness give,
And moisture, that the bowery green may live:
So keeping up an interchange of favours,
Like good men in the truth of their behaviours.
Sometimes goldfinches one by one will drop
From low hung branches; little space they stop;
But sip, and twitter, and their feathers sleek:
Then off at once, as in a wanton freak:
Or perhaps, to show their black, and golden wings,
Pausing upon their yellow flutterings.
Were I in such a place, I sure should pray
That nought less sweet, might call my thoughts away.
Than the soft rustle of a maiden's gown
Fanning away the dandelion's down;
Than the light music of her nimble toes
Patting against the sorrel as she goes.
How she would start, and blush, thus to be caught
Playing in all her innocence of thought.
O let me lead her gently o'er the brook,
Watch her half-smiling lips, and downward look;
O let me for one moment touch her wrist;
Let me one moment to her breathing list;
And as she leaves me may she often turn
Her fair eyes looking through her locks aubùrne.
What next? A tuft of evening primroses,

O'er which the mind may hover till it dozes;
O'er which it well might take a pleasant sleep,
But that 'tis ever startled by the leap
Of buds into ripe flowers; or by the flitting
Of diverse moths, that aye their rest are quitting;
Or by the moon lifting her silver rim
Above a cloud, and with a gradual swim
Coming into the blue with all her light.
O Maker of sweet poets, dear delight
Of this fair world, and all its gentle livers;
Spangler of clouds, halo of crystal rivers,
Mingler with leaves, and dew and tumbling streams,
Closer of lovely eyes to lovely dreams,
Lover of loneliness, and wandering,
Of upcast eye, and tender pondering!
Thee must I praise above all other glories
That smile us on to tell delightful stories.
For what has made the sage or poet write
But the fair paradise of Nature's light?
In the calm grandeur of a sober line,
We see the waving of the mountain pine;
And when a tale is beautifully staid,
We feel the safety of a hawthorn glade:
When it is moving on luxurious wings,
The soul is lost in pleasant smotherings:
Fair dewy roses brush against our faces,
And flowering laurels spring from diamond vases;
O'erhead we see the jasmine and sweet briar,
And bloomy grapes laughing from green attire;
While at our feet, the voice of crystal bubbles
Charms us at once away from all our troubles:
So that we feel uplifted from the world,
Walking upon the white clouds wreath'd and curl'd.
So felt he, who first told, how Psyche went
On the smooth wind to realms of wonderment;
What Psyche felt, and Love, when their full lips
First touch'd; what amorous and fondling nips
They gave each other's cheeks; with all their sighs,
And how they kist each other's tremulous eyes:
The silver lamp,—the ravishment,—the wonder—

The darkness,—loneliness,—the fearful thunder;
Their woes gone by, and both to heaven upflown,
To bow for gratitude before Jove's throne.
So did he feel, who pull'd the boughs aside,
That we might look into a forest wide,
To catch a glimpse of Fawns, and Dryades
Coming with softest rustle through the trees;
And garlands woven of flowers wild, and sweet,
Upheld on ivory wrists, or sporting feet:
Telling us how fair, trembling Syrinx fled
Arcadian Pan, with such a fearful dread.
Poor Nymph,—poor Pan,—how did he weep to find
Nought but a lovely sighing of the wind
Along the reedy stream; a half heard strain,
Full of sweet desolation—balmy pain.

What first inspired a bard of old to sing
Narcissus pining o'er the untainted spring?
In some delicious ramble, he had found
A little space, with boughs all woven round;
And in the midst of all, a clearer pool
Than e'er reflected in its pleasant cool,
The blue sky here, and there, serenely peeping
Through tendril wreaths fantastically creeping.
And on the bank a lonely flower he spied,
A meek and forlorn flower, with naught of pride,
Drooping its beauty o'er the watery clearness,
To woo its own sad image into nearness:
Deaf to light Zephyrus it would not move;
But still would seem to droop, to pine, to love.
So while the Poet stood in this sweet spot,
Some fainter gleamings o'er his fancy shot;
Nor was it long ere he had told the tale
Of young Narcissus, and sad Echo's bale.

Where had he been, from whose warm head out-flew
That sweetest of all songs, that ever new,
That aye refreshing, pure deliciousness,
Coming ever to bless
The wanderer by moonlight? to him bringing

7

Shapes from the invisible world, unearthly singing
From out the middle air, from flowery nests,
And from the pillowy silkiness that rests
Full in the speculation of the stars.
Ah! surely he had burst our mortal bars;
Into some wond'rous region he had gone,
To search for thee, divine Endymion!

He was a Poet, sure a lover too,
Who stood on Latmus' top, what time there blew
Soft breezes from the myrtle vale below;
And brought in faintness solemn, sweet, and slow
A hymn from Dian's temple; while upswelling,
The incense went to her own starry dwelling.
But though her face was clear as infant's eyes,
Though she stood smiling o'er the sacrifice,
The Poet wept at her so piteous fate,
Wept that such beauty should be desolate:
So in fine wrath some golden sounds he won,
And gave meek Cynthia her Endymion.

Queen of the wide air; thou most lovely queen
Of all the brightness that mine eyes have seen!
As thou exceedest all things in thy shine,
So every tale, does this sweet tale of thine.
O for three words of honey, that I might
Tell but one wonder of thy bridal night!

Where distant ships do seem to show their keels,
Phœbus awhile delayed his mighty wheels,
And turned to smile upon thy bashful eyes,
Ere he his unseen pomp would solemnize.
The evening weather was so bright, and clear,
That men of health were of unusual cheer;
Stepping like Homer at the trumpet's call,
Or young Apollo on the pedestal:
And lovely women were as fair and warm,
As Venus looking sideways in alarm.
The breezes were ethereal, and pure,
And crept through half closed lattices to cure

*I thought such things
were fable, fraud*

The languid sick; it cool'd their fever'd sleep,
And soothed them into slumbers full and deep.
Soon they awoke clear eyed: nor burnt with thirsting,
Nor with hot fingers, nor with temples bursting:
And springing up, they met the wond'ring sight
Of their dear friends, nigh foolish with delight;
Who feel their arms, and breasts, and kiss and stare,
And on their placid foreheads part the hair.
Young men, and maidens at each other gaz'd
With hands held back, and motionless, amaz'd
To see the brightness in each others' eyes;
And so they stood, fill'd with a sweet surprise,
Until their tongues were loos'd in poesy.
Therefore no lover did of anguish die:
But the soft numbers, in that moment spoken,
Made silken ties, that never may be broken.
Cynthia! I cannot tell the greater blisses,
That follow'd thine, and thy dear shepherd's kisses:
Was there a Poet born?—but now no more,
My wand'ring spirit must no further soar.—

SPECIMEN

OF AN

INDUCTION TO A POEM.

Lo! I must tell a tale of chivalry;
For large white plumes are dancing in mine eye.
Not like the formal crest of latter days:
But bending in a thousand graceful ways;
So graceful, that is seems no mortal hand,
Or e'en the touch of Archimago's wand,
Could charm them into such an attitude.
We must think rather, that in playful mood,
Some mountain breeze had turned its chief delight,
To show this wonder of its gentle might.
Lo! I must tell a tale of chivalry;
For while I muse, the lance points slantingly
Athwart the morning air: some lady sweet,
Who cannot feel for cold her tender feet,

9

From the worn top of some old battlement
Hails it with tears, her stout defender sent:
And from her own pure self no joy dissembling,
Wraps round her ample robe with happy trembling.
Sometimes, when the good Knight his rest would take,
It is reflected, clearly, in a lake,
With the young ashen boughs, 'gainst which it rests,
And th' half seen mossiness of linnets' nests.
Ah! shall I ever tell its cruelty,
When the fire flashes from a warrior's eye,
And his tremendous hand is grasping it,
And his dark brow for very wrath is knit?
Or when his spirit, with more calm intent,
Leaps to the honors of a tournament,
And makes the gazers round about the ring
Stare at the grandeur of the ballancing?
No, no! this is far off:—then how shall I
Revive the dying tones of minstrelsy,
Which linger yet about lone gothic arches,
In dark green ivy, and among wild larches?
How sing the splendour of the revelries,
When butts of wine are drunk off to the lees?
And that bright lance, against the fretted wall,
Beneath the shade of stately banneral,
Is slung with shining cuirass, sword, and shield,
Where ye may see a spur in bloody field?
Light-footed damsels move with gentle paces
Round the wide hall, and show their happy faces;
Or stand in courtly talk by fives and sevens:
Like those fair stars that twinkle in the heavens.
Yet must I tell a tale of chivalry:
Or wherefore comes that knight so proudly by?
Wherefore more proudly does the gentle knight,
Rein in the swelling of his ample might?

Spenser! thy brows are arched, open, kind,
And come like a clear sun-rise to my mind;
And always does my heart with pleasure dance,
When I think on thy noble countenance:
Where never yet was ought more earthly seen

Than the pure freshness of thy laurels green.
Therefore, great bard, I not so fearfully
Call on thy gentle spirit to hover nigh
My daring steps: or if thy tender care,
Thus startled unaware,
Be jealous that the foot of other wight
Should madly follow that bright path of light
Trac'd by thy lov'd Libertas; he will speak,
And tell thee that my prayer is very meek;
That I will follow with due reverence,
And start with awe at mine own strange pretence.
Him thou wilt hear; so I will rest in hope
To see wide plains, fair trees and lawny slope:
The morn, the eve, the light, the shade, the flowers;
Clear streams, smooth lakes, and overlooking towers.

CALIDORE.
A Fragment.

Young Calidore is paddling o'er the lake;
His healthful spirit eager and awake
To feel the beauty of a silent eve,
Which seem'd full loath this happy world to leave;
The light dwelt o'er the scene so lingeringly.
He bares his forehead to the cool blue sky,
And smiles at the far clearness all around,
Until his heart is well nigh overwound,
And turns for calmness to the pleasant green
Of easy slopes, and shadowy trees that lean
So elegantly o'er the waters' brim
And show their blossoms trim.
Scarce can his clear and nimble eye-sight follow
The freaks, and dartings of the black-wing'd swallow,
Delighting much, to see it half at rest,
Dip so refreshingly its wings, and breast
'Gainst the smooth surface, and to mark anon,
The widening circles into nothing gone.

And now the sharp keel of his little boat
Comes up with ripple, and with easy float,

And glides into a bed of water lillies:
Broad leav'd are they and their white canopies
Are upward turn'd to catch the heavens' dew.
Near to a little island's point they grew;
Whence Calidore might have the goodliest view
Of this sweet spot of earth. The bowery shore
Went off in gentle windings to the hoar
And light blue mountains: but no breathing man
With a warm heart, and eye prepared to scan
Nature's clear beauty, could pass lightly by
Objects that look'd out so invitingly
On either side. These, gentle Calidore
Greeted, as he had known them long before.

The sidelong view of swelling leafiness,
Which the glad setting sun, in gold doth dress;
Whence ever, and anon the jay outsprings,
And scales upon the beauty of its wings.

The lonely turret, shatter'd, and outworn, *I was*
Stands venerably proud; too proud to mourn
Its long lost grandeur: fir trees grow around,
Aye dropping their hard fruit upon the ground.

The little chapel with the cross above
Upholding wreaths of ivy; the white dove,
That on the windows spreads his feathers light,
And seems from purple clouds to wing its flight.

Green tufted islands casting their soft shades
Across the lake; sequester'd leafy glades,
That through the dimness of their twilight show
Large dock leaves, spiral foxgloves, or the glow
Of the wild cat's eyes, or the silvery stems
Of delicate birch trees, or long grass which hems
A little brook. The youth had long been viewing
These pleasant things, and heaven was bedewing
The mountain flowers, when his glad senses caught
A trumpet's silver voice. Ah! it was fraught
With many joys for him: the warder's ken

Had found white coursers prancing in the glen:
Friends very dear to him he soon will see;
So pushes off his boat most eagerly,
And soon upon the lake he skims along,
Deaf to the nightingale's first under-song;
Nor minds he the white swans that dream so sweetly:
His spirit flies before him so completely.

And now he turns a jutting point of land,
Whence may be seen the castle gloomy, and grand:
Nor will a bee buzz round two swelling peaches,
Before the point of his light shallop reaches
Those marble steps that through the water dip:
Now over them he goes with hasty trip,
And scarcely stays to ope the folding doors:
Anon he leaps along the oaken floors
Of halls and corridors.

Delicious sounds! those little bright-eyed things
That float about the air on azure wings,
Had been less heartfelt by him than the clang
Of clattering hoofs; into the court he sprang,
Just as two noble steeds, and palfreys twain,
Were slanting out their necks with lossened rein;
While from beneath the threat'ning portcullis
They brought their happy burthens. What a kiss,
What gentle squeeze he gave each lady's hand!
How tremblingly their delicate ancles spann'd!
Into how sweet a trance his soul was gone,
While whisperings of affection
Made him delay to let their tender feet
Come to the earth; with an incline so sweet
From their low palfreys o'er his neck they bent:
And whether there were tears of languishment,
Or that the evening dew had pearl'd their tresses,
He feels a moisture on his cheek, and blesses
With lips that tremble, and with glistening eye
All the soft luxury
That nestled in his arms. A dimpled hand,
Fair as some wonder out of fairy land,

Hung from his shoulder like the drooping flowers
Of whitest Cassia, fresh from summer showers:
And this he fondled with his happy cheek
As if for joy he would no further seek;
When the kind voice of good Sir Clerimond
Came to his ear, like something from beyond
His present being: so he gently drew
His warm arms, thrilling now with pulses new,
From their sweet thrall, and forward gently bending,
Thank'd heaven that his joy was never ending;
While 'gainst his forehead he devoutly press'd
A hand heaven made to succour the distress'd;
A hand that from the world's bleak promontory
Had lifted Calidore for deeds of glory.
Amid the pages, and the torches' glare,
There stood a knight, patting the flowing hair
Of his proud horse's mane: he was withal
A man of elegance, and stature tall:
So that the waving of his plumes would be
High as the berries of a wild ash tree,
Or as the winged cap of Mercury.
His armour was so dexterously wrought
In shape, that sure no living man had thought
It hard, and heavy steel: but that indeed
It was some glorious form, some splendid weed,
In which a spirit new come from the skies
Might live, and show itself to human eyes.
'Tis the far-fam'd, the brave Sir Gondibert,
Said the good man to Calidore alert;
While the young warrior with a step of grace
Came up,—a courtly smile upon his face,
And mailed hand held out, ready to greet
The large-eyed wonder, and ambitious heat
Of the aspiring boy; who as he led
Those smiling ladies, often turned his head
To admire the visor arched so gracefully
Over a knightly brow; while they went by
The lamps that from the high-roof'd hall were
    pendent,
And gave the steel a shining quite transcendent.

Soon in a pleasant chamber they are seated;
The sweet-lipp'd ladies have already greeted
All the green leaves that round the window clamber,
To show their purple stars, and bells of amber.
Sir Gondibert has doff'd his shining steel,
Gladdening in the free, and airy feel
Of a light mantle; and while Clerimond
Is looking round about him with a fond,
And placid eye, young Calidore is burning
To hear of knightly deeds, and gallant spurning
Of all unworthiness; and how the strong of arm
Kept off dismay, and terror, and alarm
From lovely woman; while brimful of this,
He gave each damsel's hand so warm a kiss,
And had such manly ardour in his eye,
That each at other look'd half staringly;
And then their features started into smiles
Sweet as blue heavens o'er enchanted isles.

Softly the breezes from the forest came,
Softly they blew aside the taper's flame;
Clear was the song from Philomel's far bower;
Grateful the incense from the lime-tree flower;
Mysterious, wild, the far-heard trumpet's tone;
Lovely the moon in ether, all alone:
Sweet too the converse of these happy mortals,
As that of busy spirits when the portals
Are closing in the west; or that soft humming
We hear around when Hesperus is coming.
Sweet be their sleep. * * * * * * * * * *

TO

SOME LADIES.

WHAT though while the wonders of nature exploring,
　　I cannot your light, mazy footsteps attend;
Nor listen to accents, that almost adoring,
　　Bless Cynthia's face, the enthusiast's friend:

Yet over the steep, whence the mountain stream rushes
  With you, kindest friends, in idea I rove;
Mark the clear tumbling crystal, its passionate gushes,
  Its spray that the wild flower kindly bedews.

Why linger you so, the wild labyrinth strolling?
  Why breathless, unable your bliss to declare?
Ah! you list to the nightingale's tender condoling,
  Responsive to sylphs, in the moonbeamy air.

'Tis morn, and the flowers with dew are yet drooping,
  I see you are treading the verge of the sea:
And now! ah, I see it—you just now are stooping
  To pick up the keep-sake intended for me.

If a cherub, on pinions of silver descending,
  Had brought me a gem from the fret-work of heaven;
And smiles, with his star-cheering voice sweetly blend-
    ing,
  The blessings of Tighe had melodiously given;

It had not created a warmer emotion
  Than the present, fair nymphs, I was blest with from
    you,
Than the shell, from the bright golden sands of the
    ocean
  Which the emerald waves at your feet gladly threw.

For, indeed, 'tis a sweet and peculiar pleasure,
  (And blissful is he who such happiness finds,)
To possess but a span of the hour of leisure,
  In elegant, pure, and aerial minds.

*On receiving a curious Shell, and a Copy of Verses,
    from the same Ladies.*

HAST thou from the caves of Golconda, a gem
  Pure as the ice-drop that froze on the mountain?
Bright as the humming-bird's green diadem,
  When it flutters in sun-beams that shine through a
    fountain?

Has thou a goblet for dark sparkling wine?
  That goblet right heavy, and massy, and gold?
And splendidly mark'd with the story divine
    Of Armida the fair, and Rinaldo the bold?

Hast thou a steed with a mane richly flowing?
  Hast thou a sword that thine enemy's smart is?
Hast thou a trumpet rich melodies blowing?
    And wear'st thou the shield of the fam'd Brito-
      martis?

What is it that hangs from thy shoulder, so brave,
  Embroidered with many a spring peering flower?
Is it a scarf that thy fair lady gave?
    And hastest thou now to that fair lady's bower?

Ah! courteous Sir Knight, with large joy thou art
    crown'd;
  Full many the glories that brighten thy youth!
I will tell thee my blisses, which richly abound
    In magical powers to bless, and to sooth.

On this scroll thou seest written in characters fair
  A sunbeamy tale of a wreath, and a chain;
And, warrior, it nurtures the property rare
    Of charming my mind from the trammels of pain.

This canopy mark: 'tis the work of a fay;
  Beneath its rich shade did King Oberon languish,
When lovely Titania was far, far away,
    And cruelly left him to sorrow, and anguish.

There, oft would he bring from his soft sighing lute
  Wild strains to which, spell-bound, the nightingales
    listened;
The wondering spirits of heaven were mute,
    And tears 'mong the dewdrops of morning oft
      glistened.

In this little dome, all those melodies strange,
  Soft, plaintive, and melting, for ever will sigh;

Nor e'er will the notes from their tenderness change;
  Nor e'er will the music of Oberon die.

So, when I am in a voluptuous vein,
  I pillow my head on the sweets of the rose,
And list to the tale of the wreath, and the chain,
  Till its echoes depart; then I sink to repose.

Adieu, valiant Eric! with joy thou art crown'd;
  Full many the glories that brighten thy youth,
I too have my blisses, which richly abound
  In magical powers, to bless and to sooth.

TO * * * *

Hadst thou liv'd in days of old,
O what wonders had been told
Of thy lively countenance,
And thy humid eyes that dance
In the midst of their own brightness;
In the very fane of lightness.
Over which thine eyebrows, leaning,
Picture out each lovely meaning:
In a dainty bend they lie,
Like to streaks across the sky,
Or the feathers from a crow,
Fallen on a bed of snow.
Of thy dark hair that extends
Into many graceful bends:
As the leaves of Hellebore
Turn to whence they sprung before.
And behind each ample curl
Peeps the richness of a pearl.
Downward too flows many a tress
With a glossy waviness;
Full, and round like globes that rise
From the censer to the skies
Through sunny air. Add too, the sweetness
Of thy honied voice; the neatness
Of thine ankle lightly turn'd:

With those beauties, scarce discern'd,
Kept with such sweet privacy,
That they seldom meet the eye
Of the little loves that fly
Round about with eager pry.
Saving when, with freshening lave,
Thou dipp'st them in the taintless wave;
Like twin water lillies, born
In the coolness of the morn.
Of, if thou hadst breathed then,
Now the Muses had been ten.
Couldst thou wish for lineage higher
Than twin sister of Thalia?
At least for ever, evermore,
Will I call the Graces four.

Hadst thou liv'd when chivalry
Lifted up her lance on high,
Tell me what thou wouldst have been?
Ah! I see the silver sheen
Of thy broidered, floating vest
Cov'ring half thine ivory breast;
Which, O heavens! I should see,
But that cruel destiny
Has placed a golden cuirass there;
Keeping secret what is fair.
Like sunbeams in a cloudlet nested
Thy locks in knightly casque are rested:
O'er which bend four milky plumes
Like the gentle lilly's blooms
Springing from a costly vase.
See with what a stately pace
Comes thine alabaster steed;
Servant of heroic deed!
O'er his loins, his trappings glow
Like the northern lights on snow.
Mount his back! thy sword unsheath!
Sign of the enchanter's death;
Bane of every wicked spell;
Silencer of dragon's yell.

Alas! thou this wilt never do:
Thou art an enchantress too,
And wilt surely never spill
Blood of those whose eyes can kill.

TO
HOPE.

WHEN by my solitary hearth I sit,
  And hateful throughts enwrap my soul in gloom;
When no fair dreams before my "mind's eye" flit,
  And the bare heath of life presents no bloom;
    Sweet Hope, ethereal balm upon me shed,
    And wave thy silver pinions o'er my head.

Whene'er I wander, at the fall of night,
  Where woven boughs shut out the moon's bright ray,
Should sad Despondency my musings fright,
  And frown, to drive fair Cheerfulness away,
    Peep with the moon-beams through the leafy roof,
    And keep that fiend Despondence far aloof.

Should Disappointment, parent of Despair,
  Strive for her son to seize my careless heart;
When, like a cloud, he sits upon the air,
  Preparing on his spell-bound prey to dart:
    Chase him away, sweet Hope, with visage bright,
    And fright him as the morning frightens night!

Whene'er the fate of those I hold most dear
  Tells to my fearful breast a tale of sorrow,
O bright-eyed Hope, my morbid fancy cheer;
  Let me awhile thy sweetest comforts borrow:
    Thy heaven-born radiance around me shed,
    And wave thy silver pinions o'er my head!

Should e'er unhappy love my bosom pain,
  From cruel parents, or relentless fair;
O let me think it is not quite in vain
  To sigh out sonnets to the midnight air!

Sweet Hope, ethereal balm upon me shed,
And wave thy silver pinions o'er my head!

In the long vista of the years to roll,
  Let me not see our country's honour fade:
O let me see our land retain her soul,
  Her pride, her freedom; and not freedom's shade.
    From thy bright eyes unusual brightness shed—
    Beneath thy pinions canopy my head!

Let me not see the patriot's high bequest,
  Great Liberty! how great in plain attire!
With the base purple of a court oppress'd,
  Bowing her head, and ready to expire:
    But let me see thee stoop from heaven on wings
    That fill the skies with silver glitterings!

And as, in sparkling majesty, a star
  Gilds the bright summit of some gloomy cloud;
Brightening the half veil'd face of heaven afar:
  So, when dark thoughts my boding spirit shroud,
    Sweet Hope, celestial influence round me shed,
    Waving thy silver pinions o'er my head.
February, 1815.

IMITATION OF SPENSER.
* * * * * * *

Now Morning from her orient chamber came,
  And her first footsteps touch'd a verdant hill;
Crowning its lawny crest with amber flame,
  Silv'ring the untainted gushes of its rill;
Which, pure from mossy beds, did down distill,
  And after parting beds of simple flowers,
By many streams a little lake did fill,
  Which round its marge reflected woven bowers,
And, in its middle space, a sky that never lowers.

There the king-fisher saw his plumage bright
Vieing with fish of brilliant dye below;

Whose silken fins, and golden scales' light
Cast upward, through the waves, a ruby glow:
There saw the swan his neck of arched snow,
And oar'd himself along with majesty;
Sparkled his jetty eyes; his feet did show
Beneath the waves like Afric's ebony,
And on his back a fay reclined voluptuously.

Ah! could I tell the wonders of an isle
That in that fairest lake had placed been,
I could e'en Dido of her grief beguile;
Or rob from aged Lear his bitter teen:
For sure so fair a place was never seen,
Of all that ever charm'd romantic eye:
It seem'd an emerald in the silver sheen
Of the bright waters; or as when on high,
Through clouds of fleecy white, laughs the cœrulean
sky.

And all around it dipp'd luxuriously
Slopings of verdure through the glossy tide,
Which, as it were in gentle amity,
Rippled delighted up the flowery side;
As if to glean the ruddy tears, it tried,
Which fell profusely from the rose-tree stem!
Haply it was the workings of its pride,
In strife to throw upon the shore a gem
Outvieing all the buds in Flora's diadem.

* * * * * * *
════════

WOMAN! when I behold thee flippant, vain,
    Inconstant, childish, proud, and full of fancies;
    Without that modest softening that enhances
The downcast eye, repentant of the pain
That its mild light creates to heal again:
    E'en then, elate, my spirit leaps, and prances,
    E'en then my soul with exultation dances
For that to love, so long, I've dormant lain:
But when I see thee meek, and kind, and tender,
    Heavens! how desperately do I adore

Thy winning graces;—to be thy defender
  I hotly burn—to be a Calidore—
A very Red Cross Knight—a stout Leander—
  Might I be loved by thee like these of yore.

Light feet, dark violet eyes, and parted hair;
  Soft dimpled hands, white neck, and creamy breast,
  Are things on which the dazzled senses rest
Till the fond, fixed eyes, forget they stare.
From such fine pictures, heavens! I cannot dare
  To turn my admiration, though unpossess'd
  They be of what is worthy,—though not drest
In lovely modesty, and virtues rare.
Yet these I leave as thoughtless as a lark;
  These lures I straight forget,—e'en ere I dine,
Or thrice my palate moisten: but when I mark
  Such charms with mild intelligences shine,
My ear is open like a greedy shark,
  To catch the tunings of a voice divine.

Ah! who can e'er forget so fair a being?
  Who can forget her half retiring sweets?
  God! she is like a milk-white lamb that bleats
For man's protection. Surely the All-seeing,
Who joys to see us with his gifts agreeing,
  Will never give him pinions, who intreats
  Such innocence to ruin,—who vilely cheats
A dove-like bosom. In truth there is no freeing
One's thoughts from such a beauty; when I hear
  A lay that once I saw her hand awake,
Her form seems floating palpable, and near;
  Had I e'er seen her from an arbour take
A dewy flower, oft would that hand appear,
  And o'er my eyes the trembling moisture shake.

EPISTLES

TO
GEORGE FELTON MATHEW.

SWEET are the pleasures that to verse belong,
And doubly sweet a brotherhood in song;
Nor can remembrance, Mathew! bring to view
A fate more pleasing, a delight more true
Than that in which the brother Poets joy'd,
Who with combined powers, their wit employ'd
To raise a trophy to the drama's muses.
The thought of this great partnership diffuses
Over the genius loving heart, a feeling
Of all that's high, and great, and good, and healing.

Too partial friend! fain would I follow thee
Past each horizon of fine poesy;
Fain would I echo back each pleasant note
As o'er Sicilian seas, clear anthems float
'Mong the light skimming gondolas far parted,
Just when the sun his farewell beam has darted:
But 'tis impossible; far different cares
Beckon me sternly from soft "Lydian airs,"
And hold my faculties so long in thrall,
That I am oft in doubt whether at all
I shall again see Phœbus in the morning:
Or flush'd Aurora in the roseate dawning!
Or a white Naiad in a rippling stream;
Or a rapt seraph in a moonlight beam;
Or again witness what with thee I've seen,
The dew by fairy feet swept from the green,
After a night of some quaint jubilee
Which every elf and fay had come to see:
When bright processions took their airy march
Beneath the curved moon's triumphal arch.

But might I now each passing moment give
To the coy muse, with me she would not live
In this dark city, nor would condescend
'Mid contradictions her delights to lend.
Should e'er the fine-eyed maid to me be kind,
Ah! surely it must be whene'er I find
Some flowery spot, sequester'd, wild, romantic,
That often must have seen a poet frantic;
Where oaks, that erst the Druid knew, are growing,
And flowers, the glory of one day, are blowing;
Where the dark-leav'd laburnum's drooping clusters
Reflect athwart the stream their yellow lustres,
And intertwined the cassia's arms unite,
With its own drooping buds, but very white.
Where on one side are covert branches hung,
'Mong which the nightingales have always sung
In leafy quiet; where to pry, aloof,
Atween the pillars of the sylvan roof,
Would be to find where violet beds were nestling,
And where the bee with cowslip bells was wrestling.
There must be too a ruin dark, and gloomy,
To say "joy not too much in all that's bloomy."

Yet this is vain—O Mathew lend thy aid
To find a place where I may greet the maid—
Where we may soft humanity put on,
And sit, and rhyme and think on Chatterton;
And that warm-hearted Shakspeare sent to meet him
Four laurell'd spirits, heaven-ward to intreat him.
With reverence would we speak of all the sages
Who have left streaks of light athwart their ages:
And thou shouldst moralize on Milton's blindness,
And mourn the fearful dearth of human kindness
To those who strove with the bright golden wing
Of genius, to flap away each sting
Thrown by the pitiless world. We next could tell
Of those who in the cause of freedom fell;
Of our own Alfred, of Helvetian Tell;
Of him whose name to ev'ry heart's a solace,
High-minded and unbending William Wallace.

25

While to the rugged north our musing turns
We well might drop a tear for him, and Burns.

Felton! without incitements such as these,
How vain for me the niggard Muse to tease:
For thee, she will thy every dwelling grace,
And make "a sunshine in a shady place:"
For thou wast once a flowret blooming wild,
Close to the source, bright, pure, and undefil'd,
Whence gush the streams of song: in happy hour
Came chaste Diana from her shady bower,
Just as the sun was from the east uprising;
And, as for him some gift she was devising,
Beheld thee, pluck'd thee, cast thee in the stream
To meet her glorious brother's greeting beam.
I marvel much that thou hast never told
How, from a flower, into a fish of gold
Apollo chang'd thee; how thou next didst seem
A black-eyed swan upon the widening stream;
And when thou first didst in that mirror trace
The placid features of a human face:
That thou hast never told thy travels strange,
And all the wonders of the mazy range
O'er pebbly crystal, and o'er golden sands;
Kissing thy daily food from Naiad's pearly hands.
November, 1815.

TO
MY BROTHER GEORGE.

FULL many a dreary hour have I past,
My brain bewilder'd, and my mind o'ercast
With heaviness; in seasons when I've thought
No sphery strains by me could e'er be caught
From the blue dome, though I to dimness gaze
On the far depth where sheeted lightning plays;
Or, on the wavy grass outstretch'd supinely,
Pry 'mong the stars, to strive to think divinely:
That I should never hear Apollo's song,
Though feathery clouds were floating all along

The purple west, and, two bright streaks between,
The golden lyre itself were dimly seen:
That the still murmur of the honey bee
Would never teach a rural song to me:
That the bright glance from beauty's eyelids slanting
Would never make a lay of mine enchanting,
Or warm my breast with ardour to unfold
Some tale of love and arms in time of old.

But there are times, when those that love the bay,
Fly from all sorrowing far, far away;
A sudden glow comes on them, nought they see
In water, earth, or air, but poesy.
It has been said, dear George, and true I hold it,
(For knightly Spenser to Libertas told it,)
That when a Poet is in such a trance,
In air he sees white coursers paw, and prance,
Bestridden of gay knights, in gay apparel,
Who at each other tilt in playful quarrel,
And what we, ignorantly, sheet-lightning call,
Is the swift opening of their wide portal,
When the bright warder blows his trumpet clear,
Whose tones reach nought on earth but Poet's ear.
When these enchanted portals open wide,
And through the light the horsemen swiftly glide,
The Poet's eye can reach those golden halls,
And view the glory of their festivals:
Their ladies fair, that in the distance seem
Fit for the silv'ring of a seraph's dream;
Their rich brimm'd goblets, that incessant run
Like the bright spots that move about the sun;
And, when upheld, the wine from each bright jar
Pours with the lustre of a falling star.
Yet further off, are dimly seen their bowers,
Of which, no mortal eye can reach the flowers;
And 'tis right just, for well Apollo knows
'Twould make the Poet quarrel with the rose.
All that's reveal'd from that far seat of blisses,
Is, the clear fountains' interchanging kisses,
As gracefully descending, light and thin,

Like silver streaks across a dolphin's fin,
When he upswimmeth from the coral caves,
And sports with half his tail above the waves.

These wonders strange he sees, and many more,
Whose head is pregnant with poetic lore.
Should he upon an evening ramble fare
With forehead to the soothing breezes bare,
Would he naught see but the dark, silent blue
With all its diamonds trembling through and through?
Or the coy moon, when in the waviness
Of whitest clouds she does her beauty dress,
And staidly paces higher up, and higher,
Like a sweet nun in holy-day attire?
Ah, yes! much more would start into his sight—
The revelries, and mysteries of night:
And should I ever see them, I will tell you
Such tales as needs must with amazement spell you.
These are the living pleasures of the bard:
But richer far posterity's award.
What does he murmur with his latest breath,
While his proud eye looks through the film of death?
"What though I leave this dull, and earthly mould,
"Yet shall my spirit lofty converse hold
"With after times.—The patriot shall feel
"My stern alarum, and unsheath his steel;
"Or, in the senate thunder out my numbers
"To startle princes from their easy slumbers.
"The sage will mingle with each moral theme
"My happy thoughts sententious; he will teem
"With lofty periods when my verses fire him,
"And then I'll stoop from heaven to inspire him.
"Lays have I left of such a dear delight
"That maids will sing them on their bridal night.
"Gay villagers, upon a morn of May,
"When they have tired their gentle limbs with play,
"And form'd a snowy circle on the grass,
"And plac'd in midst of all that lovely lass
"Who chosen is their queen,—with her fine head
"Crowned with flowers purple, white, and red:

28

"For there the lily, and the musk-rose, sighing,
"Are emblems true of hapless lovers dying:
"Between her breasts, that never yet felt trouble,
"A bunch of violets full blown, and double,
"Serenely sleep:—she from a casket takes
"A little book,—and then a joy awakes
"About each youthful heart,—with stifled cries,
"And rubbing of white hands, and sparkling eyes:
"For she's to read a tale of hopes, and fears;
"One that I foster'd in my youthful years:
"The pearls, that on each glist'ning circlet sleep,
"Gush ever and anon with silent creep,
"Lured by the innocent dimples. To sweet rest
"Shall the dear babe, upon its mother's breast,
"Be lull'd with songs of mine. Fair world, adieu!
"Thy dales, and hills, are fading from my view:
"Swiftly I mount, upon wide spreading pinions,
"Far from the narrow bounds of thy dominions.
"Full joy I feel, while thus I cleave the air,
"That my soft verse will charm thy daughters fair,
"And warm thy sons!" Ah, my dear friend and brother,
Could I, at once, my mad ambition smother,
For tasting joys like these, sure I should be
Happier, and dearer to society.
At times 'tis true, I've felt relief from pain
When some bright thought has darted through my
      brain:
Through all that day I've felt a greater pleasure
Than if I'd brought to light a hidden treasure.
As to my sonnets, though none else should heed them,
I feel delighted, still, that you should read them.
Of late, too, I have had much calm enjoyment,
Stretch'd on the grass at my best lov'd employment
Of scribbling lines for you. These things I thought
While, in my face, the freshest breeze I caught.
E'en now I'm pillow'd on a bed of flowers
That crowns a lofty clift, which proudly towers
Above the ocean-waves. The stalks, and blades,
Chequer my tablet with their quivering shades.
On one side is a field of drooping oats,

Through which the poppies show their scarlet coats;
So pert and useless, that they bring to mind
The scarlet coats that pester human-kind.
And on the other side, outspread, is seen
Ocean's blue mantle streak'd with purple, and green.
Now 'tis I see a canvass'd ship, and now
Mark the bright silver curling round her prow.
I see the lark down-dropping to his nest,
And the broad winged sea-gull never at rest;
For when no more he spreads his feathers free,
His breast is dancing on the restless sea.
Now I direct my eyes into the west,
Which at this moment is in sunbeams drest:
Why westward turn? 'Twas but to say adieu!
'Twas but to kiss my hand, dear George, to you!
August, 1816.

TO
CHARLES COWDEN CLARKE.

OFT have you seen a swan superbly frowning,
And with proud breast his own white shadow crowning,
He slants his neck beneath the waters bright
So silently, it seems a beam of light
Come from the galaxy: anon he sports,—
With outspread wings the Naiad Zephyr courts,
Or ruffles all the surface of the lake
In striving from its crystal face to take
Some diamond water drops, and them to treasure
In milky nest, and sip them off at leisure.
But not a moment can he there insure them,
Nor to such downy rest can he allure them;
For down they rush as though they would be free,
And drop like hours into eternity.
Just like that bird am I in loss of time,
Whene'er I venture on the stream of rhyme;
With shatter'd boat, oar snapt, and canvass rent,
I slowly sail, scarce knowing my intent;
Still scooping up the water with my fingers,
In which a trembling diamond never lingers.

30

By this, friend Charles, you may full plainly see
Why I have never penn'd a line to thee:
Because my thoughts were never free, and clear,
And little fit to please a classic ear;
Because my wine was of too poor a savour
For one whose palate gladdens in the flavour
Of sparkling Helicon:—small good it were
To take him to a desert rude, and bare,
Who had on Baiæ's shore reclin'd at ease,
While Tasso's page was floating in a breeze
That gave soft music from Armida's bowers,
Mingled with fragrance from her rarest flowers:
Small good to one who had by Mulla's stream
Fondled the maidens with the breasts of cream;
Who had beheld Belphœbe in a brook,
And lovely Una in a leafy nook,
And Archimago leaning o'er his book:
Who had of all that's sweet tasted, and seen,
From silv'ry ripple, up to beauty's queen;
From the sequester'd haunts of gay Titania,
To the blue dwelling of divine Urania:
One, who, of late, had ta'en sweet forest walks
With him who elegantly chats, and talks—
The wrongd' Libertas,—who has told you storie
Of laurel chaplets, and Apollo's glories;
Of troops chivalrous prancing through a city,
And tearful ladies made for love, and pity:
With many else which I have never known.
Thus have I thought; and days on days have flown
Slowly, or rapidly—unwilling still
For you to try my dull, unlearned quill.
Nor should I now, but that I've known you long;
That you first taught me all the sweets of song:
The grand, the sweet, the terse, the free, the fine;
What swell'd with pathos, and what right divine:
Spenserian vowels that elope with ease,
And float along like birds o'er summer seas;
Miltonian storms, and more, Miltonian tenderness;
Michael in arms, and more, meek Eve's fair slenderness.
Who read for me the sonnet swelling loudly

Up to its climax and then dying proudly?
Who found for me the grandeur of the ode,
Growing, like Atlas, stronger from its load?
Who let me taste that more than cordial dram,
The sharp, the rapier-pointed epigram?
Shew'd me that epic was of all the king,
Round, vast, and spanning all like Saturn's ring?
You too upheld the veil from Clio's beauty,
And pointed out the patriot's stern duty;
The might of Alfred, and the shaft of Tell;
The hand of Brutus, that so grandly fell
Upon a tyrant's head. Ah! had I never seen,
Or known your kindness, what might I have been?
What my enjoyments in my youthfus years,
Bereft of all that now my life endears?
And can I e'er these benefits forget?
And can I e'er repay the friendly debt?
No, doubly no;—yet should these rhymings please,
I shall roll on the grass with two-fold ease:
For I have long time been my fancy feeding
With hopes that you would one day think the reading
Of my rough verses not an hour misspent;
Should it e'er be so, what a rich content!
Some weeks have pass'd since last I saw the spires
In lucent Thames reflected:—warm desires
To see the sun o'er peep the eastern dimness,
And morning shadows streaking into slimness
Across the lawny fields, and pebbly water;
To mark the time as they grow broad, and shorter;
To feel the air that plays about the hills,
And sips its freshness from the little rills;
To see high, golden corn wave in the light
When Cynthia smiles upon a summer's night,
And peers among the cloudlet's jet and white,
As though she were reclining in a bed
Of bean blossoms, in heaven freshly shed.
No sooner had I stepp'd into these pleasures
Than I began to think of rhymes and measures:
The air that floated by me seem'd to say
"Write! thou wilt never have a better day."

And so I did. When many lines I'd written,
Though with their grace I was not oversmitten,
Yet, as my hand was warm, I thought I'd better
Trust to my feelings, and write you a letter.
Such an attempt required an inspiration
Of a peculiar sort,—a consummation;—
Which, had I felt, these scribblings might have been
Verses from which the soul would never wean:
But many days have past since last my heart
Was warm'd luxuriously by divine Mozart;
By Arne delighted, or by Handel madden'd;
Or by the song of Erin pierc'd and sadden'd:
What time you were before the music sitting,
And the rich notes to each sensation fitting.
Since I have walk'd with you through shady lanes
That freshly terminate in open plains,
And revel'd in a chat that ceased not
When at night-fall among your books we got:
No, nor when supper came, nor after that,—
Nor when reluctantly I took my hat;
No, nor till cordially you shook my hand
Mid-way between our homes:—your accents bland
Still sounded in my ears, when I no more
Could hear your footsteps touch the grav'ly floor.
Sometimes I lost them, and then found again;
You chang'd the footpath for the grassy plain.
In those still moments I have wish'd you joys
That well you know to honour:—"Life's very toys
"With him," said I, "will take a pleasant charm;
"It cannot be that ought will work him harm."
These thoughts now come o'er me with all their might:
Again I shake your hand,—friend Charles, good night.

September, 1816.

SONNETS.

I.
TO MY BROTHER GEORGE.

MANY the wonders I this day have seen:
  The sun, when first he kist away the tears
  That fill'd the eyes of morn;—the laurel'd peers
Who from the feathery gold of evening lean;—
The ocean with its vastness, its blue green,
  Its ships, its rocks, its caves, its hopes, its fears,—
  Its voice mysterious, which whoso hears
Must think on what will be, and what has been.
E'en now, dear George, while this for you I write,
  Cynthia is from her silken curtains peeping
So scantly, that it seems her bridal night,
  And she her half-discover'd revels keeping.
But what, without the social thought of thee,
Would be the wonders of the sky and sea?

II.
TO * * * * * *

HAD I a man's fair form, then might my sighs
  Be echoed swiftly through that ivory shell
  Thine ear, and find thy gentle heart; so well
Would passion arm me for the enterprize:
But ah! I am no knight whose foeman dies;
  No cuirass glistens on my bosom's swell;
  I am no happy shepherd of the dell
Whose lips have trembled with a maiden's eyes.
Yet must I doat upon thee,—call thee sweet,
  Sweeter by far than Hybla's honied roses
  When steep'd in dew rich to intoxication.
Ah! I will taste that dew, for me 'tis meet,
  And when the moon her pallid face discloses,
    I'll gather some by spells, and incantation.

III.

Written on the day that Mr. Leigh Hunt left Prison.

WHAT though, for showing truth to flatter'd state,
 Kind Hunt was shut in prison, yet has he,
 In his immortal spirit, been as free
As the sky-searching lark, and as elate.
Minion of grandeur! think you he did wait?
 Think you he nought but prison walls did see,
 Till, so unwilling, thou unturn'dst the key?
Ah, no! far happier, nobler was his fate!
In Spenser's halls he strayed, and bowers fair,
 Culling enchanted flowers; and he flew
With daring Milton through the fields of air:
 To regions of his own his genius true
Took happy flights. Who shall his fame impair
 When thou art dead, and all thy wretched crew?

IV.

How many bards gild the lapses of time!
 A few of them have ever been the food
 Of my delighted fancy,—I could brood
Over their beauties, earthly, or sublime:
And often, when I sit me down to rhyme,
 These will in throngs before my mind intrude:
 But no confusion, no disturbance rude
Do they occasion; 'tis a pleasing chime.
So the unnumber'd sounds that evening store;
 The songs of birds—the whisp'ring of the leaves—
The voice of waters—the great bell that heaves
 With solemn sound,—and thousand others more,
That distance of recognizance bereaves,
 Make pleasing music, and not wild uproar.

V.

To a Friend who sent me some Roses.

As late I rambled in the happy fields,
 What time the sky-lark shakes the tremulous dew
 From his lush clover covert;—when anew

35

Adventurous knights take up their dinted shields:
I saw the sweetest flower wild nature yields,
  A fresh-blown musk-rose; 'twas the first that threw
  Its sweets upon the summer: graceful it grew
As is the wand that queen Titania wields.
And, as I feasted on its fragrancy,
  I thought the garden-rose it far excell'd:
But when, O Wells! thy roses came to me
  My sense with their deliciousness was spell'd:
Soft voices had they, that with tender plea
  Whisper'd of peace, and truth, and friedliness un-
    quell'd.

VI.

To G. A. W.

NYMPH of the downward smile, and sidelong glance,
  In what diviner moments of the day
  Art thou most lovely? When gone far astray
Into the labyrinths of sweet utterance?
Or when serenely wand'ring in a trance
  Of sober thought? Or when starting away,
  With careless robe, to meet the morning ray,
Thou spar'st the flowers in thy mazy dance?
Haply 'tis when thy ruby lips part sweetly,
  And so remain, because thou listenest:
But thou to please wert nurtured so completely
  That I can never tell what mood is best.
I shall as soon pronounce which grace more neatly
  Trips it before Apollo than the rest.

VII.

O SOLITUDE! if I must with thee dwell,
  Let it not be among the jumbled heap
  Of murky buildings; climb with me the steep,—
Nature's observatory—whence the dell,
Its flowery slopes, its river's crystal swell,
  May seem a span; let me thy vigils keep
  'Mongst boughs pavillion'd, where the deer's swift
    leap
Startles the wild bee from the fox-glove bell,

But though I'll gladly trace these scenes with thee,
   Yet the sweet converse of an innocent mind,
Whose words are images of thoughts refin'd,
   Is my soul's pleasure; and it sure must be
Almost the highest bliss of human-kind,
   When to thy haunts two kindred spirits flee.

VIII.
TO MY BROTHERS.

SMALL, busy flames play through the fresh laid coals,
   And their faint cracklings o'er our silence creep
   Like whispers of the household gods that keep
A gentle empire o'er fraternal souls.
And while, for rhymes, I search around the poles,
   Your eyes are fix'd, as in poetic sleep,
   Upon the lore so voluble and deep,
That aye at fall of night our care condoles.
This is your birth-day Tom, and I rejoice
   That thus it passes smoothly, quietly.
Many such eves of gently whisp'ring noise
   May we together pass, and calmly try
What are this world's true joys,—ere the great voice,
   From its fair face, shall bid our spirits fly.
November, 18, 1816.

IX.

KEEN, fitful gusts are whisp'ring here and there
   Among the bushes half leafless, and dry;
   The stars look very cold about the sky,
And I have many miles on foot to fare.
Yet feel I little of the cool bleak air,
   Or of the dead leaves rustling drearily,
   Or of those silver lamps that burn on high,
Or of the distance from home's pleasant lair:
For I am brimfull of the friendliness
   That in a little cottage I have found;
Of fair-hair'd Milton's eloquent distress,
   And all his love for gentle Lycid drown'd;
Of lovely Laura in her light green dress,
   And faithful Petrarch gloriously crown'd.

X.

To one who has been long in city pent,
　'Tis very sweet to look into the fair
　And open face of heaven,—to breathe a prayer
Full in the smile of the blue firmament.
Who is more happy, when, with heart's content,
　Fatigued he sinks into some pleasant lair
　Of wavy grass, and reads a debonair
And gentle tale of love and languishment?
Returning home at evening, with an ear
　Catching the notes of Philomel,—an eye
Watching the sailing cloudlet's bright career,
　He mourns that day so soon has glided by:
E'en like the passage of an angel's tear
　That falls through the clear ether silently.

XI.

On first looking into Chapman's Homer.

MUCH have I travell'd in the realms of gold,
　And many goodly states and kingdoms seen;
　Round many western islands have I been
Which bards in fealty to Apollo hold.
Oft of one wide expanse had I been told
　That deep-brow'd Homer ruled as his demesne;
　Yet did I never breathe its pure serene
Till I heard Chapman speak out loud and bold:
Then felt I like some watcher of the skies
　When a new planet swims into his ken;
Or like stout Cortez when with eagle eyes
　He star'd at the Pacific—and all his men
Look'd at each other with a wild surmise—
　Silent, upon a peak in Darien.

XII.

On leaving some Friends at an early Hour.

GIVE me a golden pen, and let me lean
　On heap'd up flowers, in regions clear, and far;
　Bring me a tablet whiter than a star,

Or hand of hymning, angel when 'tis seen
The silver strings of heavenly harp atween:
    And let there glide by many a pearly car,
    Pink robes, and wavy hair, and diamond jar,
And half discovered wings, and glances keen.
The while let music wander round my ears,
    And as it reaches each delicious ending,
        Let me write down a line of glorious tone,
And full of many wonders of the spheres:
    For what a height my spirit is contending!
        'Tis not content so soon to be alone.

XIII.
ADDRESSED TO HAYDON.

HIGHMINDEDNESS, a jealousy for good,
    A loving-kindness for the great man's fame,
    Dwells here and there with people of no name,
In noisome alley, and in pathless wood:
And where we think the truth least understood,
    Oft may be found a "singleness of aim,"
    That ought to frighten into hooded shame
A money mong'ring, pitiable brood.
How glorious this affection for the cause
    Of stedfast genius, toiling gallantly!
What when a stout unbending champion awes
    Envy, and Malice to their native sty?
Unnumber'd souls breathe out a still applause,
    Proud to behold him in his country's eye.

XIV.
ADDRESSED TO THE SAME.

GREAT spirits now on earth are sojourning;
    He of the cloud, the cataract, the lake,
    Who on Helvellyn's summit, wide awake,
Catches his freshness from Archangel's wing:
He of the rose, the violet, the spring.
    The social smile, the chain for Freedom's sake:
    And lo!—whose stedfastness would never take

A meaner sound than Raphael's whispering.
And other spirits there are standing apart
  Upon the forehead of the age to come;
These, these will give the world another heart,
  And other pulses. Hear ye not the hum
Of mighty workings?————
  Listen awhile ye nations, and be dumb.

XV.

On the Grasshopper and Cricket.

THE poetry of earth is never dead:
  When all the birds are faint with the hot sun,
  And hide in cooling trees, a voice will run
From hedge to hedge about the new-mown mead;
That is the Grasshopper's—he takes the lead
  In summer luxury,—he has never done
  With his delights; for when tired out with fun
He rests at ease beneath some pleasant weed.
The poetry of earth is ceasing never:
  On a lone winter evening, when the frost
    Has wrought a silence, from the stove there shrills
  The Cricket's song, in warmth increasing ever,
  And seems to one in drowsiness half lost,
    The Grasshopper's among some grassy hills.
December, 30, 1816.

XVI.

TO KOSCIUSKO.

GOOD Kosciusko, thy great name alone
  Is a full harvest whence to reap high feeling;
  It comes upon us like the glorious pealing
Of the wide spheres—an everlasting tone.
And now it tells me, that in worlds unknown,
  The names of heroes, burst from clouds concealing,
  And changed to harmonies, for ever stealing
Through cloudless blue, and round each silver throne.
It tells me too, that on a happy day,
  When some good spirit walks upon the earth,
  Thy name with Alfred's, and the great of yore

Gently commingling, gives tremendou s irth
To a loud hymn, that sounds far, faraway
    To where the great God lives for evermore.

XVII.

Happy is England! I could be content
    To see no other verdure than its own;
    To feel no other breezes than are blown
Through its tall woods with high romances blent:
Yet do I sometimes feel a languishment
    For skies Italian, and an inward groan
    To sit upon an Alp as on a throne,
And half forget what world or worldling meant.
Happy is England, sweet her artless daughters;
    Enough their simple loveliness for me,
        Enough their whitest arms in silence clinging:
    Yet do I often warmly burn to see
        Beauties of deeper glance, and hear their singing,
And float with them about the summer waters.

SLEEP AND POETRY.

"As I lay in my bed slepe full unmete
"Was unto me, but why that I ne might
"Rest I ne wist, for there n'as erthly wight
"[As I suppose] had more of hertis ese
"Than I, for I n'ad sicknesse nor disese."
                                        CHAUCER.

WHAT is more gentle than a wind in summer?
What is more soothing than the pretty hummer
That stays one moment in an open flower,
And buzzes cheerily from bower to bower?
What is more tranquil than a musk-rose blowing
In a green island, far from all men's knowing?
More healthful than the leafiness of dales?
More secret than a nest of nightingales?
More serene than Cordelia's countenance?
More full of visions than a high romance?
What, but thee Sleep? Soft closer of our eyes!

Low murmurer of tender lullabies!
Light hoverer around our happy pillows!
Wreather of poppy buds, and weeping willows!
Silent entangler of a beauty's tresses!
Most happy listener! when the morning blesses
Thee for enlivening all the cheerful eyes
That glance so brightly at the new sun-rise.

But what is higher beyond thought than thee?
Fresher than berries of a mountain tree?
More strange, more beautiful, more smooth, more regal,
Than wings of swans, than doves, than dim-seen eagle?
What is it? And to what shall I compare it?
It has a glory, and nought else can share it:
The thought thereof is awful, sweet, and holy,
Chacing away all worldliness and folly;
Coming sometimes like fearful claps of thunder,
Or the low rumblings earth's regions under;
And sometimes like a gentle whispering
Of all the secrets of some wond'rous thing
That breathes about us in the vacant air;
So that we look around with prying stare,
Perhaps to see shapes of light, aerial limning,
And catch soft floatings from a faint-heard hymning;
To see the laurel wreath, on high suspended,
That is to crown our name when life is ended.
Sometimes it gives a glory to the voice,
And from the heart up-springs, rejoice! rejoice!
Sounds which will reach the Framer of all things,
And die away in ardent mutterings.

No one who once the glorious sun has seen,
And all the clouds, and felt his bosom clean
For his great Maker's presence, but must know
What 'tis I mean, and feel his being glow:
Therefore no insult will I give his spirit,
By telling what he sees from native merit.

O Poesy! for thee I hold my pen
That am not yet a glorious denizen

Of thy wide heaven—Should I rather kneel
Upon some mountain-top until I feel
A glowing splendour round about me hung,
And echo back the voice of thine own tongue?
O Poesy! for thee I grasp my pen
That am not yet a glorious denizen
Of thy wide heaven; yet, to my ardent prayer,
Yield from thy sanctuary some clear air,
Smoothed for intoxication by the breath
Of flowering bays, that I may die a death
Of luxury, and my young spirit follow
The morning sunbeams to the great Apollo
Like a fresh sacrifice; or, if I can bear
The o'erwhelming sweets, 'twill bring me to the fair
Visions of all places: a bowery nook
Will be elysium—an eternal book
Whence I may copy many a lovely saying
About the leaves, and flowers—about the playing
Of nymphs in woods, and fountains; and the shade
Keeping a silence round a sleeping maid;
And many a verse from so strange influence
That we must ever wonder how, and whence
It came. Also imaginings will hover
Round my fire-side, and haply there discover
Vistas of solemn beauty, where I'd wander
In happy silence, like the clear meander
Through its lone vales; and where I found a spot
Of awfuller shade, or an enchanted grot,
Or a green hill o'erspread with chequered dress
Of flowers, and fearful from its loveliness,
Write on my tablets all that was permitted,
All that was for our human senses fitted.
Then the events of this wide world I'd seize
Like a strong giant, and my spirit teaze
Till at its shoulders it should proudly see
Wings to find out an immortality.

Stop and consider! life is but a day;
A fragile dew-drop on its perilous way
From a tree's summit; a poor Indian's sleep

While his boat hastens to the monstrous steep
Of Montmorenci. Why so sad a moan?
Life is the rose's hope while yet unblown;
The reading of an ever-changing tale;
The light uplifting of a maiden's veil;
A pigeon tumbling in clear summer air;
A laughing school-boy, without grief or care,
Riding the springy branches of an elm.

O for ten years, that I may overwhelm
Myself in poesy; so I may do the deed
That my own soul has to itself decreed.
Then I will pass the countries that I see
In long perspective, and continually
Taste their pure fountains. First the realm I'll pass
Of Flora, and old Pan: sleep in the grass,
Feed upon apples red, and strawberries,
And choose each pleasure that my fancy sees;
Catch the white-handed nymphs in shady places,
To woo sweet kisses from averted faces,—
Play with their fingers, touch their shoulders white
Into a pretty shrinking with a bite
As hard as lips can make it: till agreed,
A lovely tale of human life we'll read.
And one will teach a tame dove how it best
May fan the cool air gently o'er my rest;
Another, bending o'er her nimble tread,
Will set a green robe floating round her head,
And still will dance with ever varied ease,
Smiling upon the flowers and the trees:
Another will entice me on, and on
Through almond blossoms and rich cinnamon;
Till in the bosom of a leafy world
We rest in silence, like two gems upcurl'd
In the recesses of a pearly shell.

And can I ever bid these joys farewell?
Yes, I must pass them for a nobler life,
Where I may find the agonies, the strife
Of human hearts: for lo! I see afar,

O'er sailing the blue cragginess, a car
And steeds with streamy manes—the charioteer
Looks out upon the winds with glorious fear:
And now the numerous tramplings quiver lightly
Along a huge cloud's ridge; and now with sprightly
Wheel downward come they into fresher skies,
Tipt round with silver from the sun's bright eyes.
Still downward with capacious whirl they glide;
And now I see them on a green-hill's side
In breezy rest among the nodding stalks.
The charioteer with wond'rous gesture talks
To the trees and mountains; and there soon appear
Shapes of delight, of mystery, and fear,
Passing along before a dusky space
Made by some mighty oaks: as they would chase
Some ever-fleeting music on they sweep.
Lo! how they murmur, laugh, and smile, and weep:
Some with upholden hand and mouth severe;
Some with their faces muffled to the ear
Between their arms; some, clear in youthful bloom,
Go glad and smilingly athwart the gloom;
Some looking back, and some with upward gaze;
Yes, thousands in a thousand different ways
Flit onward—now a lovely wreath of girls
Dancing their sleek hair into tangled curls;
And now broad wings. Most awfully intent
The driver of those steeds is forward bent,
And seems to listen: O that I might know
All that he writes with such a hurrying glow.

The visions all are fled—the car is fled
Into the light of heaven, and in their stead
A sense of real things comes doubly strong,
And, like a muddy stream, would bear along
My soul to nothingness: but I will strive
Against all doubtings, and will keep alive
The thought of that same chariot, and the strange
Journey it went.

               Is there so small a range
In the present strength of manhood, that the high

Imagination cannot freely fly
As she was wont of old? prepare her steeds,
Paw up against the light, and do strange deeds
Upon the clouds? Has she not shewn us all?
From the clear space of ether, to the small
Breath of new buds unfolding? From the meaning
Of Jove's large eye-brow, to the tender greening
Of April meadows? Here her altar shone,
E'en in this isle; and who could paragon
The fervid choir that lifted up a noise
Of harmony, to where it aye will poise
Its mighty self of convoluting sound,
Huge as a planet, and like that roll round,
Eternally around a dizzy void?
Ay, in those days the Muses were nigh cloy'd
With honors; nor had any other care
Than to sing our and sooth their wavy hair.

Could all this be forgotten? Yes, a schism
Nurtured by foppery and barbarism,
Made great Apollo blush for this his land.
Men were thought wise who could not understand
His glories: with a puling infant's force
They sway'd about upon a rocking horse,
And thought it Pegasus. Ah dismal soul'd!
The winds of heaven blew, the ocean roll'd
Its gathering waves—ye felt it not. The blue
Bared its eternal bosom, and the dew
Of summer nights collected still to make
The morning precious: beauty was awake!
Why were ye not awake? But ye were dead
To things ye knew not of,—were closely wed
To musty laws lined out with wretched rule
And compass vile: so that ye taught a school
Of dolts to smooth, inlay, and clip, and fit,
Till, like the certain wands of Jacob's wit,
Their verses tallied. Easy was the task:
A thousand handicraftsmen wore the mask
Of Poesy. Ill-fated, impious race!
That blasphemed the bright Lyrist to his face,

And did not know it,—no, they went about,
Holding a poor, decrepit standard out
Mark'd with most flimsy mottos, and in large
The name of one Boileau!

                O ye whose charge
It is to hover round our pleasant hills!
Whose congregated majesty so fills
My boundly reverence, that I cannot trace
Your hallowed names, in this unholy place,
So near those common folk; did not their shames
Affright you? Did our old lamenting Thames
Delight you? Did ye never cluster round
Delicious Avon, with a mournful sound,
And weep? Or did ye wholly bid adieu
To regions where no more the laurel grew?
Or did ye stay to give a welcoming
To some lone spirits who could proudly sing
Their youth away, and die? 'Twas even so:
But let me think away those times of woe:
Now 'tis fairer season; ye have breathed
Rich benedictions o'er us; ye have wreathed
Fresh garlands: for sweet music has been heard
In many places;—some has been upstirr'd
From out its crystal dwelling in a lake,
By a swan's ebon bill; from a thick brake,
Nested and quiet in a valley mild,
Bubbles a pipe; fine sounds are floating wild
About the earth: happy are ye and glad.
These things are doubtless: yet in truth we've had
Strange thunders from the potency of song;
Mingled indeed with what is sweet and strong,
From majesty: but in clear truth the themes
Are ugly clubs, the Poets Polyphemes
Disturbing the grand sea. A drainless shower
Of light is posy; 'tis the supreme of power;
'Tis might half slumb'ring on its own right arm.
The very archings of her eye-lids charm
A thousand willing agents to obey,
And still she governs with the mildest sway:

But strength alone though of the Muses born
Is like a fallen angel: trees uptorn,
Darkness, and worms, and shrouds, and sepulchres
Delight it; for it feeds upon the burrs,
And thorns of life; forgetting the great end
Of poesy, that it should be a friend
To sooth the cares, and lift the thoughts of man.

Yet I rejoice: a myrtle fairer than
E'er grew in Paphos, from the bitter weeds
Lifts its sweet head into the air, and feeds
A silent space with ever sprouting green.
All tenderest birds there find a pleasant screen,
Creep through the shade with jaunty fluttering,
Nibble the little cupped flowers and sing.
Then let us clear away the choaking thorns
From round its gentle stem; let the young fawns,
Yeaned in after times, when we are flown,
Find a fresh sward beneath it, overgrown
With simple flowers: let there nothing be
More boisterous than a lover's bended knee;
Nought more ungentle than the placid look
Of one who leans upon a closed book;
Nought more untranquil than the grassy slopes
Between two hills. All hail delightful hopes!
As she was wont, th' imagination
Into most lovely labyrinths will be gone,
And they shall be accounted poet kings
Who simply tell the most heart-easing things.
O may these joys be ripe before I die.
Will not some day that I presumptuously
Have spoken? that from hastening disgrace
T'were better far to hide my foolish face?
That whining boyhood should with reverence bow
Ere the dread thunderbolt could reach? How!
If I do hide myself, it sure shall be
In the very fane, the light of Poesy:
If I do fall, at least I will be laid
Beneath the silence of a poplar shade;
And over me the grass shall be smooth shaven;

And there shall be a kind memorial graven.
But off Despondence! miserable bane!
They should not know thee, who athirst to gain
A noble end, are thirsty every hour.
What though I am not wealthy in the dower
Of spanning wisdom; though I do not know
The shiftings of the mighty winds that blow
Hither and thither all the changing thoughts
Of man: though no great minist'ring reason sorts
Out the dark mysteries of human souls
To clear conceiving: yet there ever rolls
A vast idea before me, and I glean
Therefrom my liberty; thence too I've seen
The end and aim of Poesy. 'Tis clear
As anything most true; as that the year
Is made of the four seasons—manifest
As a large cross, some old cathedral's crest,
Lifted to the white clouds. Therefore should I
Be but the essence of deformity,
A coward, did my very eye-lids wink
At speaking out what I have dared to think.
Ah! rather let me like a madman run
Over some precipice; let the hot sun
Melt my Dedalian wings, and drive me down
Convuls'd and headlong! Stay! an inward frown
Of conscience bids me be more calm awhile.
An ocean dim, sprinkled with many an isle,
Spreads awfully before me. How much toil!
How many days! what desperate turmoil!
Ere I can have explored its widenesses.
Ah, what a task! upon my bended knees,
I could unsay those—no, impossible!
Impossible!

For sweet relief I'll dwell
On humbler thoughts, and let this strange assay
Begun in gentleness die so away.
E'en now all tumult from my bosom fades:
I turn full hearted to the friendly aids
That smooth the path of honour; brotherhood,

And friendliness the nurse of mutual good.
The hearty grasp that sends a pleasant sonnet
Into the brain ere one can think upon it;
The silence when some rhymes are coming out;
And when they're come, the very pleasant rout:
The message certain to be done to-morrow.
'Tis perhaps as well that it should be to borrow
Some precious book from out its snug retreat,
To cluster round it when we next shall meet.
Scarce can I scribble on; for lovely airs.
Are fluttering round the room like doves in pairs;
Many delights of that glad day recalling,
When first my senses caught their tender falling.
And with these airs come forms of elegance
Stooping their shoulders o'er a horse's prance,
Careless, and grand—fingers soft and round
Parting luxuriant curls;—and the swift bound
Of Bacchus from his chariot, when his eye
Made Ariadne's cheek look blushingly.
Thus I remember all the pleasant flow
Of words at opening a portfolio.

Things such as these are ever harbingers
To trains of peaceful images: the stirs
Of a swan's neck unseen among the rushes:-
A linnet starting all about the bushes:
A butterfly, with golden wings broad parted
Nestling a rose, convuls'd as though it smarted
With over pleasure—many, many more,
Might I indulge at large in all my store
Of luxuries: yet I must not forget
Sleep, quiet with his poppy coronet:
For what there may be worthy in these rhymes
I partly owe to him: and thus, the chimes
Of friendly voices had just given place
To as sweet a silence, when I 'gan retrace
The pleasant day, upon a couch at ease.
It was a poet's house who keeps the keys
Of pleasure's temple. Round about were hung
The glorious features of the bards who sung

In other ages—cold and sacred busts
Smiled at each other. Happy he who trusts
To clear Futurity his darling fame!
Then there were fauns and satyrs taking aim
At swelling apples with a frisky leap
And reaching fingers, 'mid a luscious heap
Of vine leaves. Then there rose to view a fane
Of liny marble, and thereto a train
Of nymphs approaching fairly o'er the sward:
One, loveliest, holding her white hand toward
The dazzling sunrise: two sisters sweet
Bending their graceful figures till they meet
Over the trippings of a little child:
And some are hearing, eagerly, the wild
Thrilling liquidity of dewy piping.
See, in another picture, nymphs are wiping
Cherishingly Diana's timorous limbs;—
A fold of lawny mantle dabbling swims
At the bath's edge, and keeps a gentle motion
With the subsiding crystal: as when ocean
Heaves calmly its broad swelling smoothiness o'er
Its rocky marge, and balances once more
The patient weeds; that now unshent by foam
Feel all about their undulating home.

Sappho's meek head was there half smiling down
At nothing; just as though the earnest frown
Of over thinking had that moment gone
From off her brow, and left her all alone.

Great Alfred's too, with anxious, pitying eyes,
As if he always listened to the sighs
Of the goaded world; and Kosciusko's worn
By horrid suffrance—mightily forlorn.
Petrarch, outstepping from the shady green,
Starts at the sight of Laura; nor can wean
His eyes from her sweet face. Most happy they!
For over them was seen a free display
Of out-spread wings, and from between them shone
The face of Poesy: from off her throne

She overlook'd things that I scarce could tell.
The very sense of where I was might well
Keep Sleep aloof: but more than that there came
Thought after thought to nourish up the flame
Within my breast; so that the morning light
Surprised me even from a sleepless night;
And up I rose refresh'd, and glad, and gay,
Resolving to begin that very day
These lines; and howsoever they be done,
I leave them as a father does his son.

FINIS

[PUBLISHED 1818]

ENDYMION:

A Poetic Romance.

"THE STRETCHED METRE OF AN ANTIQUE SONG."

INSCRIBED
TO THE MEMORY
OF
THOMAS CHATTERTON.

PREFACE.

KNOWING within myself the manner in which this Poem has been produced, it is not without a feeling of regret that I make it public.

What manner I mean, will be quite clear to the reader, who must soon perceive great inexperience, immaturity, and every error denoting a feverish attempt, rather than a deed accomplished. The two first books, and indeed the two last, I feel sensible are not of such completion as to warrant their passing the press; nor should they if I thought a year's castigation would do them any good;—it will not: the foundations are too sandy. It is just that this youngster should die away: a sad thought for me, if I had not some hope that while it is dwindling I may be plotting, and fitting myself for verses fit to live.

This may be speaking too presumptuously, and may deserve a punishment: but no feeling man will be forward to inflict it: he will leave me alone, with the conviction that there is not a fiercer hell than the failure in a great object. This is not written with the least atom of purpose to forestall criticisms of course, but from the desire I have to conciliate men who are competent to look, and who do look with a zealous eye, to the honour of English literature.

The imagination of a boy is healthy, and the mature imagination of a man is healthy; but there is a space of life between, in which the soul is in a ferment, the character undecided, the way of life uncertain, the ambition thick-sighted: thence proceeds mawkishness, and all the thousand bitters which those men I speak of must necessarily taste in going over the following pages.

I hope I have not in too late a day touched the beautiful mythology of Greece, and dulled its brightness: for I wish to try once more, before I bid it farewel.

Teignmouth,
April 10, 1818.

ENDYMION.

BOOK I.

A thing of beauty is a joy for ever:
Its loveliness increases; it will never
Pass into nothingness; but still will keep
A bower quiet for us, and a sleep
Full of sweet dreams, and health, and quiet breathing.
Therefore, on every morrow, are we wreathing
A flowery band to bind us to the earth,
Spite of despondence, of the inhuman dearth
Of noble natures, of the gloomy days,
Of all the unhealthy and o'er-darkened ways
Made for our searching: yes, in spite of all,
Some shape of beauty moves away the pall
From our dark spirits. Such the sun, the moon,
Trees old and young, sprouting a shady boon
For simple sheep; and such are daffodils
With the green world they live in; and clear rills
That for themselves a cooling covert make
'Gainst the hot season; the mid forest brake,
Rich with a sprinkling of fair musk-rose blooms:
And such too is the grandeur of the dooms
We have imagined for the mighty dead;
All lovely tales that we have heard or read:
An endless fountain of immortal drink,
Pouring unto us from the heaven's brink.

Nor do we merely feel these essences
For one short hour; no, even as the trees
That whisper round a temple become soon
Dear as the temple's self, so does the moon,
The passion poesy, glories infinite,

Haunt us till they become a cheering light
Unto our souls, and bound to us so fast,
That whether there be shine, or gloom o'ercast,
They alway must be with us, or we die.

Therefore, 'tis with full happiness that I
Will trace the story of Endymion.
The very music of the name has gone
Into my being, and each pleasant scene
Is growing fresh before me as the green
Of our own vallies: so I will begin
Now while I cannot hear the city's din;
Now while the early budders are just new,
And run in mazes of the youngest hue
About old forests; while the willow trails
Its delicate amber; and the dairy pails
Bring home increase of milk. And, as the year
Grows lush in juicy stalks, I'll smoothly steer
My little boat, for many quiet hours,
With streams that deepen freshly into bowers.
Many and many a verse I hope to write,
Before the daisies, vermeil rimm'd and white,
Hide in deep herbage; and ere yet the bees
Hum about globes of clover and sweet peas,
I must be near the middle of my story.
O may no wintry season, bare and hoary,
See it half finished: but let Autumn bold,
With universal tinge of sober gold,
Be all about me when I make an end.
And now at once, adventuresome, I send
My herald thought into a wilderness:
There let its trumpet blow, and quickly dress
My uncertain path with green, that I may speed
Easily onward, thorough flowers and weed.

Upon the sides of Latmos was outspread
A mighty forest; for the moist earth fed
So plenteously all weed-hidden roots
Into o'er-hanging boughs, and precious fruits.
And it had gloomy shades, sequestered deep,

Where no man went; and if from shepherd's keep
A lamp strayed far a-down those inmost glens,
Never again saw he the happy pens
Whither his brethren, bleating with content,
Over the hills at every nightfall went.
Among the shepherds, 'twas believed ever,
That not one fleecy lamb which thus did sever
From the white flock, but pass'd unworried
By angry wolf, or pard with prying head,
Until it came to some unfooted plains
Where fed the herds of Pan: ay great his gains
Who thus one lamb did lose. Paths there were many,
Winding through palmy fern, and rushes fenny,
And ivy banks; all leading pleasantly
To a wide lawn, whence one could only see
Stems thronging all around between the swell
Of turf and slanting branches: who could tell
The freshness of the space of heaven above,
Edg'd round with dark tree tops? through which a dove
Would often beat its wings, and often too
A little cloud would move across the blue.

Full in the middle of this pleasantness
There stood a marble altar, with a tress
Of flowers budded newly; and the dew
Had taken fairy phantasies to strew
Daisies upon the sacred sward last eve,
And so the dawned light in pomp receive.
For 'twas the morn: Apollo's upward fire
Made every eastern cloud a silvery pyre
Of brightness so unsullied, that therein
A melancholy spirit well might win
Oblivion, and melt out his essence fine
Into the winds: rain-scented eglantine
Gave temperate sweets to that well-wooing sun;
The lark was lost in him; cold springs had run
To warm their chilliest bubbles in the grass;
Man's voice was on the mountains; and the mass
Of nature's lives and wonders puls'd tenfold,
To feel this sunrise and its glories old.

Now while the silent workings of the dawn
Were busiest, into that self-same lawn
All suddenly, with joyful cries, there sped
A troop of little children garlanded;
Who gathering round the altar, seemed to pry
Earnestly round as wishing to espy
Some folk of holiday: nor had they waited
For many moments, ere their ears were sated
With a faint breath of music, which ev'n then
Fill'd out its voice, and died away again.
Within a little space again it gave
Its airy swellings, with a gentle wave,
To light-hung leaves, in smoothest echos breaking
Through copse-clad vallies,—ere their death, o'ertaking
The surgy murmurs of the lonely sea.

And now, as deep into the wood as we
Might mark a lynx's eye, there glimmered light
Fair faces and a rush of garments white,
Plainer and plainer shewing, till at last
Into the widest alley they all past,
Making directly for the woodland altar.
O kindly muse! let not my weak tongue falter
In telling of this goodly company,
Of their old piety, and of their glee:
But let a portion of ethereal dew
Fall on my head, and presently unmew
My soul; that I may dare, in wayfaring,
To stammer where old Chaucer used to sing.

Leading the way, young damsels danced along
Bearing the burden of a shepherd song;
Each having a white wicker over brimm'd
With April's tender younglings: next, well trimm'd,
A crowd of shepherds with as sunburnt looks
As may be read of in Arcadian books;
Such as sat listening round Apollo's pipe,
When the great deity, for earth too ripe,
Let his divinity o'er-flowing die
In music, through the vales of Thessaly:

Some idly trailed their sheep-hooks on the ground,
And some kept up a shrilly mellow sound
With ebon-tipped flutes: close after these,
Now coming from beneath the forest trees,
A venerable priest full soberly,
Begirt with ministring looks: alway his eye
Stedfast upon the matted turf he kept,
And after him his sacred vestments swept.
From his right hand there swung a vase, milk-white,
Of mingled wine, out-sparkling generous light;
And in his left he held a basket full
Of all sweet herbs that searching eye could cull:
Wild thyme, and valley-lilies whiter still
Than Leda's love, and cresses from the rill.
His aged head, crowned with beechen wreath,
Seem'd like a poll of ivy in the teeth
Of winter hoar. Then came another crowd
Of shepherds, lifting in due time aloud
Their share of the ditty. After them appear'd,
Up-followed by a multitude that rear'd
Their voices to the clouds, a fair wrought car,
Easily rolling so as scarce to mar
The freedom of three steeds of dapple brown:
Who stood therein did seem of great renown
Among the throng. His youth was fully blown,
Shewing like Ganymede to manhood grown;
And, for those simple times, his garments were
A chieftain king's: beneath his breast, half bare,
Was hung a silver bugle, and between
His nervy knees there lay a boar-spear keen.
A smile was on his countenance; he seem'd,
To common lookers on, like one who dream'd
Of idleness in groves Elysian:
But there were some who feelingly could scan
A lurking trouble in his nether lip,
And see that oftentimes the reins would slip
Through his forgotten hands: then would they sigh,
And think of yellow leaves, of owlets cry,
Of logs piled solemnly.—Ah, well-a-day,
Why should our young Endymion pine away!

Soon the assembly, in a circle rang'd,
Stood silent round the shrine: each look was
    chang'd
To sudden veneration: women meek
Beckon'd their sons to silence; while each cheek
Of virgin bloom paled gently for slight fear.
Endymion too, without a forest peer,
Stood, wan, and pale, and with an awed face,
Among his brothers of the mountain chase.
In midst of all, the venerable priest
Eyed them with joy from greatest to the least,
And, after lifting up his aged hands,
Thus spake he: "Men of Latmos! shepherd bands!
Whose care it is to guard a thousand flocks:
Whether descended from beneath the rocks
That overtop your mountains; whether come
From vallies where the pipe is never dumb;
Or from your swelling downs, where sweet air stirs
Blue hare-bells lightly, and where prickly furze
Buds lavish gold; or ye, whose precious charge
Nibble their fill at ocean's very marge,
Whose mellow reeds are touch'd with sounds for-
    lorn
By the dim echoes of old Triton's horn:
Mothers and wives! who day by day prepare
The scrip, with needments, for the mountain air;
And all ye gentle girls who foster up
Udderless lambs, and in a little cup
Will put choice honey for a favoured youth:
Yea, every one attend! for in good truth
Our vows are wanting to our great god Pan.
Are not our lowing heifers sleeker than
Night-swollen mushrooms? Are not our wide plains
Speckled with countless fleeces? Have not rains
Green'd over April's lap? No howling sad
Sickens our fearful ewes; and we have had
Great bounty from Endymion our lord.
The earth is glad: the merry lark has pour'd
His early song against yon breezy sky,
That spreads so clear o'er our solemnity."

Thus ending, on the shrine he heap'd a spire
Of teeming sweets, enkindling sacred fire;
Anon he stain'd the thick and spongy sod
With wine, in honour of the shepherd-god.
Now while the earth was drinking it, and while
Bay leaves were crackling in the fragrant pile,
And gummy frankincense was sparkling bright
'Neath smothering parsley, and a hazy light
Spread greyly eastward, thus a chorus sang:

"O THOU, whose mighty palace roof doth hang
From jagged trunks, and overshadoweth
Eternal whispers, glooms, the birth, life, death
Of unseen flowers in heavy peacefulness;
Who lov'st to see the hamadryads dress
Their ruffled locks where meeting hazels darken;
And through whole solemn hours dost sit, and hearken
The dreary melody of bedded reeds—
In desolate places, where dank moisture breeds
The pipy hemlock to strange overgrowth;
Bethinking thee, how melancholy loth
Thou wast to lose fair Syrinx—do thou now,
By thy love's milky brow!
By all the trembling mazes that she ran,
Hear us, great Pan!

"O thou, for whose soul-soothing quiet, turtles
Passion their voices cooingly 'mong myrtles,
What time thou wanderest at eventide
Through sunny meadows, that outskirt the side
Of thine enmossed realms: O thou, to whom
Broad leaved fig trees even now foredoom
Their ripen'd fruitage; yellow girted bees
Their golden honeycombs; our village leas
Their fairest-blossom'd beans and poppied corn;
The chuckling linnet its five young unborn,
To sing for thee; low creeping strawberries
Their summer coolness; pent up butterflies
Their freckled wings; yea, the fresh budding year
All its completions—be quickly near,

By every wind that nods the mountain pine,
O forester divine!

"Thou, to whom every fawn and satyr flies
For willing service; whether to surprise
The squatted hare while in half sleeping fit;
Or upward ragged precipices flit
To save poor lambkins from the eagle's maw;
Or by mysterious enticement draw
Bewildered shepherds to their path again;
Or to tread breathless round the frothy main,
And gather up all fancifullest shells
For thee to tumble into Naiads' cells,
And, being hidden, laugh at their out-peeping;
Or to delight thee with fantastic leaping,
The while they pelt each other on the crown
With silvery oak apples, and fir cones brown—
By all the echoes that about thee ring,
Hear us, O satyr king!

"O Hearkener to the loud clapping shears,
While ever and anon to his shorn peers
A ram goes bleating: Winder of the horn,
When snouted wild-boars routing tender corn
Anger our huntsman: Breather round our farms,
To keep off mildews, and all weather harms:
Strange ministrant of undescribed sounds,
That come a swooning over hollow grounds,
And wither drearily on barren moors:
Dread opener of the mysterious doors
Leading to universal knowledge—see,
Great son of Dryope,
The many that are come to pay their vows
With leaves about their brows!

Be still the unimaginable lodge
For solitary thinkings; such as dodge
Conception to the very bourne of heaven,
Then leave the naked brain: be still the leaven,
That spreading in this dull and clodded earth

Gives it a touch ethereal—a new birth:
Be still a symbol of immensity;
A firmament reflected in a sea;
An element filling the space between;
An unknown—but no more: we humbly screen
With uplift hands our foreheads, lowly bending,
And giving out a shout most heaven rending,
Conjure thee to receive our humble Pæan,
Upon thy Mount Lycean!

Even while they brought the burden to a close,
A shout from the whole multitude arose,
That lingered in the air like dying rolls
Of abrupt thunder, when Ionian shoals
Of dolphins bob their noses through the brine.
Meantime, on shady levels, mossy fine,
Young companies nimbly began dancing
To the swift treble pipe, and humming string.
Aye, those fair living forms swam heavenly
To tunes forgotten—out of memory:
Fair creatures! whose young children's children bred
Thermopylæ its heroes—not yet dead,
But in old marbles ever beautiful.
High genitors, unconscious did they cull
Time's sweet first-fruits—they danc'd to weariness,
And then in quiet circles did they press
The hillock turf, and caught the latter end
Of some strange history, potent to send
A young mind from its bodily tenement.
Or they might watch the quoit-pitchers, intent
On either side; pitying the sad death
Of Hyacinthus, when the cruel breath
Of Zephyr slew him,—Zephyr penitent,
Who now, ere Phœbus mounts the firmament,
Fondles the flower amid the sobbing rain.
The archers too, upon a wider plain,
Beside the feathery whizzing of the shaft,
And the dull twanging bowstring, and the raft
Branch down sweeping from a tall ash top,
Call'd up a thousand thoughts to envelope

Those who would watch. Perhaps, the trembling knee
And frantic gape of lonely Niobe,
Poor, lonely Niobe! when her lovely young
Were dead and gone, and her caressing tongue
Lay a lost thing upon her paly lip,
And very, very deadliness did nip
Her motherly cheeks. Arous'd from this sad mood
By one, who at a distance loud halloo'd,
Uplifting his strong bow into the air,
Many might after brighter visions stare:
After the Argonauts, in blind amaze
Tossing about on Neptune's restless ways,
Until, from the horizon's vaulted side,
There shot a golden splendour far and wide,
Spangling those million poutings of the brine
With quivering ore: 'twas even an awful shine
From the exaltation of Apollo's bow;
A heavenly beacon in their dreary woe.
Who thus were ripe for high contemplating,
Might turn their steps towards the sober ring
Where sat Endymion and the aged priest
'Mong shepherds gone in eld, whose looks increas'd
The silvery setting of their mortal star.
There they discours'd upon the fragile bar
That keeps us from our homes ethereal;
And what our duties there: to nightly call
Vesper, the beauty-crest of summer weather;
To summon all the downiest clouds together
For the sun's purple couch; to emulate
In ministring the potent rule of fate
With speed of fire-tailed exhalations;
To tint her pallid cheek with bloom, who cons
Sweet poesy by moonlight: besides these,
A world of other unguess'd offices.
Anon they wander'd, by divine converse,
Into Elysium; vieing to rehearse
Each one his own anticipated bliss.
One felt heart-certain that he could not miss
His quick gone love, among fair blossom'd boughs,
Where every zephyr-sigh pouts, and endows

Her lips with music for the welcoming.
Another wish'd, mid that eternal spring,
To meet his rosy child, with feathery sails,
Sweeping, eye-earnestly, through almond vales:
Who, suddenly, should stoop through the smooth wind,
And with the balmiest leaves his temples bind;
And, ever after, through those regions be
His messenger, his little Mercury.
Some were athirst in soul to see again
Their fellow huntsmen o'er the wide champaign
In times long past; to sit with them, and talk
Of all the chances in their earthly walk;
Comparing, joyfully, their plenteous stores
Of happiness, to when upon the moors,
Benighted, close they huddled from the cold,
And shar'd their famish'd scrips. Thus all out-told
Their fond imaginations,—saving him
Whose eyelids curtain'd up their jewels dim,
Endymion: yet hourly had he striven
To hide the cankering venom, that had riven
His fainting recollections. Now indeed
His senses had swoon'd off: he did not heed
The sudden silence, or the whispers low,
Or the old eyes dissolving at his woe,
Or anxious calls, or close of trembling palms,
Or maiden's sigh, that grief itself embalms:
But in the self-same fixed trance he kept,
Like one who on the earth had never stept.
Aye, even as dead-still as a marble man,
Frozen in that old tale Arabian.

Who whispers him so pantingly and close?
Peona, his sweet sister: of all those,
His friends, the dearest. Hushing signs she made,
And breath'd a sister's sorrow to persuade
A yielding up, a cradling on her care.
Her eloquence did breathe away the curse:
She led him, like some midnight spirit nurse
Of happy changes in emphatic dreams,
Along a path between two little streams,—

Guarding his forehead, with her round elbow,
From low-grown branches, and his footsteps slow
From stumbling over stumps and hillocks small;
Until they came to where these streamlets fall,
With mingled bubblings and a gentle rush,
Into a river, clear, brimful, and flush
With crystal mocking of the trees and sky.
A little shallop, floating there hard by,
Pointed its beak over the fringed bank;
And soon it lightly dipt, and rose, and sank,
And dipt again, with the young couple's weight,—
Peona guiding, through the water straight,
Towards a bowery island opposite;
Which gaining presently, she steered light
Into a shady, fresh, and ripply cove,
Where nested was an arbour, overwove
By many a summer's silent fingering;
To whose cool bosom she was used to bring
Her playmates, with their needle broidery,
And minstrel memories of times gone by.

So she was gently glad to see him laid
Under her favourite bower's quiet shade,
On her own couch, new made of flower leaves,
Dried carefully on the cooler side of sheaves
When last the sun his autumn tresses shook,
And the tann'd harvesters rich armfuls took.
Soon was he quieted to slumbrous rest:
But, ere it crept upon him, he had prest
Peona's busy hand against his lips,
And still, a sleeping, held her finger-tips
In tender pressure. And as a willow keeps
A patient watch over the stream that creeps
Windingly by it, so the quiet maid
Held her in peace: so that a whispering blade
Of grass, a wailful gnat, a bee bustling
Down in the blue-bells, or a wren light rustling
Among sear leaves and twigs, might all be heard.

O magic sleep! O comfortable bird,
That broodest o'er the troubled sea of the mind

Till it is hush'd and smooth! O unconfin'd
Restraint! imprisoned liberty! great key
To golden palaces, strange minstrelsy,
Fountains grotesque, new trees, bespangled caves,
Echoing grottos, full of tumbling waves
And moonlight; aye, to all the mazy world
Of silvery enchantment!—who, upfurl'd
Beneath thy drowsy wing a triple hour,
But renovates and lives?—Thus, in the bower,
Endymion was calm'd to life again.
Opening his eyelids with a healthier brain,
He said: "I feel this thine endearing love
All through my bosom: thou art as a dove
Trembling its closed eyes and sleeked wings
About me; and the pearliest dew not brings
Such morning incense from the fields of May,
As do those brighter drops that twinkling stray
From those kind eyes,—the very home and haunt
Of sisterly affection. Can I want
Aught else, aught nearer heaven, than such tears?
Yet dry them up, in bidding hence all fears
That, any longer, I will pass my days
Alone and sad. No, I will once more raise
My voice upon the mountain-heights; once more
Make my horn parley from their foreheads hoar:
Again my trooping hounds their tongues shall loll
Around the breathed boar: again I'll poll
The fair-grown yew tree, for a chosen bow:
And, when the pleasant sun is getting low,
Again I'll linger in a sloping mead
To hear the speckled thrushes, and see feed
Our idle sheep. So be thou cheered sweet,
And, if thy lute is here, softly intreat
My soul to keep in its resolved course."

Hereat Peona, in their silver source,
Shut her pure sorrow drops with glad exclaim,
And took a lute, from which there pulsing came
A lively prelude, fashioning the way.
In which her voice should wander. 'Twas a lay

More subtle cadenced, more forest wild
Than Dryope's lone lulling of her child;
And nothing since has floated in the air
So mournful strange. Surely some influence rare
Went, spiritual, through the damsel's hand;
For still, with Delphic emphasis, she spann'd
The quick invisible strings, even though she saw
Endymion's spirit melt away and thaw
Before the deep intoxication.
But soon she came, with sudden burst, upon
Her self-possession—swung the lute aside,
And earnestly said: "Brother, 'tis vain to hide
That thou dost know of things mysterious,
Immortal, starry; such alone could thus
Weigh down thy nature. Hast thou sinn'd in aught
Offensive to the heavenly powers? Caught
A Paphian dove upon a message sent?
Thy deathful bow against some deer-herd bent,
Sacred to Dian? Haply, thou hast seen
Her naked limbs among the alders green;
And that, alas! is death. No, I can trace
Something more high perplexing in thy face!"

Endymion look'd at her, and press'd her hand,
And said, "Art thou so pale, who wast so bland
And merry in our meadows? How is this?
Tell me thine ailment: tell me all amiss!—
Ah! thou hast been unhappy at the change
Wrought suddenly in me. What indeed more strange?
Or more complete to overwhelm surmise?
Ambition is no sluggard: 'tis no prize,
That toiling years would put within my grasp,
That I have sigh'd for: with so deadly gasp
No man e'er panted for a mortal love.
So all have set my heavier grief above
These things which happen. Rightly have they done:
I, who still saw the horizontal sun
Heave his broad shoulder o'er the edge of the world,
Out-facing Lucifer, and then had hurl'd
My spear aloft, as signal for the chace—

I, who, for very sport of heart, would race
With my own steed from Araby; pluck down
A vulture from his towery perching; frown
A lion into growling, loth retire—
To lose, at once, all my toil breeding fire,
And sink thus low! but I will ease my breast
Of secret grief, here in this bowery nest.

"This river does not see the naked sky,
Till it begins to progress silverly
Around the western border of the wood,
Whence, from a certain spot, its winding flood
Seems at the distance like a crescent moon:
And in that nook, the very pride of June,
Had I been used to pass my weary eves;
The rather for the sun unwilling leaves
So dear a picture of his sovereign power,
And I could witness his most kingly hour,
When he doth lighten up the golden reins,
And paces leisurely down amber plains
His snorting four. Now when his chariot last
Its beams against the zodiac-lion cast,
There blossom'd suddenly a magic bed
Of sacred ditamy, and poppies red:
At which I wondered greatly, knowing well
That but one night had wrought this flowery spell;
And, sitting down close by, began to muse
What it might mean. Perhaps, thought I, Morpheus,
In passing here, his owlet pinions shook;
Or, it may be, ere matron Night uptook
Her ebon urn, young Mercury, by stealth,
Had dipt his rod in it: such garland wealth
Came not by common growth. Thus on I thought,
Until my head was dizzy and distraught.
Moreover, through the dancing poppies stole
A breeze, most softly lulling to my soul;
And shaping visions all about my sight
Of colours, wings, and bursts of spangly light;
The which became more strange, and strange, and dim,
And then were gulph'd in a tumultuous swim:

And then I fell asleep. Ah, can I tell
The enchantment that afterwards befel?
Yet it was but a dream: yet such a dream
That never tongue, although it overteem
With mellow utterance, like a cavern spring,
Could figure out and to conception bring
All I beheld and felt. Methought I lay
Watching the zenith, where the milky way
Among the stars in virgin splendour pours;
And travelling my eye, until the doors
Of heaven appear'd to open for my flight,
I became loth and fearful to alight
From such high soaring by a downward glance:
So kept me stedfast in that airy trance,
Spreading imaginary pinions wide.
When, presently, the stars began to glide,
And faint away, before my eager view:
At which I sigh'd that I could not pursue,
And dropt my vision to the horizon's verge;
And lo! from opening clouds, I saw emerge
The loveliest moon, that ever silver'd o'er
A shell for Neptune's goblet: she did soar
So passionately bright, my dazzled soul
Commingling with her argent spheres did roll
Through clear and cloudy, even when she went
At last into a dark and vapoury tent—
Whereat, methought, the lidless-eyed train
Of planets all were in the blue again.
To commune with those orbs, once more I rais'd
My sight right upward: but it was quite dazed
By a bright something, sailing down apace,
Making me quickly veil my eyes and face:
Again I look'd and, O ye deities,
Who from Olympus watch our destinies!
Whence that completed form of all completeness?
Whence came that high perfection of all sweetness?
Speak, stubborn earth, and tell me where, O where
Hast thou a symbol of her golden hair?
Not oat-sheaves drooping in the western sun;
Not—thy soft hand, fair sister! let me shun

Such follying before thee—yet she had,
Indeed, locks bright enough to make me mad;
And they were simply gordian'd up and braided,
Leaving, in naked comeliness, unshaded,
Her pearl round ears, white neck, and orbed brow;
The which were blended in, I know not how,
With such a paradise of lips and eyes,
Blush-tinted cheeks, half smiles, and faintest sighs,
That, when I think thereon, my spirit clings
And plays about its fancy, till the stings
Of human neighbourhood envenom all.
Unto what awful power shall I call?
To what high fane?—Ah! see her hovering feet,
More bluely vein'd, more soft, more whitely sweet
Than those of sea-born Venus, when she rose
From out her cradle shell. The wind out-blows
Her scarf into a fluttering pavilion;
'Tis blue, and over-spangled with a million
Of little eyes, as though thou wert to shed,
Over the darkest, lushest blue-bell bed,
Handfuls of daisies."—"Endymion, how strange!
Dream within dream!"—"She took an airy range,
And then, towards me, like a very maid,
Came blushing, waning, willing, and afraid,
And press'd me by the hand: Ah! 'twas too much;
Methought I fainted at the charmed touch,
Yet held my recollection, even as one
Who dives three fathoms where the waters run
Gurgling in beds of coral: for anon,
I felt upmounted in that region
Where falling stars dart their artillery forth,
And eagles struggle with the buffeting north
That balances the heavy meteor-stone;—
Felt too, I was not fearful, nor alone,
But lapp'd and lull'd along the dangerous sky.
Soon, as it seem'd, we left our journeying high,
And straightway into frightful eddies swoop'd;
Such as ay muster where grey time has scoop'd
Huge dens and caverns in a mountain's side:
There hollow sounds arous'd me, and I sigh'd

To faint once more by looking on my bliss—
I was distracted; madly did I kiss
The wooing arms which held me, and did give
My eyes at once to death: but 'twas to live,
To take in draughts of life from the gold fount
Of kind and passionate looks; to count, and count
The moments, by some greedy help that seem'd
A second self, that each might be redeem'd
And plunder'd of its load of blessedness.
Ah, desperate mortal! I ev'n dar'd to press
Her very cheek against my crowned lip,
And, at that moment, felt my body dip
Into a warmer air: a moment more,
Our feet were soft in flowers. There was store
Of newest joys upon that alp. Sometimes
A scent of violets, and blossoming limes,
Loiter'd around us; then of honey cells,
Made delicate from all white-flower bells;
And once, above the edges of our nest,
An arch face peep'd,—an Oread as I guess'd.

"Why did I dream that sleep o'er-power'd me
In midst of all this heaven? Why not see,
Far off, the shadows of his pinions dark,
And stare them from me? But no, like a spark
That needs must die, although its little beam
Reflects upon a diamond, my sweet dream
Fell into nothing—into stupid sleep.
And so it was, until a gentle creep,
A careful moving caught my waking ears,
And up I started: Ah! my sighs, my tears,
My clenched hands;—for lo! the poppies hung
Dew-dabbled on their stalks, the ouzel sung
A heavy ditty, and the sullen day
Had chidden herald Hesperus away,
With leaden looks: the solitary breeze
Bluster'd, and slept, and its wild self did teaze
With wayward melancholy; and I thought,
Mark me, Peona! that sometimes it brought
Faint fare-thee-wells, and sigh-shrilled adieus!—

Away I wander'd—all the pleasant hues
Of heaven and earth had faded: deepest shades
Were deepest dungeons; heaths and sunny glades
Were full of pestilent light; our taintless rills
Seem'd sooty, and o'er-spread with upturn'd gills
Of dying fish; the vermeil rose had blown
In frightful scarlet, and its thorns out-grown
Like spiked aloe. If an innocent bird
Before my heedless footsteps stirr'd, and stirr'd
In little journeys, I beheld in it
A disguis'd demon, missioned to knit
My soul with under darkness; to entice
My stumblings down some monstrous precipice:
Therefore I eager followed, and did curse
The disappointment. Time, that aged nurse,
Rock'd me to patience. Now, thank gentle heaven!
These things, with all their comfortings, are given
To my down-sunken hours, and with thee,
Sweet sister, help to stem the ebbing sea
Of weary life."

                    Thus ended he, and both
Sat silent: for the maid was very loth
To answer; feeling well that breathed words
Would all be lost, unheard, and vain as swords
Against the enchased crocodile, or leaps
Of grasshoppers against the sun. She weeps,
And wonders; struggles to devise some blame;
To put on such a look as would say, *Shame
On this poor weakness*! but, for all her strife,
She could as soon have crush'd away the life
From a sick dove. At length, to break the pause,
She said with trembling chance: "Is this the cause?
This all? Yet it is strange, and sad, alas!
That one who through this middle earth should pass
Most like as sojourning demi-god, and leave
His name upon the harp-string, should achieve
No higher bard than simple maidenhood,
Singing alone, and fearfully,—how the blood
Left his young cheek; and how he used to stray

He knew not where; and how he would say, *nay*,
If any said 'twas love: and yet 'twas love;
What could it be but love? How a ring-dove
Let fall a sprig of yew tree in his path;
And how he died: and then, that love doth scathe,
The gentle heart, as northern blasts do roses;
And then the ballad of his sad life closes
With sighs, and an alas!—Endymion!
Be rather in the trumpet's mouth,—anon
Among the winds at large—that all may hearken!
Although, before the crystal heavens darken,
I watch and dote upon the silver lakes
Pictur'd in western cloudiness, that takes
The semblance of gold rocks and bright gold sands,
Islands, and creeks, and amber-fretted strands
With horses prancing o'er them, palaces
And towers of amethyst,—would I so tease
My pleasant days, because I could not mount
Into those regions? The Morphean fount
Of that fine element that visions, dreams,
And fitful whims of sleep are made of, streams
Into its airy channels with so subtle,
So thin a breathing, not the spider's shuttle,
Circled a million times within the space
Of a swallow's nest-door, could delay a trace,
A tinting of its quality: how light
Must dreams themselves be; seeing they're more slight
Than the mere nothing that engenders them!
Then wherefore sully the entrusted gem
Of high and noble life with thoughts so sick?
Why pierce high-fronted honour to the quick
For nothing but a dream?" Hereat the youth
Look'd up: a conflicting of shame and ruth
Was in his plaited brow: yet his eyelids
Widened a little, as when Zephyr bids
A little breeze to creep between the fans
Of careless butterflies: amid his pains
He seem'd to taste a drop of manna-dew,
Full palatable; and a colour grew
Upon his cheek, while thus he lifeful spake.

"Peona! ever have I long'd to slake
My thirst for the world's praises: nothing base,
No merely slumberous phantasm, could unlace
The stubborn canvas for my voyage prepar'd—
Though now 'tis tatter'd; leaving my bark bar'd
And sullenly drifting: yet my higher hope
Is of too wide, too rainbow-large a scope,
To fret at myriads of earthly wrecks.
Wherein lies happiness? In that which becks
Our ready minds to fellowship divine,
A fellowship with essence; till we shine,
Full alchemiz'd, and free of space. Behold
The clear religion of heaven! Fold
A rose leaf round thy finger's taperness,
And soothe thy lips: hist, when the airy stress
Of music's kiss impregnates the free winds,
And with a sympathetic touch unbinds
Eolian magic from their lucid wombs:
Then old songs waken from enclouded tombs;
Old ditties sigh above their father's grave;
Ghosts of melodious prophecyings rave
Round every spot where trod Apollo's foot;
Bronze clarions awake, and faintly bruit,
Where long ago a giant battle was;
And, from the turf, a lullaby doth pass
In every place where infant Orpheus slept.
Feel we these things?—that moment have we stept
Into a sort of oneness, and our state
Is like a floating spirit's. But there are
Richer entanglements, enthralments far
More self-destroying, leading, by degrees,
To the chief intensity: the crown of these
Is made of love and friendship, and sits high
Upon the forehead of humanity.
All its more ponderous and bulky worth
Is friendship, whence there ever issues forth
A steady splendour; but at the tip-top,
There hangs by unseen film, an orbed drop
Of light, and that is love: its influence,
Thrown in our eyes, genders a novel sense,·

At which we start and fret; till in the end,
Melting into its radiance, we blend,
Mingle, and so become a part of it,—
Nor with aught else can our souls interknit
So wingedly: when we combine therewith,
Life's self is nourish'd by its proper pith,
And we are nurtured like a pelican brood.
Aye, so delicious is the unsating food,
That men, who might have tower'd in the van
Of all the congregated world, to fan
And winnow from the coming step of time
All chaff of custom, wipe away all slime
Left by men-slugs and human serpentry,
Have been content to let occasion die,
Whilst they did sleep in love's elysium.
And, truly, I would rather be struck dumb,
Than speak against this ardent listlessness:
For I have ever thought that it might bless
The world with benefits unknowingly;
As does the nightingale, upperched high,
And cloister'd among cool and bunched leaves—
She sings but to her love, nor e'er conceives
How tiptoe Night holds back her dark-grey hood.
Just so may love, although 'tis understood
The mere commingling of passionate breath,
Produce more than our searching witnesseth:
What I know not: but who, of men, can tell
That flowers would bloom, or that green fruit would
    swell
To melting pulp, that fish would have bright mail,
The earth its dower of river, wood, and vale,
The meadows runnels, runnels pebble-stones,
The seed its harvest, or the lute its tones,
Tones ravishment, or ravishment its sweet,
If human souls did never kiss and greet?

    "Now, if this earthly love has power to make
Men's being mortal, immortal; to shake
Ambition from their memories, and brim
Their measure of content; what merest whim,

Seems all this poor endeavour after fame,
To one, who keeps within his stedfast aim
A love immortal, an immortal too.
Look not so wilder'd; for these things are true,
And never can be born of atomies
That buzz about our slumbers, like brain-flies,
Leaving us fancy-sick. No, no, I'm sure,
My restless spirit never could endure
To brood so long upon one luxury,
Unless it did, though fearfully, espy
A hope beyond the shadow of a dream.
My sayings will the less obscured seem,
When I have told thee how my waking sight
Has made me scruple whether that same night
Was pass'd in dreaming. Hearken, sweet Peona!
Beyond the matron-temple of Latona,
Which we should see but for these darkening boughs,
Lies a deep hollow, from whose ragged brows
Bushes and trees do lean all round athwart,
And meet so nearly, that with wings outraught,
And spreaded tail, a vulture could not glide
Past them but he must brush on every side.
Some moulder'd steps lead into this cool cell,
Far as the slabbed margin of a well,
Whose patient level peeps its crystal eye
Right upward, through the bushes, to the sky.
Oft have I brought thee flowers, on their stalks set
Like vestal primroses, but dark velvet
Edges them round, and they have golden pits:
'Twas there I got them, from the gaps and slits
In a mossy stone, that sometimes was my seat,
When all above was faint with mid-day heat.
And there in strife no burning thoughts to heed,
I'd bubble up the water through a reed;
So reaching back to boy-hood: make me ships
Of moulted feathers, touchwood, alder chips,
With leaves stuck in them; and the Neptune be
Of their petty ocean. Oftener, heavily,
When love-lorn hours had left me less a child,
I sat contemplating the figures wild

Of o'er-head clouds melting the mirror through.
Upon a day, while thus I watch'd, by flew
A cloudy Cupid, with his bow and quiver;
So plainly character'd, no breeze would shiver
The happy chance: so happy, I was fain
To follow it upon the open plain,
And, therefore, was just going; when, behold!
A wonder, fair as any I have told—
The same bright face I tasted in my sleep,
Smiling in the clear well. My heart did leap
Through the cool depth.—It moved as if to flee—
I started up, when lo! refreshfully,
There came upon my face, in plenteous showers,
Dew-drops, and dewy buds, and leaves, and flowers,
Wrapping all objects from my smothered sight,
Bathing my spirit in a new delight.
Aye, such a breathless honey-feel of bliss
Alone preserved me from the drear abyss
Of death; for the fair form had gone again.
Pleasure is oft a visitant; but pain
Clings cruelly to us, like the gnawing sloth
On the deer's tender haunches: late, and loth,
'Tis scar'd away by slow returning pleasure.
How sickening, how dark the dreadful leisure
Of weary days, made deeper exquisite,
By a fore-knowledge of unslumbrous night!
Like sorrow came upon me, heavier still,
Than when I wander'd from the poppy hill:
And a whole age of lingering moments crept
Sluggishly by, ere more contentment swept
Away at once the deadly yellow spleen.
Yes, thrice have I this fair enchantment seen;
Once more been tortured with renewed life.
When last the wintry gusts gave over strife
With the conquering sun of spring, and left the skies
Warm and serene, but yet with moistened eyes
In pity of the shatter'd infant buds,—
That time thou didst adorn, with amber studs,
My hunting cap, because I laugh'd and smil'd,
Chatted with thee, and many days exil'd

All torment from my breast;—'twas even then,
Straying about, yet, coop'd up in the den
Of helpless discontent,—hurling my lance
From place to place, and following at chance,
At last, by hap, through some young trees it struck,
And, plashing among bedded pebbles, stuck
In the middle of a brook,—whose silver ramble
Down twenty little falls, through reeds and bramble,
Tracing along, it brought me to a cave,
Whence it ran brightly forth, and white did lave
The nether sides of mossy stones and rock,—
'Mong which it gurgled blythe adieus, to mock
Its own sweet grief at parting. Overhead,
Hung a lush screen of drooping weeds, and spread
Thick, as to curtain up some wood-nymph's home.
"Ah! impious mortal, whither do I roam?"
Said I, low voic'd: "Ah, whither! 'Tis the grot
Of Proserpine, when Hell, obscure and hot,
Doth her resign; and where her tender hands
She dabbles, on the cool and sluicy sands:
Or 'tis the cell of Echo, where she sits,
And babbles thorough silence, till her wits
Are gone in tender madness, and anon,
Faints into sleep, with many a dying tone
Of sadness. O that she would take my vows,
And breathe them sighingly among the boughs,
To sue her gentle ears for whose fair head,
Daily, I pluck sweet flowerets from their bed,
And weave them dyingly—send honey-whispers
Round every leaf, that all those gentle lispers
May sigh my love unto her pitying!
O charitable echo! hear, and sing
This ditty to her!—tell her"—so I stay'd
My foolish tongue, and listening, half afraid,
Stood stupefied with my own empty folly,
And blushing for the freaks of melancholy.
Salt tears were coming, when I heard my name
Most fondly lipp'd, and then these accents came:
"Endymion! the cave is secreter
Than the isle of Delos. Echo hence shall stir

No sighs but sigh-warm kisses, or light noise
Of thy combing hand, the while it travelling cloys
And trembles through my labyrinthine hair."
At that oppress'd I hurried in.—Ah! where
Are those swift moments? Whither are they fled?
I'll smile no more, Peona; nor will wed
Sorrow the way to death: but patiently
Bear up against it: so farewel, sad sigh;
And come instead demurest meditation,
To occupy me wholly, and to fashion
My pilgrimage for the world's dusky brink.
No more will I count over, link by link,
My chain of grief: no longer strive to find
A half-forgetfulness in mountain wind
Blustering about my ears: aye, thou shalt see,
Dearest of sisters, what my life shall be;
What a calm round of hours shall make my days.
There is a paly flame of hope that plays
Where'er I look: but yet, I'll say 'tis naught—
And here I bid it die. Have not I caught,
Already, a more healthy countenance?
By this the sun is setting; we may chance
Meet some of our near-dwellers with my car."

This said, he rose, faint-smiling like a star
Through autumn mists, and took Peona's hand:
They stept into the boat, and launch'd from land.

ENDYMION.

BOOK II.

O SOVEREIGN power of love! O grief! O balm!
All records, saving thine, come cool, and calm,
And shadowy, through the mist of passed years:
For others, good or bad, hatred and tears
Have become indolent; but touching thine,
One sigh doth echo, one poor sob doth pine,
One kiss brings honey-dew from buried days.
The woes of Troy, towers smothering o'er their blaze,

Stiff-holden shields, far-piercing spears, keen blades,
Struggling, and blood, and shrieks—all dimly fades
Into some backward corner of the brain;
Yet, in our very souls, we feel amain
The close of Troilus and Cressid sweet.
Hence, pageant history! hence, gilded cheat!
Swart planet in the universe of deeds!
Wide sea, that one continuous murmur breeds
Along the pebbled shore of memory!
Many old rotten-timber'd boats there be
Upon thy vaporous bosom, magnified
To goodly vessels; many a sail of pride,
And golden keel'd is left unlaunch'd and dry.
But wherefore this? What care, though owl did fly
About the great Athenian admiral's mast?
What care, though striding Alexander past
The Indus with his Macedonian numbers?
Though old Ulysses tortured from his slumbers
The glutted Cyclops, what care?—Juliet leaning
Amid her window-flowers,—sighing,—weaning
Tenderly her fancy from its maiden snow,
Doth more avail than these: the silver flow
Of Hero's tears, the swoon of Imogen,
Fair Pastorella in the bandit's den,
Are things to brood on with more ardency
Than the death-day of empires. Fearfully
Must such conviction come upon his head,
Who, thus far, discontent has dared to tread,
Without one muse's smile, or kind behest,
The path of love and poesy. But rest,
In chaffing restlessness, is yet more drear
Than to be crush'd ,in striving to uprear
Love's standard on the battlements of song.
So once more days and nights aid me along,
Like legion'd soldiers.

                    Brain-sick shepherd-prince,
What promise hast thou faithful guarded since
The day of sacrifice? Or, have new sorrows
Come with the constant dawn upon thy morrows?

Alas! 'tis his old grief. For many days,
Has he been wandering in uncertain ways:
Through wilderness, and woods of mossed oaks
Counting his woe-worn minutes, by the strokes
Of the lone woodcutter; and listening still,
Hour after hour, to each lush-leav'd rill.
Now he is sitting by a shady spring,
And elbow-deep with feverous fingering
Stems the upbursting cold: a wild rose tree
Pavilions him in bloom, and he doth see
A bud which snares his fancy: lo! but now
He plucks it, dips its stalk in the water: how!
It swells, it buds, it flowers beneath his sight;
And, in the middle, there is softly pight
A golden butterfly; upon whose wings
There must be surely character'd strange things,
For with wide eye he wonders, and smiles oft.

Lightly this little herald flew aloft,
Follow'd by glad Endymion's clasped hands:
Onward it flies. From langour's sullen bands
His limbs are loos'd, and eager, on he hies
Dazzled to trace it in the sunny skies.
It seem'd he flew, the way so easy was;
And like a new-born spirit did he pass
Through the green evening quiet in the sun,
O'er many a heath, through many a woodland dun,
Through buried paths, where sleepy twilight dreams
The summer time away. One track unseams
A wooded cleft, and, far away, the blue
Of ocean fades upon him; then, anew,
He sinks adown a solitary glen,
Where there was never sound of mortal men,
Saving, perhaps, some snow-light cadences
Melting to silence, when upon the breeze
Some holy bark let forth an anthem sweet,
To cheer itself to Delphi. Still his feet
Went swift beneath the merry-winged guide,
Until it reached a splashing foutain's side
That, near a cavern's mouth, for ever pour'd

Unto the temperate air: then high it soar'd,
And, downward, suddenly began to dip,
As if, athirst with so much toil, 'twould sip
The crystal spout-head: so it did, with touch
Most delicate, as though afraid to smutch
Even with mealy gold the waters clear.
But, at that very touch, to disappear
So fairy-quick, was strange! Bewildered,
Endymion sought around, and shook each bed
Of covert flowers in vain; and then he flung
Himself along the grass. What gentle tongue,
What whisperer disturb'd his gloomy rest?
It was a nymph uprisen to the breast
In the fountain's pebbly margin, and she stood
'Mong lilies like the youngest of the brood.
To him her dripping hand she softly kist,
And anxiously began to plait and twist
Her ringlets round her fingers, saying: "Youth!
Too long, alas, hast thou starv'd on the ruth,
The bitterness of love: too long indeed,
Seeing thou art so gentle. Could I weed
Thy soul of care, by heavens, I would offer
All the bright riches of my crystal coffer
To Amphitrite; all my clear-eyed fish,
Golden, or rainbow-sided, or purplish,
Vermilion-tail'd, or finn'd with silvery gauze;
Yea, or my veined pebble-floor, that draws
A virgin light to the deep; my grotto-sands
Tawny and gold, ooz'd slowly from far lands
By my diligent springs; my level lilies, shells,
My charming rod, my potent river spells;
Yes, every thing, even to the pearly cup
Meander gave me,—for I bubbled up
To fainting creatures in a desert wild.
But woe is me, I am but as a child
To gladden thee; and all I dare to say,
Is, that I pity thee; that on this day
I've been thy guide; that thou must wander far
In other regions, past the scanty bar
To mortal steps, before thou can'st be ta'en

From every wasting sigh, from every pain,
Into the gentle bosom of thy love.
Why it is thus, one knows in heaven above:
But, a poor Naiad, I guess not. Farewel!
I have a ditty for my hollow cell."

Hereat, she vanished from Endymion's gaze,
Who brooded o'er the water in amaze:
The dashing fount pour'd on, and where its pool
Lay, half asleep, in grass and rushes cool,
Quick waterflies and gnats were sporting still,
And fish were dimpling, as if good nor ill
Had fallen out that hour. The wanderer,
Holding his forehead, to keep off the burr
Of smothering fancies, patiently sat down;
And, while beneath the evening's sleepy frown
Glow-worms began to trim their starry lamps,
Thus breath'd he to himself: "Whoso encamps
To take a fancied city of delight,
O what a wretch is he! and when 'tis his,
After long toil and travelling, to miss
The kernel of his hopes, how more than vile:
Yet, for him there's refreshment even in toil;
Another city doth he set about,
Free from the smallest pebble-bead of doubt
That he will seize on trickling honey-combs:
Alas, he finds them dry; and then he foams,
And onward to another city speeds.
But this is human life: the war, the deeds,
The disappointment, the anxiety,
Imagination's struggles, far and nigh,
All human; bearing in themselves this good,
That they are still the air, the subtle food,
To make us feel existence, and to shew
How quiet death is. Where soil is men grow,
Whether to weeds or flowers; but for me,
There is no depth to strike in: I can see
Nought earthly worth my compassing; so stand
Upon a misty, jutting head of land—
Alone? No, no; and by the Orphean lute,

When mad Eurydice is listening to 't;
I'd rather stand upon this misty peak,
With not a thing to sigh for, or to seek,
But the soft shadow of my thrice-seen love,
Than be—I care not what. O meekest dove
Of heaven! O Cynthia, ten-times bright and fair!
From thy blue throne, now filling all the air,
Glance but one little beam of temper'd light
Into my bosom, that the dreadful might
And tyranny of love be somewhat scar'd!
Yet do not so, sweet queen; one torment spar'd,
Would give a pang to jealous misery,
Worse than the torment's self: but rather tie
Large wings upon my shoulders, and point out
My love's far dwelling. Though the playful rout
Of Cupids shun thee, too divine art thou,
Too keen in beauty, for thy silver prow
Not to have dipp'd in love's most gentle stream.
O be propitious nor severely deem
My madness impious; for, by all the stars
That tend thy bidding, I do think the bars
That kept my spirit in are burst—that I
Am sailing with thee through the dizzy sky!
How beautiful thou art! The world how deep!
How tremulous-dazzlingly the wheels sweep
Around their axle! Then these gleaming reins,
How lithe! When this thy chariot attains
Its airy goal, haply some bower veils
Those twilight eyes? Those eyes!—my spirit fails—
Dear goddess, help! or the wide-gaping air
Will gulph me—help!"—At this with madden'd stare,
And lifted hands, and trembling lips he stood;
Like old Deucalion mountain'd o'er the flood,
Or blind Orion hungry for the morn.
And, but from the deep cavern there was borne
A voice, he had been froze to senseless stone;
Nor sigh of his, nor plaint, nor passion'd moan
Had more been heard. Thus swell'd it forth: "Descend,
Young mountaineer! descend where alleys bend
Into the sparry hollows of the world!

Oft hast thou seen bolts of the thunder hurl'd
As from thy threshold; day by day hast been
A little lower than the chilly sheen
Of icy pinnacles, and dipp'dst thine arms
Into the deadening ether that still charms
Their marble being: now, as deep profound
As those are high, descend! He ne'er is crown'd
With immortality, who fears to follow
Where airy voices lead: so through the hollow,
The silent mysteries of earth, descend!"

He heard but the last words, nor could contend
One moment in reflection: for he fled
Into the fearful deep, to hide his head
From the clear moon, the trees, and coming madness.

'Twas far too strange, and wonderful for sadness;
Sharpening, by degrees, his appetite
To dive into the deepest. Dark, nor light,
The region; nor bright, nor sombre wholly,
But mingled up; a gleaming melancholy;
A dusky empire and its diadems;
One faint eternal eventide of gems.
Aye, millions sparkled on a vein of gold,
Along whose track the prince quick footsteps told,
With all its lines abrupt and angular:
Out-shooting sometimes, like a meteor-star,
Through a vast antre; then the metal woof,
Like Vulcan's rainbow, with some monstrous roof
Curves hugely: now, far in the deep abyss,
It seems an angry lightning, and doth hiss
Fancy into belief: anon it leads
Through winding passages, where sameness breeds
Vexing conceptions of some sudden change;
Whether to silver grots, or giant range
Of sapphire columns, or fantastic bridge
Athwart a flood of crystal. On a ridge
Now fareth he, that o'er the vast beneath
Towers like an ocean-cliff, and whence he seeth
A hundred waterfalls, whose voices come
But as the murmuring surge. Chilly and numb

His bosom grew, when first he, far away,
Descried an orbed diamond, set to fray
Old darkness from his throne: t'was like the sun
Uprisen o'er chaos: and with such a stun
Came the amazement, that, absorb'd in it,
He saw not fiercer wonders—past the wit
Of any spirit to tell, but one of those
Who, when this planet's sphering time doth close,
Will be its high remembrancers: who they?
The mighty ones who have made eternal day
For Greece and England. While astonishment
With deep-drawn sighs was quieting, he went
Into a marble gallery, passing through
A mimic temple, so complete and true
In sacred custom, that he well nigh fear'd
To search it inwards; whence far off appear'd,
Through a long pillar'd vista, a fair shrine,
And, just beyond, on light tiptoe divine,
A quiver'd Dian. Stepping awfully,
The youth approach'd; oft turning his veil'd eye
Down sidelong aisles, and into niches old.
And when, more near against the marble cold
He had touch'd his forehead, he began to thread
All courts and passages, where silence dead
Rous'd by his whispering footsteps murmured faint:
And long he travers'd to and fro, to acquaint
Himself with every mystery, and awe;
Till, weary, he sat down before the maw
Of a wide outlet, fathomless and dim
To wild uncertainty and shadows grim.
There, when new wonders ceas'd to float before,
And thoughts of self came on, how crude and sore
The journey homeward to habitual self!
A mad pursuing of the fog-born elf,
Whose flitting lantern, through rude nettle-briar,
Cheats us into a swamp, into a fire,
Into the bosom of a hated thing.

What misery most drowningly doth sing
In lone Endymion's ear, now he has caught

The goal of consciousness? Ah, 'tis the thought,
The deadly feel of solitude: for lo!
He cannot see the heavens, nor the flow
Of rivers, nor hill-flowers running wild
In pink and purple chequer, nor, up-pil'd,
The cloudy rack slow journeying in the west,
Like herded elephants; nor felt, nor prest
Cool grass, nor tasted the fresh slumberous air;
But far from such companionship to wear
An unknown time, surcharg'd with grief, away,
Was now his lot. And must he patient stay,
Tracing fantastic figures with his spear?
"No!" exclaimed he, "why should I tarry here?"
No! loudly echoed times innumerable.
At which he straightway started, and 'gan tell
His paces back into the temple's chief;
Warming and glowing strong in the belief
Of help from Dian: so that when again
He caught her airy form, thus did he plain,
Moving more near the while. "O Haunter chaste
Of river sides, and woods, and heathy waste,
Where with thy silver bow and arrows keen
Art thou now forested? O woodland Queen,
What smoothest air thy smoother forehead woos?
Where dost thou listen to the wide halloos
Of thy disparted nymphs? Through what dark tree
Glimmers thy crescent? Wheresoe'er it be,
'Tis in the breath of heaven: thou dost taste
Freedom as none can taste it, nor dost waste
Thy loveliness in dismal elements;
But, finding in our green earth sweet contents,
There livest blissfully. Ah, if to thee
It feels Elysian how rich to me,
An exil'd mortal, sounds its pleasant name!
Within my breast there lives a choking flame—
O let me cool it among the zephyr-boughs!
A homeward fever parches up my tongue—
O let me slake it at the running springs!
Upon my ear a noisy nothing springs—
O let me once more hear the linnet's note!

Before mine eyes thick films and shadows float—
O let me 'noint them with the heaven's light!
Dost thou now lave thy feet and ankles white?
O think how sweet to me the freshening sluice!
Dost thou now please thy thirst with berry-juice?
O think how this dry palate would rejoice!
If in soft slumber thou dost hear my voice,
Oh think how I should love a bed of flowers!—
Young goddess! let me see my native bowers!
Deliver me from this rapacious deep!"

Thus ending loudly, as he would o'erleap
His destiny, alert he stood: but when
Obstinate silence came heavily again,
Feeling about for its old couch of space
And airy cradle, lowly bow'd his face
Desponding, o'er the marble floor's cold thrill.
But 'twas not long; for, sweeter than the rill
To its old channel, or a swollen tide
To margin sallows, were the leaves he spied,
And flowers, and wreaths, and ready myrtle crowns
Up heaping through the slab: refreshment drowns
Itself, and strives its own delights to hide—
Nor in one spot alone; the floral pride
In a long whispering birth enchanted grew
Before his footsteps; as when heav'd anew
Old ocean rolls a lengthened wave to the shore,
Down whose green back the short-liv'd foam, all hoar,
Bursts gradual, with a wayward indolence.

Increasing still in heart, and pleasant sense,
Upon his fairy journey on he hastes;
So anxious for the end, he scarcely wastes
One moment with his hand among the sweets:
Onward he goes—he stops—his bosom beats
As plainly in his ear, as the faint charm
Of which the throbs were born. This still alarm,
This sleepy music, forc'd him walk tiptoe:
For it came more softly than the east could blow
Arion's magic to the Atlantic isles;

Or than the west, made jealous by the smiles
Of thron'd Apollo, could breathe back the lyre
To seas Ionian and Tyrian.

O did he ever live, that lonely man,
Who lov'd—and music slew not? 'Tis the pest
Of love, that fairest joys give most unrest;
That things of delicate and tenderest worth
Are swallow'd all, and made a seared dearth,
By one consuming flame: it doth immerse
And suffocate true blessings in a curse.
Half-happy, by comparison of bliss,
Is miserable. 'Twas even so with this
Dew-dropping melody, in the Carian's ear;
First heaven, then hell, and then forgotten clear,
Vanish'd in elemental passion.

And down some swart abysm he had gone,
Had not a heavenly guide benignant led
To where thick myrtle branches, 'gainst his head
Brushing, awakened: then the sounds again
Went noiseless as a passing noontide rain
Over a bower, where little space he stood;
For as the sunset peeps into a wood
So saw he panting light, and towards it went
Through winding alleys; and lo, wonderment!
Upon soft verdure saw, one here, one there,
Cupids a slumbering on their pinions fair.

After a thousand mazes overgone,
At last, with sudden step, he came upon
A chamber, myrtle wall'd, embowered high,
Full of light, incense, tender minstrelsy,
And more of beautiful and strange beside:
For on a silken couch of rosy pride,
In midst of all, there lay a sleeping youth
Of fondest beauty; fonder, in fair sooth,
Than sighs could fathom, or contentment reach:
And coverlids gold-tinted like the peach,
Or ripe October's faded marigolds,

Fell sleek about him in a thousand folds—
Not hiding up an Apollonian curve
Of neck and shoulder, nor the tenting swerve
Of knee from knee, nor ankles pointing light;
But rather, giving them to the filled sight
Officiously. Sideway his face repos'd
On one white arm, and tenderly unclos'd,
By tenderest pressure, a faint damask mouth
To slumbery pout; just as the morning south
Disparts a dew-lipp'd rose. Above his head,
Four lily stalks did their white honours wed
To make a coronal; and round him grew
All tendrils green, of every bloom and hue,
Together intertwin'd and trammel'd fresh:
The vine of glossy sprout; the ivy mesh,
Shading its Ethiop berries; and woodbine,
Of velvet leaves and bugle-blooms divine;
Convolvulus in streaked vases flush;
The creeper, mellowing for an autumn blush;
And virgin's bower trailing airily;
With others of the sisterhood. Hard by,
Stood serene Cupids watching silently.
One, kneeling to a lyre, touch'd the strings,
Muffling to death the pathos with his wings;
And, ever and anon, uprose to look
At the youth's slumber; while another took
A willow-bough, distilling odorous dew,
And shook it on his hair; another flew
In through the woven roof, and fluttering-wise
Rain'd violets upon his sleeping eyes.

At these enchantments, and yet many more,
The breathless Latmian wonder'd o'er and o'er;
Until, impatient in embarrassment,
He forthright pass'd, and lightly treading went
To that same feather'd lyrist, who straightway,
Smiling, thus whisper'd: "Though from upper day
Thou art a wanderer, and thy pressence here
Might seem unholy, be of happy cheer!
For 'tis the nicest touch of human honour,

When some ethereal and high-favouring donor
Presents immortal bowers to mortal sense;
As now 'tis done to thee, Endymion. Hence
Was I in no wise startled. So recline
Upon these living flowers. Here is wine,
Alive with sparkles—never, I aver,
Since Ariadne was a vintager,
So cool a purple: taste these juicy pears,
Sent me by sad Vertumnus,when his fears
Were high about Pomona: here is cream,
Deepening to richness from a snowy gleam;
Sweeter than that nurse Amalthea skimm'd
For the boy Jupiter: and here, undimm'd
By any touch, a bunch of blooming plums
Ready to melt between an infant's gums:
And here is manna pick'd from Syrian trees,
In starlight, by the three Hesperides.
Feast on, and meanwhile I will let thee know
Of all these things around us." He did so,
Still brooding o'er the cadence of his lyre;
And thus: "I need not any hearing tire
By telling how the sea-born goddess pin'd
For a mortal youth, and how she strove to bind
Him all in all unto her doting self.
Who would not be so prison'd? but, fond elf,
He was content to let her amorous plea
Faint throught his careless arms; content to see
An unseiz'd heaven dying at his feet;
Content, O fool! to make a cold retreat,
When on the pleasant grass such love, lovelorn,
Lay sorrowing; when every tear was born
Of diverse passion; when her lips and eyes
Were clos'd in sullen moisture, and quick sighs
Came vex'd and pettish through her nostrils small.
Hush! no exclaim—yet, justly mightst thou call
Curses upon his head.—I was half glad,
But my poor mistress went distract and mad,
When the boar tusk'd him: so away she flew
To Jove's high throne, and by her plainings drew
Immortal tear-drops down the thunderer's beard;

Whereon, it was decreed he should be rear'd
Each summer time to life. Lo! this is he,
That same Adonis, safe in the privacy
Of this still region all his winter-sleep.
Aye, sleep; for when our love-sick queen did weep
Over his waned corse, the tremulous shower
Heal'd up the wound, and, with a balmy power,
Medicined death to a lengthened drowsiness:
The which she fills with visions, and doth dress
In all this quiet luxury; and hath set
Us young immortals, without any let,
To watch his slumber through. 'Tis well nigh pass'd,
Even to a moment's filling up, and fast
She scuds with summer breezes, to pant through
The first long kiss, warm firstling, to renew
Embower'd sports in Cytherea's isle.
Look! how those winged listeners all this while
Stand anxious: see! behold!"—This clamant word
Broke through the careful silence; for they heard
A rustling noise of leaves, and out there flutter'd
Pigeons and doves: Adonis something mutter'd,
The while one hand, that erst upon his thigh
Lay dormant, mov'd convuls'd and gradually
Up to his forehead. Then there was a hum
Of sudden voices, echoing, "Come! come!
Arise! awake! Clear summer has forth walk'd
Unto the clover-sward, and she has talk'd
Full soothingly to every nested finch:
Rise, Cupids! or we'll give the blue-bell pinch
To your dimpled arms. Once more sweet life begin!"
At this, from every side they hurried in,
Rubbing their sleepy eyes with lazy wrists,
And doubling overhead their little fists
In backward yawns. But all were soon alive:
For as delicious wine doth, sparkling, dive
In nectar'd clouds and curls through water fair,
So from the arbour roof down swell'd an air
Odorous and enlivening; making all
To laugh, and play, and sing, and loudly call
For their sweet queen: when lo! the wreathed green

Disparted, and far upward could be seen
Blue heaven, and a silver car, air-borne,
Whose silent wheels, fresh wet from clouds of morn,
Spun off a drizzling dew,—which falling chill
On soft Adonis' shoulders, made him still
Nestle and turn uneasily about.
Soon were the white doves plain, with necks stretch'd
    out,
And silken traces lighten'd in descent;
And soon, returning from love's banishment,
Queen Venus leaning downward open arm'd:
Her shadow fell upon his breast, and charm'd
A tumult to his heart, and a new life
Into his eyes. Ah, miserable strife,
But for her comforting! unhappy sight,
But meeting her blue orbs! Who, who can write
Of these first minutes? The unchariest muse
To embracements warm as theirs makes coy excuse.

O it has ruffled every spirit there,
Saving love's self, who stands superb to share
The general gladness: awfully he stands;
A sovereign quell is in his waving hands;
No sight can bear the lightning of his bow;
His quiver is mysterious, none can know
What themselves think of it; from forth his eyes
There darts strange light of varied hues and dyes:
A scowl is sometimes on his brow, but who
Look full upon it feel anon the blue
Of his fair eyes run liquid through their souls.
Endymion feels it, and no more controls
The burning prayer within him; so, bent low,
He had begun a plaining of his woe.
But Venus, bending forward, said: "My child,
Favour this gentle youth; his days are wild
With love—he—but alas! too well I see
Thou know'st the deepness of his misery.
Ah, smile not so, my son: I tell thee true,
That when through heavy hours I used to rue
The endless sleep of this new-born Adon',

This stranger ay I pitied. For upon
A dreary morning once I fled away
Into the breezy clouds, to weep and pray
For this my love: for vexing Mars had teaz'd
Me even to tears: thence, when a little eas'd,
Down-looking, vacant, through a hazy wood,
I saw this youth as he despairing stood:
Those same dark curls blown vagrant in the wind:
Those same full fringed lids a constant blind
Over his sullen eyes: I saw him throw
Himself on wither'd leaves, even as though
Death had come sudden; for no jot he mov'd,
Yet mutter'd wildly. I could hear he lov'd
Some fair immortal, and that his embrace
Had zoned her through the night. There is no trace
Of this in heaven: I have mark'd each cheek,
And find it is the vainest thing to seek;
And that of all things 'tis kept secretest.
Endymion! one day thou wilt be blest:
So still obey the guiding hand that fends
Thee safely through these wonders for sweet ends.
'Tis a concealment needful in extreme;
And if I guess'd not so, the sunny beam
Thou shouldst mount up to with me. Now adieu!
Here must we leave thee." — At these words up flew
The impatient doves, up rose the floating car,
Up went the hum celestial. High afar
The Latmian saw them minish into nought;
And, when all were clear vanish'd, still he caught
A vivid lightning from that dreadful bow.
When all was darkened, with Etnean throe
The earth clos'd—gave a solitary moan—
And left him once again in twilight lone.

He did not rave, he did not stare aghast,
For all those visions were o'ergone, and past,
And he in loneliness: he felt assur'd
Of happy times, when all he had endur'd
Would seem a feather to the mighty prize.
So, with unusual gladness, on he hies

Through caves, and palaces of mottled ore,
Gold dome, and crystal wall, and turquois floor,
Black polish'd porticos of awful shade,
And, at the last, a diamond balustrade,
Leading afar past wild magnificence,
Spiral through ruggedest loopholes, and thence
Stretching across a void, then guiding o'er
Enormous chasms, where, all foam and roar,
Streams subterranean tease their granite beds;
Then heighten'd just above the silvery heads
Of a thousand fountains, so that he could dash
The waters with his spear; but at the splash,
Done heedlessly, those spouting columns rose
Sudden a poplar's height, and 'gan to enclose
His diamond path with fretwork, streaming round
Alive, and dazzling cool, and with a sound,
Haply, like dolphin tumults, when sweet shells
Welcome the float of Thetis. Long he dwells
On this delight; for, every minute's space,
The streams with changed magic interlace:
Sometimes like delicatest lattices,
Cover'd with crystal vines; then weeping trees,
Moving about as in a gentle wind,
Which, in a wink, to watery gauze refin'd,
Pour'd into shapes of curtain'd canopies,
Spangled, and rich with liquid broideries
Of flowers, peacocks, swans, and naiads fair.
Swifter than lightning went these wonders rare;
And then the water, into stubborn streams
Collecting, mimick'd the wrought oaken beams,
Pillars, and frieze, and high fantasic roof,
Of those dusk places in times far aloof
Cathedrals call'd. He bade a loth farewel
To these founts Protean, passing gulph, and dell,
And torrent, and ten thousand jutting shapes,
Half seen through deepest gloom, and grisly gapes,
Blackening on every side, and overhead
A vaulted dome like Heaven's, far bespread
With starlight gems: aye, all so huge and strange,
The solitary felt a hurried change

Working within him into something dreary,—
Vex'd like a morning eagle, lost, and weary,
And purblind amid foggy, midnight wolds.
But he revives at once: for who beholds
New sudden things, nor casts his mental slough?
Forth from a rugged arch, in the dusk below,
Came mother Cybele! alone—alone—
In sombre chariot; dark foldings thrown
About her majesty, and front death-pale,
With turrets crown'd. Four maned lions hale
The sluggish wheels; solemn their toothed maws,
Their surly eyes brow-hidden, heavy paws
Uplifted drowsily, and nervy tails
Cowering their tawny brushes. Silent sails
This shadowy queen athwart, and faints away
In another gloomy arch.

              Wherefore delay,
Young traveller, in such a mournful place?
Art thou wayworn, or canst not further trace
The diamond path? And does it indeed end
Abrupt in middle air? Yet earthward bend
Thy forehead, and to Jupiter cloud-borne
Call ardently! He was indeed wayworn;
Abrupt, in middle air, his way was lost;
To cloud-borne Jove he bowed, and there crost
Towards him a large eagle, 'twixt whose wings,
Without one impious word, himself he flings,
Committed to the darkness and the gloom;
Down, down, uncertain to what pleasant doom,
Swift as a fathoming plummet down he fell
Through unknown things; till exhaled asphodel,
And rose, with spicy fannings interbreath'd,
Came swelling forth where little caves were wreath'd
So thick with leaves and mosses, that they seem'd
Large honey-combs of green, and freshly teem'd
With airs delicious. In the greenest nook
The eagle landed him, and farewel took.

  It was a jasmine bower, all bestrown
With golden moss. His every sense had grown

Ethereal for pleasure; 'bove his head
Flew a delight half-graspable; his tread
Was Hesperean; to his capable ears
Silence was music from the holy spheres;
A dewy luxury was in his eyes;
The little flowers felt his pleasant sighs
And stirr'd them faintly. Verdant cave and cell
He wander'd through, of wondering at such swell
Of sudden exaltation: but, "Alas!
Said he, "will all this gush of feeling pass
Away in solitude? And must they wane,
Like melodies upon a sandy plain,
Without an echo? Then shall I be left
So sad, so melancholy, so bereft!
Yet still I feel immortal! O my love,
My breath of life, where art thou? High above,
Dancing before the morning gates of heaven?
Or keeping watch among those starry seven,
Old Atlas' children? Art a maid of the waters,
One of shell-winding Triton's bright-hair'd daughters?
Or art, impossible! a nymph of Dian's,
Weaving a coronal of tender scions
For very idleness? Where'er thou art,
Methinks it now is at my will to start
Into thine arms; to scare Aurora's train,
And snatch thee from the morning; o'er the main
To scud like a wild bird, and take thee off
From thy sea-foamy cradle; or to doff
Thy shepherd vest, and woo thee mid fresh leaves.
No, no, too eagerly my soul deceives
Its powerless self: I know this cannot be.
O let me then by some sweet dreaming flee
To her entrancements: hither sleep awhile!
Hither most gentle sleep! and soothing foil
For some few hours the coming solitude."

Thus spake he, and that moment felt endued
With power to dream deliciously; so wound
Through a dim passage, searching till he found
The smoothest mossy bed and deepest, where

He threw himself, and just into the air
Stretching his indolent arms, he took, O bliss!
A naked waist: "Fair Cupid, whence is this?"
A well-known voice sigh'd, "Sweetest, here am I!"
At which soft ravishment, with doating cry
They trembled to each other.—Helicon!
O fountain'd hill! Old Homer's Helicon!
That thou wouldst spout a little streamlet o'er
These sorry pages; then the verse would soar
And sing above this gentle pair, like lark
Over his nested young: but all is dark
Around thine aged top, and thy clear fount
Exhales in mists to heaven. Aye, the count
Of mighty Poets is made up; the scroll
Is folded by the Muses; the bright roll
Is in Apollo's hand: our dazed eyes
Have seen a new tinge in the western skies:
The world has done its duty. Yet, oh yet,
Although the sun of poesy is set,
These lovers did embrace, and we must weep
That there is no old power left to steep
A quill immortal in their joyous tears.
Long time in silence did their anxious fears
Question that thus it was; long time they lay
Fondling and kissing every doubt away;
Long time ere soft caressing sobs began
To mellow into words, and then there ran
Two bubbling springs of talk from their sweet lips.
"O known Unknown! from whom my being sips
Such darling essence, wherefore may I not
Be ever in these arms? in this sweet spot
Pillow my chin for ever? ever press
These toying hands and kiss their smooth excess?
Why not for ever and for ever feel
That breath about my eyes? Ah, thou wilt steal
Away from me again, indeed, indeed—
Thou wilt be gone away, and wilt not heed
My lonely madness. Speak, my kindest fair!
Is—is it to be so? No! Who will dare
To pluck thee from me? And, of thine own will,

Full well I feel thou wouldst not leave me. Still
Let·me entwine thee surer, surer—now
How can we part? Elysium! who art thou?
Who, that thou canst not be for ever here,
Or lift me with thee to some starry sphere?
Enchantress! tell me by this soft embrace,
By the most soft completion of thy face,
Those lips, O slippery blisses, twinkling eyes,
And by these tenderest, milky sovereignties—
These tenderest, and by the nectar-wine,
The passion"————"O lov'd Ida the divine!
Endymion! dearest! Ah, unhappy me!
His soul will 'scape us—O felicity!
How he does love me! His poor temples beat
To the very tune of love—how sweet, sweet, sweet.
Revive, dear youth, or I shall faint and die;
Revive, or these soft hours will hurry by
In tranced dulness; speak, and let that spell
Affright this lethargy! I cannot quell
Its heavy pressure, and will press at least
My lips to thine, that they may richly feast
Until we taste the life of love again.
What! dost thou move? dost kiss? O bliss! O pain!
I love thee, youth, more than I can conceive;
And so long absence from thee doth bereave
My soul of any rest: yet must I hence:
Yet, can I not to starry eminence
Uplift thee; nor for very shame can own
Myself to thee. Ah, dearest, do not groan
Or thou wilt force me from this secrecy,
And I must blush in heaven. O that I
Had done it already; that the dreadful smiles
At my lost brightness, my impassion'd wiles,
Had waned from Olympus' solemn height,
And from all serious Gods; that our delight
Was quite forgotten, save of us alone!
And wherefore so ashamed? 'Tis but to atone
For endless pleasure, by some coward blushes:
Yet must I be a coward!—Horror rushes
Too palpable before me—the sad look

Of Jove—Minerva's start—no bosom shook
With awe of purity—no Cupid pinion
In reverence veiled—my crystaline dominion
Half lost, and all old hymns made nullity!
But what is this to love? O I could fly
With thee into the ken of heavenly powers,
So thou wouldst thus, for many sequent hours,
Press me so sweetly. Now I swear at once
That I am wise, that Pallas is a dunce—
Perhaps her love like mine is but unknown—
O I do think that I have been alone
In chastity: yes, Pallas has been sighing,
While every eve saw me my hair uptying
With fingers cool as aspen leaves. Sweet love,
I was as vague as solitary dove,
Nor knew that nests were built. Now a soft kiss—
Aye, by that kiss, I vow an endless bliss,
An immortality of passion's thine:
Ere long I will exalt thee to the shine
Of heaven ambrosial; and we will shade
Ourselves whole summers by a river glade;
And I will tell thee stories of the sky,
And breathe thee whispers of its minstrelsy.
My happy love will overwing all bounds!
O let me melt into thee; let the sounds
Of our close voices marry at their birth;
Let us entwine hoveringly—O dearth
Of human words! roughness of mortal speech!
Lispings empyrean will I sometime teach
Thine honied tongue—lute-breathings, which I gasp
To have thee understand, now while I clasp
Thee thus, and weep for fondness—I am pain'd,
Endymion: woe! woe! is grief contain'd
In the very deeps of pleasure, my sole life?"—
Hereat, with many sobs, her gentle strife
Melted into a languor. He return'd
Entranced vows and tears.

                        Ye who have yearn'd
With too much passion, will here stay and pity,

For the mere sake of truth; as 'tis a ditty
Not of these days, but long ago 'twas told
By a cavern wind unto a forest old;
And then the forest told it in a dream
To a sleeping lake, whose cool and level gleam
A poet caught as he was journeying
To Phœbus' shrine; and in it he did fling
His weary limbs, bathing an hour's space,
And after, straight in that inspired place
He sang the story up into the air,
Giving it universal freedom. There
Has it been ever sounding for those ears
Whose tips are glowing hot. The legend cheers
Yon centinel stars; and he who listens to it
Must surely be self-doomed or he will rue it:
For quenchless burnings come upon the heart,
Made fiercer by a fear lest any part
Should be engulphed in the eddying wind,
As much as here is penn'd doth always find
A resting place, thus much comes clear and plain;
Anon the strange voice is upon the wane—
And 'tis but echo'd from departing sound,
That the fair visitant at last unwound
Her gentle limbs, and left the youth asleep.—
Thus the tradition of the gusty deep.

Now turn we to our former chroniclers.—
Endymion awoke, that grief of hers
Sweet paining on his ear: he sickly guess'd
How lone he was once more, and sadly press'd
His empty arms together, hung his head,
And most forlorn upon that widow'd bed
Sat silently. Love's madness he had known:
Often with more than tortured lion's groan
Moanings had burst from him; but now that rage
Had pass'd away: no longer did he wage
A rough-voic'd war against the dooming stars.
No, he had felt too much for such harsh jars:
The lyre of his soul Eolian tun'd
Forgot all violence, and but commun'd

With melancholy thought: O he had swoon'd
Drunken from pleasure's nipple; and his love
Henceforth was dove-like.—Loth was he to move
From the imprinted couch, and when he did,
'Twas with slow, languid paces, and face hid
In muffling hands. So temper'd, out he stray'd
Half seeing visions that might have dismay'd
Alecto's serpents; ravishments more keen
Than Hermes' pipe, when anxious he did lean
Over eclipsing eyes: and at the last
It was a sounding grotto, vaulted, vast,
O'er studded with a thousand, thousand pearls,
And crimson mouthed shells with stubborn curls,
Of every shape and size, even to the bulk
In which whales arbour close, to brood and sulk
Against an endless storm. Moreover too,
Fish-semblances, of green and azure hue,
Ready to snort their streams. In this cool wonder
Endymion sat down, and 'gan to ponder
On all his life: his youth, up to the day
When 'mid acclaim, and feasts, and garlands gay,
He stept upon his shepherd throne: the look
Of his white palace in wild forest nook,
And all the revels he had lorded there:
Each tender maiden whom he once thought fair,
With every friend and fellow-woodlander—
Pass'd like a dream before him. Then the spur
Of the old bards to mighty deeds: his plans
To nurse the golden age 'mong shepherd clans:
That wondrous night: the great Pan-festival:
His sister's sorrow; and his wanderings all,
Until into the earth's deep maw he rush'd:
Then all its buried magic, till it flush'd
High with excessive love. "And now," thought he,
"How long must I remain in jeopardy
Of blank amazements that amaze no more?
Now I have tasted her sweet soul to the core
All other depths are shallow: essences,
Once spiritual, are like muddy lees,
Meant but to fertilize my earthly root,

And make my branches lift a golden fruit
Into the bloom of heaven: other light,
Though it be quick and sharp enough to blight
The Olympian eagle's vision, is dark,
Dark as the parentage of chaos. Hark!
My silent thoughts are echoing from these shells;
Or they are but the ghosts, the dying swells
Of noises far away?—list!"—Hereupon
He kept an anxious ear. The humming tone
Came louder, and behold, there as he lay,
On either side outgush'd, with misty spray,
A copious spring; and both together dash'd
Swift, mad, fantastic round the rocks, and lash'd
Among the conchs and shells of the lofty grot,
Leaving a trickling dew. At last they shot
Down from the ceiling's height, pouring a noise
As of some breathless racers whose hopes poise
Upon the last few steps, and with spent force
Along the ground they took a winding course.
Endymion follow'd—for it seem'd that one
Ever pursued, the other strove to shun—
Follow'd their languid mazes, till well nigh
He had left thinking of the mystery,—
And was now rapt in tender hoverings
Over the vanish'd bliss. Ah! what is it sings
His dream away? What melodies are these?
They sound as through the whispering of trees,
Not native in such barren vaults. Give ear!

    "O Arethusa, peerless nymph! why fear
Such tenderness as mine? Great Dian, why,
Why didst thou hear her prayer? O that I
Were rippling round her dainty fairness now,
Circling about her waist, and striving how
To entice her to a dive! then stealing in
Between her luscious lips and eyelids thin.
O that her shining hair was in the sun,
And I distilling from it thence to run
In amorous rillets down her shrinking form!
To linger on her lily shoulders, warm

Between her kissing breasts, and every charm
Touch raptur'd!—See how painfully I flow:
Fair maid, be pitiful to my great woe,
Stay, stay thy weary course, and let me lead,
A happy wooer, to the flowery mead
Where all that beauty snar'd me."—"Cruel god,
Desist! or my offended mistress' nod
Will stagnate all thy fountains:—tease me not
With syren word—Ah, have I really got
Such power to madden thee? And is it true—
Away, away, or I shall dearly rue
My very thoughts: in mercy then away,
Kindest Alpheus, for should I obey
My own dear will, 'twould be a deadly bane."—
"O, Oread-Queen! would that thou hadst a pain
Like this of mine, then would I fearless turn
And be a criminal."—"Alas, I burn,
I shudder—gentle river, get thee hence.
Alpheus! thou enchanter! every sense
Of mine was once made perfect in these woods.
Fresh breezes, bowery lawns, and innocent floods,
Ripe fruits, and lonely couch, contentment gave;
But ever since I heedlessly did lave
In thy deceitful stream, a panting glow
Grew strong within me: wherefore serve me so,
And call it love? Alas, 'twas cruelty.
Not once more did I close my happy eyes
Amid the thrush's song. Away! Avaunt!
O 'twas a cruel thing."—"Now thou dost taunt
So softly, Arethusa, that I think
If thou wast playing on my shady brink,
Thou wouldst bathe once again. Innocent maid!
Stifle thine heart no more;—nor be afraid
Of angry powers: there are deities
Will shade us with their wings. Those fitful sighs
'Tis almost death to hear: O let me pour
A dewy balm upon them!—fear no more,
Sweet Arethusa! Dian's self must feel
Sometimes these very pangs. Dear maiden, steal
Blushing into my soul, and let us fly

These dreary caverns for the open sky.
I will delight thee all my winding course,
From the green sea up to my hidden source
About Arcadian forests; and will shew
The channels where my coolest waters flow
Through mossy rocks; where, 'mid exuberant green,
I roam in pleasant darkness, more unseen
Than Saturn in his exile; where I brim
Round flowery islands, and take thence a skim
Of mealy sweets, which myriads of bees
Buzz from their honied wings: and thou shouldst please
Thyself to choose the richest, where we might
Be incense-pillow'd every summer night.
Doff all sad fears, thou white deliciousness,
And let us be thus comforted; unless
Thou couldst rejoice to see my hopeless stream
Hurry distracted from Sol's temperate beam,
And pour to death along some hungry sands."—
"What can I do, Alpheus? Dian stands
Severe before me: persecuting fate!
Unhappy Arethusa! thou wast late
A huntress free in"—At this, sudden fell
Those two sad streams adown a fearful dell.
The Latmian listen'd, but he heard no more,
Save echo, faint repeating o'er and o'er
The name of Arethusa. On the verge
Of that dark gulph he wept, and said: "I urge
Thee, gentle Goddess of my pilgrimage,
By our eternal hopes, to soothe, to assuage,
If thou art powerful, these lovers pains;
And make them happy in some happy plains.

He turn'd—there was a whelming sound—he stept,
There was a cooler light; and so he kept
Towards it by a sandy path, and lo!
More suddenly than doth a moment go,
The visions of the earth were gone and fled—
He saw the giant sea above his head.

ENDYMION.

BOOK III.

THERE are who lord it o'er their fellow-men
With most prevailing tinsel: who unpen
Their baaing vanities, to browse away
The comfortable green and juicy hay
From human pastures; or, O torturing fact!
Who, through an idiot blink, will see unpack'd
Fire-branded foxes to sear up and singe
Our gold and ripe-ear'd hopes. With not one tinge
Of sanctuary splendour, not a sight
Able to face an owl's, they still are dight
By the blear-eyed nations in empurpled vests,
And crowns and turbans. With unladen breasts,
Save of blown self-applause, they proudly mount
To their spirit's perch, their being's high account,
Their tiptop nothings, their dull skies, their thrones—
Amid the fierce intoxicating tones
Of trumpets, shoutings, and belabour'd drums,
And sudden cannon. Ah! how all this hums,
In wakeful ears, like uproar past and gone—
Like thunder clouds that spake to Babylon,
And set those old Chaldeans to their tasks.—
Are then regalities all gilded masks?
No, there are throned seats unscalable
But by a patient wing, a constant spell,
Or by ethereal things that, unconfin'd,
Can make a ladder of the eternal wind,
And poise about in cloudy thunder-tents
To watch the abysm-birth of elements.
Aye, 'bove the withering of old-lipp'd Fate
A thousand Powers keep religious state,
In water, fiery realm, and airy bourne;
And, silent as a consecrated urn,
Hold sphery sessions for a season due.
Yet few of these far majesties, ah, few!
Have bared their operations to this globe—
Few, who with gorgeous pageantry enrobe
Our piece of heaven—whose benevolence

Shakes hand with our own Ceres; every sense
Filling with spiritual sweets to plenitude,
As bees gorge full their cells. And, by the feud
'Twixt Nothing and Creation, I here swear,
Eterne Apollo! that thy Sister fair
Is of all these the gentlier-mightiest.
When thy gold breath is misting in the west,
She unobserved steals unto her throne,
And there she sits most meek and most alone;
As if she had not pomp subservient;
As if thine eye, high Poet! was not bent
Towards her with the Muses in thine heart;
As if the ministring stars kept not apart,
Waiting for silver-footed messages.
O Moon! the oldest shades 'mong oldest trees
Feel palpitations when thou lookest in:
O Moon! old boughs lisp forth a holier din
The while they feel thine airy fellowship.
Thou dost bless every where, with silver lip
Kissing dead things to life. The sleeping kine,
Couched in thy brightness, dream of fields divine:
Innumerable mountains rise, and rise,
Ambitious for the hallowing of thine eyes;
And yet thy benediction passeth not
One obscure hiding-place, one little spot
Where pleasure may be sent: the nested wren
Has thy fair face within its tranquil ken,
And from beneath a sheltering ivy leaf
Takes glimpses of thee; thou art a relief
To the poor patient oyster, where it sleeps
Within its pearly house.—The mighty deeps,
The monstrous sea is thine—the myriad sea!
O Moon! far-spooming Ocean bows to thee,
And Tellus feels his forehead's cumbrous load.

Cynthia! where art thou now? What far abode
Of green or silvery bower doth enshrine
Such utmost beauty? Alas, thou dost pine
For one as sorrowful: thy cheek is pale
For one whose cheek is pale: thou dost bewail

His tears, who weeps for thee. Where dost thou sigh?
Ah! surely that light peeps from Vesper's eye,
Or what a thing is love! 'Tis She, but lo!
How chang'd, how full of ache, how gone in woe!
She dies at the thinnest cloud; her loveliness
Is wan on Neptune's blue: yet there's a stress
Of love-spangles, just off yon cape of trees,
Dancing upon the waves, as if to please
The curly foam with amorous influence.
O, not so idle: for down-glancing thence
She fathoms eddies, and runs wild about
O'erwhelming water-courses; scaring out
The thorny sharks from hiding-holes, and fright'ning
Their savage eyes with unaccustomed lightning.
Where will the splendor be content to reach?
O love! how potent hast thou been to teach
Strange journeyings! Wherever beauty dwells,
In gulf or aerie, mountains or deep dells,
In light, in gloom, in star or blazing sun,
Thou pointest out the way, and straight 'tis won.
Amid his toil thou gav'st Leander breath;
Thou leddest Orpheus through the gleams of death;
Thou madest Pluto bear thine element;
And now, O winged Chieftain! thou hast sent
A moon-beam to the deep, deep water-world,
To find Endymion.

                On gold sand impearl'd
With lily shells, and pebbles milky white,
Poor Cynthia greeted him, and sooth'd her light
Against his pallid face: he felt the charm
To breathlessness, and suddenly a warm
Of his heart's blood: 'twas very sweet; he stay'd
His wandering steps, and half-entranced laid
His head upon a tuft of straggling weeds,
To taste the gentle moon, and freshening beads,
Lashed from the crystal roof by fishes' tails.
And so he kept, until the rosy veils
Mantling the east, by Aurora's peering hand
Were lifted from the water's breast, and fann'd

Into sweet air; and sober'd morning came
Meekly through billows:—when like taper-flame
Left sudden by a dallying breath of air,
He rose in silence, and once more 'gan fare
Along his fated way.

                    Far had he roam'd,
With nothing save the hollow vast, that foam'd
Above, around, and at his feet; save things
More dead than Morpheus' imaginings:
Old rusted anchors, helmets, breast-plates large
Of gone sea-warriors; brazen beaks and targe;
Rudders that for a hundred years had lost
The sway of human hand; gold vase emboss'd
With long-forgotten story, and wherein
No reveller had ever dipp'd a chin
But those of Saturn's vintage; mouldering scrolls,
Writ in the tongue of heaven, by those souls
Who first were on the earth; and sculptures rude
In ponderous stone, developing the mood
Of ancient Nox;—then skeletons of man,
Of beast, behemoth, and leviathan,
And elephant, and eagle, and huge jaw
Of nameless monster. A cold leaden awe
These secrets struck into him; and unless
Dian had chased away that heaviness,
He might have died: but now, with cheered feel,
He onward kept: wooing these thoughts to steal
About the labyrinth in his soul of love.

   "What is there in thee, Moon! that thou shouldst
      move
My heart so potently? When yet a child
I oft have dried my tears when thou hast smil'd.
Thou seem'dst my sister: hand in hand we went
From eve to morn across the firmament.
No apples would I gather from the tree,
Till thou hadst cool'd their cheeks deliciously:
No tumbling water ever spake romance,
But when my eyes with thine thereon could dance:

110

No woods were green enough, no bower divine,
Until thou liftedst up thine eyelids fine:
In sowing time ne'er would I dibble take,
Or drop a seed, till thou wast wide awake;
And, in the summer tide of blossoming,
No one but thee hath heard me blithely sing
And mesh my dewy flowers all the night.
No melody was like a passing spright
If it went not to solemnize thy reign.
Yes, in my boyhood, every joy and pain
By thee were fashion'd to the self-same end;
And as I grew in years still didst thou blend
With all my ardours: thou wast the deep glen;
Thou wast the mountain-top—the sage's pen—
The poet's harp—the voice of friends—the sun;
Thou wast the river—thou wast glory won;
Thou wast my clarion's blast—thou wast my steed—
My goblet full of wine—my topmost deed:—
Thou wast the charm of women, lovely Moon!
O what a wild and harmonized tune
My spirit struck from all the beautiful!
On some bright essence could I lean, and lull
Myself to immortality: I prest
Nature's soft pillow in a wakeful rest.
But, gentle Orb! there came a nearer bliss—
My strange love came—Felicity's abyss!
She came, and thou didst fade, and fade away—
Yet not entirely; no, thy starry sway
Has been an under-passion to this hour.
Now I begin to feel thine orby power
Is coming fresh upon me: O be kind,
Keep back thine influence, and do not blind
My sovereign vision.—Dearest love, forgive
That I can think away from thee and live!—
Pardon me, airy planet, that I prize
One thought beyond thine argent luxuries!
How far beyond!" At this a surpris'd start
Frosted the springing verdure of his heart;
For as he lifted up his eyes to swear
How his own goddess was past all things fair,

He saw far in the concave green of the sea
An old man sitting calm and peacefully.
Upon a weeded rock this old man sat,
And his white hair was awful, and a mat
Of weeds were cold beneath his cold thin feet;
And, ample as the largest winding-sheet,
A cloak of blue wrapp'd up his aged bones,
O'erwrought with symbols by the deepest groans
Of ambitious magic: every ocean-form
Was woven in with black distinctness; storm,
And calm, and whispering, and hideous roar
Were emblem'd in the woof; with every shape
That skims, or dives, or sleeps, 'twixt cape and cape.
The gulping whale was like a dot in the spell,
Yet look upon it, and 'twould size and swell
To its huge self; and the minutest fish
Would pass the very hardest gazer's wish,
And show his little eye's anatomy.
Then there was pictur'd the regality
Of Neptune; and the sea nymphs round his state,
In beauteous vassalage, look up and wait.
Beside this old man lay a pearly wand,
And in his lap a book, the which he conn'd
So stedfastly, that the new denizen
Had time to keep him in amazed ken,
To mark these shadowings, and stand in awe.

The old man rais'd his hoary head and saw
The wilder'd stranger—seeming not to see,
His features were so lifeless. Suddenly
He woke as from a trance; his snow-white brows
Went arching up, and like two magic ploughs
Furrow'd deep wrinkles in his forehead large,
Which kept as fixedly as rocky marge,
Till round his wither'd lips had gone a smile.
Then up he rose, like one whose tedious toil
Had watch'd for years in forlorn hermitage,
Who had not from mid-life to utmost age
Eas'd in one accent his o'er-burden'd soul,
Even to the trees. He rose: he grasp'd his stole,

With convuls'd clenches waving it abroad,
And in a voice of solemn joy, that aw'd
Echo into oblivion, he said:—

"Thou art the man! Now shall I lay my head
In peace upon my watery pillow: now
Sleep will come smoothly to my weary brow.
O Jove! I shall be young again, be young!
O shell-borne Neptune, I am pierc'd and stung
With new-born life! What shall I do? Where go,
When I have cast this serpent-skin of woe?—
I'll swim to the syrens, and one moment listen
Their melodies, and see their long hair glisten;
Anon upon that giant's arm I'll be,
That writhes about the roots of Sicily:
To northern seas I'll in a twinkling sail,
And mount upon the snortings of a whale
To some black cloud; thence down I'll madly sweep
On forked lightning, to the deepest deep,
Where through some sucking pool I will be hurl'd
With rapture to the other side of the world!
O, I am full of gladness! Sisters three,
I bow full hearted to your old decree!
Yes, every god be thank'd, and power benign,
For I no more shall wither, droop, and pine.
Thou art the man!" Endymion started back
Dismay'd; and, like a wretch from whom the rack
Tortures hot breath, and speech of agony,
Mutter'd: "What lonely death am I to die
In this cold region? Will he let me freeze,
And float my brittle limbs o'er seas?
Or will he touch me with his searing hand,
And leave a black memorial on the sand?
Or tear me piece-meal with a bony saw,
And keep me as a chosen food to draw
His magian fish through hated fire and flame?
O misery of hell! resistless, tame,
Am I to be burnt up? No, I will shout,
Until the gods through heaven's blue look out!—
O Tartarus! but some few days agone

Her soft arms were entwining me, and on
Her voice I hung like fruit among green leaves:
Her lips were all my own, and—ah, ripe sheaves
Of happiness! ye on the stubble droop,
But never may be garner'd. I must stoop
My head, and kiss death's foot. Love! love, farewel!
Is there no hope from thee? This horrid spell
Would melt at thy sweet breath.—By Dian's hind
Feeding from her white fingers, on the wind
I see thy streaming hair! and now, by Pan,
I care not for this old mysterious man!"

He spake, and walking to that aged form,
Look'd high defiance. Lo! his heart 'gan warm
With pity, for the grey-hair'd creature wept.
Had he then wrong'd a heart where sorrow kept?
Had he, though blindly contumelious, brought
Rheum to kind eyes, a sting to human thought,
Convulsion to a mouth of many years?
He had in truth; and he was ripe for tears.
The penitent shower fell, as down he knelt
Before that care-worn sage, who trembling felt
About his large dark locks, and faultering spake:

"Arise, good youth, for sacred Phœbus' sake!
I know thine inmost bosom, and I feel
A very brother's yearning for thee steal
Into mine own: for why? thou openest
The prison gates that have so long opprest
My weary watching. Though thou know'st it not,
Thou art commission'd to this fated spot
For great enfranchisement. O weep no more;
I am a friend to love, to loves of yore:
Aye, hadst thou never lov'd an unknown power
I had been grieving at this joyous hour
But even now most miserable old,
I saw thee, and my blood no longer cold
Gave mighty pulses: in this tottering case
Grew a new heart, which at this moment plays
As dancingly as thine. Be not afraid,

For thou shalt hear this secret all display'd,
Now as we speed towards our joyous task."

So saying, this young soul in age's mask
Went forward with the Carian side by side:
Resuming quickly thus; while ocean's tide
Hung swollen at their backs, and jewel'd sands
Took silently their foot-prints.

                              "My soul stands
Now past the midway from mortality,
And so I can prepare without a sigh
To tell thee briefly all my joy and pain.
I was a fisher once, upon this main,
And my boat danc'd in every creek and bay;
Rough billows were my home by night and day,—
The sea-gulls not more constant; for I had
No housing from the storm and tempests mad,
But hollow rocks,—and they were palaces
Of silent happiness, of slumberous ease:
Long years of misery have told me so.
Aye, thus it was one thousand years ago.
One thousand years! Is it then possible
To look so plainly through them? to dispel
A thousand years with backward glance sublime?
To breathe away as 'twere all scummy slime
From off a crystal pool, to see its deep,
And one's own image from the bottom peep?
Yes: now I am no longer wretched thrall,
My long captivity and moanings all
Are but a slime, a thin-pervading scum,
The which I breathe away, and thronging come
Like things of yesterday my youthful pleasures.

"I touch'd no lute, I sang not, trod no measures:
I was a lonely youth on desert shores.
My sports were lonely, 'mid continuous roars,
And craggy isles, and sea-mew's plaintive cry
Plaining discrepant between sea and sky.
Dolphins were still my playmates; shapes unseen

Would let me feel their scales of gold and green,
Nor be my desolation; and, full oft,
When a dread waterspout had rear'd aloft
Its hungry hugeness, seeming ready ripe
To burst with hoarsest thunderings, and wipe
My life away like a vast sponge of fate,
Some friendly monster, pitying my sad state,
Has dived to its foundations, gulph'd it down,
And left me tossing safely. But the crown
Of all my life was utmost quietude;
More did I love to lie in cavern rude,
Keeping in wait whole days for Neptune's voice,
And if it came at last, hark, and rejoice!
There blush'd no summer eve but I would steer
My skiff along green shelving coasts, to hear
The shepherd's pipe come clear from aery steep,
Mingled with ceaseless bleatings of his sheep:
And never was a day of summer shine,
But I beheld its birth upon the brine:
For I would watch all night to see unfold
Heaven's gates, and Æthon snort his morning gold
Wide o'er the swelling streams: and constantly
At brim of day-tide, on some grassy lea,
My nets would be spread out, and I at rest.
The poor folk of the sea-country I blest
With daily boon of fish most delicate:
They knew not whence this bounty, and elate
Would strew sweet flowers on a sterile beach.

"Why was I not contented? Wherefore reach
At things which, but for thee, O Latmian!
Had been my dreary death? Fool! I began
To feel distemper'd longings: to desire
The utmost privilege that ocean's sire
Could grant in benediction: to be free
Of all his kingdom. Long in misery
I wasted, ere in one extremest fit
I plung'd for life or death. To interknit
One's senses with so dense a breathing stuff
Might seem a work of pain; so not enough

Can I admire how crystal-smooth it felt,
And buoyant round my limbs. At first I dwelt
Whole days and days in sheer astonishment;
Forgetful utterly of self-intent;
Moving but with the mighty ebb and flow.
Then, like a new fledg'd bird that first doth shew
His spreaded feathers to the morrow chill,
I tried in fear the pinions of my will.
'Twas freedom! and at once I visited
The ceaseless wonders of this ocean-bed.
No need to tell thee of them, for I see
That thou hast been a witness—it must be
For these I know thou canst not feel a drouth,
By the melancholy corners of that mouth.
So I will in my story straightway pass
To more immediate matter. Woe, alas!
That love should be my bane! Ah, Scylla fair!
Why did poor Glaucus ever—ever dare
To sue thee to his heart? Kind stranger-youth!
I lov'd her to the very white of truth,
And she would not conceive it. Timid thing!
She fled me swift as sea-bird on the wing,
Round every isle, and point, and promontory,
From where large Hercules wound up his story
Far as Egyptian Nile. My passion grew
The more, the more I saw her dainty hue
Gleam delicately through the azure clear:
Until 'twas too fierce agony to bear;
And in that agony, across my grief
It flash'd, that Circe might find some relief—
Cruel enchantress! So above the water
I rear'd my head, and look'd for Phœbus' daughter.
Æææa's isle was wondering at the moon:—
It seem'd to whirl around me, and a swoon
Left me dead-drifting to that fatal power.

"When I awoke, 'twas in a twilight bower;
Just when the light of morn, with hum of bees,
Stole through its verdurous matting of fresh trees.
How sweet, and sweeter! for I heard a lyre,

And over it a sighing voice expire.
It ceased—I caught light footsteps; and anon
The fairest face that morn e'er look'd upon
Push'd through a screen of roses. Starry Jove!
With tears, and smiles, and honey-words she wove
A net whose thraldom was more bliss than all
The range of flower'd Elysium. Thus did fall
The dew of her rich speech: "Ah! Art awake?
O let me hear thee speak, for Cupid's sake!
I am so oppress'd with joy! Why, I have shed
An urn of tears, as though thou wert cold dead;
And now I find thee living, I will pour
From these devoted eyes their silver store,
Until exhausted of the latest drop,
So it will pleasure thee, and force thee stop
Here, that I too may live: but if beyond
Such cool and sorrowful offerings, thou art fond
Of soothing warmth, of dalliance supreme;
If thou art ripe to taste a long love dream;
If smiles, if dimples, tongues for ardour mute,
Hang in thy vision like a tempting fruit,
O let me pluck it for thee." Thus she link'd
Her charming syllables, till indistinct
Their music came to my o'er-sweeten'd soul;
And then she hover'd over me, and stole
So near, that if no nearer it had been
This furrow'd visage thou hadst never seen.

"Young man of Latmos! thus particular
Am I, that thou may'st plainly see how far
This fierce temptation went: and thou may'st not
Exclaim, How then, was Scylla quite forgot?

"Who could resist? Who in this universe?
She did so breathe ambrosia; so immerse
My fine existence in a golden clime.
She took me like a child of suckling time,
And cradled me in roses. Thus condemn'd,
The current of my former life was stemm'd,
And to this arbitrary queen of sense

I bow'd a tranced vassal: nor would thence
Have mov'd, even though Amphion's harp had woo'd
Me back to Scylla o'er the billows rude.
For as Apollo each eve doth devise
A new appareling for western skies;
So every eve, nay every spendthrift hour
Shed balmy consciousness within that bower.
And I was free of haunts umbrageous;
Could wander in the mazy forest-house
Of squirrels, foxes shy, and antler'd deer,
And birds from coverts innermost and drear
Warbling for very joy mellifluous sorrow—
To me new born delights!

     "Now let me borrow,
For moments few, a temperament as stern
As Pluto's sceptre, that my words not burn
These uttering lips, while I in calm speech tell
How specious heaven was changed to real hell.

 "One morn she left me sleeping: half awake
I sought for her smooth arms and lips, to slake
My greedy thirst with nectarous camel-draughts;
But she was gone. Whereat the barbed shafts
Of disappointment stuck in me so sore,
That out I ran and search'd the forest o'er.
Wandering about in pine and cedar gloom
Damp awe assail'd me; for there 'gan to boom
A sound of moan, an agony of sound,
Sepulchral from the distance all around.
Then came a conquering earth-thunder, and rumbled
That fierce complain to silence: while I stumbled
Down a precipitous path, as if impell'd.
I came to a dark valley.—Groanings swell'd
Poisonous about my ears, and louder grew,
The nearer I approach'd a flame's gaunt blue,
That glar'd before me through a thorny brake.
This fire, like the eye of gordian snake,
Bewitch'd me towards; and I soon was near
A sight too fearful for the feel of fear:

In thicket hid I curs'd the haggard scene—
The banquet of my arms, my arbour queen,
Seated upon an uptorn forest root;
And all around her shapes, wizard and brute,
Laughing, and wailing, groveling, serpenting,
Shewing tooth, tusk, and venom-bag, and sting!
O such deformities! Old Charon's self,
Should he give up awhile his penny pelf,
And take a dream 'mong rushes Stygian,
It could not be so phantasied. Fierce, wan,
And tyrannizing was the lady's look,
As over them a gnarled staff she shook.
Oft-times upon the sudden she laugh'd out,
And from a basket emptied to the rout
Clusters of grapes, the which they raven'd quick
And roar'd for more; with many a hungry lick
About their shaggy jaws. Avenging, slow,
Anon she took a branch of mistletoe,
And emptied on't a black dull-gurgling phial:
Groan'd one and all, as if some piercing trial
Was sharpening for their pitiable bones.
She lifted up the charm: appealing groans
From their poor breasts went sueing to her ear
In vain; remorseless as an infant's bier
She whisk'd against their eyes the sooty oil.
Whereat was heard a noise of painful toil,
Increasing gradual to a tempest rage,
Shrieks, yells, and groans of torture-pilgrimage;
Until their grieved bodies 'gan to bloat
And puff from the tail's end to stifled throat:
Then was appalling silence: then a sight
More wildering than all that hoarse affright;
For the whole herd, as by a whirlwind writhen,
Went through the dismal air like one huge Python
Antagonizing Boreas,—and so vanish'd.
Yet there was not a breath of wind: she banish'd
These phantoms with a nod. Lo! from the dark
Came waggish fauns, and nymphs, and satyrs stark,
With dancing and loud revelry,—and went
Swifter than centaurs after rapine bent.—

Sighing an elephant appear'd and bow'd
Before the fierce witch, speaking thus aloud
In human accent: "Potent goddess! chief
Of pains resistless! make my being brief,
Or let me from this heavy prison fly:
Or give me to the air, or let me die!
I sue not for my happy crown again;
I sue not for my phalanx on the plain;
I sue not for my lone, my widow'd wife;
I sue not for my ruddy drops of life,
My children fair, my lovely girls and boys!
I will forget them; I will pass these joys;
Ask nought so heavenward, so too—too high:
Only I pray, as fairest boon, to die,
Or be deliver'd from this cumbrous flesh,
From this gross, detestable, filthy mesh,
And merely given to the cold bleak air.
Have mercy, Goddess! Circe, feel my prayer!"

That curst magician's name fell icy numb
Upon my wild conjecturing: truth had come
Naked and sabre-like against my heart.
I saw a fury whetting a death-dart;
And my slain spirit, overwrought with fright,
Fainted away in that dark lair of night.
Think, my deliverer, how desolate
My waking must have been! disgust, and hate,
And terrors manifold divided me
A spoil amongst them. I prepar'd to flee
Into the dungeon core of that wild wood:
I fled three days—when lo! before me stood
Glaring the angry witch. O Dis, even now,
A clammy dew is beading on my brow,
At mere remembering her pale laugh, and curse.
"Ha! ha! Sir Dainty! there must be a nurse
Made of rose leaves and thistledown, express,
To cradle thee my sweet, and lull thee: yes,
I am too flinty-hard for thy nice touch:
My tenderest squeeze is but a giant's clutch.
So, fairy-thing, it shall have lullabies

Unheard of yet; and it shall still its cries
Upon some breast more lily-feminine.
Oh, no—it shall not pine, and pine, and pine
More than one pretty, trifling thousand years;
And then 'twere pity, but fate's gentle shears
Cut short its immortality. Sea-flirt!
Young dove of the waters! truly I'll not hurt
One hair of thine: see how I weep and sigh,
That our heart-broken parting is so nigh.
And must we part? Ah, yes, it must be so.
Yet ere thou leavest me in utter woe,
Let me sob over thee my last adieus,
And speak a blessing: Mark me! thou hast thews
Immortal, for thou art of heavenly race:
But such a love is mine, that here I chase
Eternally away from thee all bloom
Of youth, and destine thee towards a tomb.
Hence shalt thou quickly to the watery vast;
And there, ere many days be overpast,
Disabled age shall seize thee; and even then
Thou shalt not go the way of aged men;
But live and wither, cripple and still breathe
Ten hundred years: which gone, I then bequeath
Thy fragile bones to unknown burial.
Adieu, sweet love, adieu!"—As shot stars fall,
She fled ere I could groan for mercy. Stung
And poisoned was my spirit: despair sung
A war-song of defiance 'gainst all hell.
A hand was at my shoulder to compel
My sullen steps; another 'fore my eyes
Moved on with pointed finger. In this guise
Enforced, at the last by ocean's foam
I found me; by my fresh, my native home.
Its tempering coolness, to my life akin,
Came salutary as I waded in;
And, with a blind voluptuous rage, I gave
Battle to the swollen billow-ridge, and drave
Large froth before me, while there yet remain'd
Hale strength, nor from my bones all marrow
    drain'd.

"Young lover, I must weep—such hellish spite
With dry cheek who can tell? While thus my might
Proving upon this element, dismay'd,
Upon a dead thing's face my hand I laid;
I look'd—'twas Scylla! Cursed, cursed Circe!
O vulture-witch, hast never heard of mercy?
Could not thy harshest vengeance be content,
But thou must nip this tender innocent
Because I lov'd her?—Cold, O cold indeed
Were her fair limbs, and like a common weed
The sea-swell took her hair. Dead as she was
I clung about her waist, nor ceas'd to pass
Fleet as an arrow through unfathom'd brine,
Until there shone a fabric crystalline,
Ribb'd and inlaid with coral, pebble, and pearl.
Headlong I darted; at one eager swirl
Gain'd its bright portal, enter'd, and behold!
'Twas vast, and desolate, and icy-cold;
And all around—But wherefore this to thee
Who in few minutes more thyself shalt see?—
I left poor Scylla in a niche and fled.
My fever'd parchings up, my scathing dread
Met palsy half way: soon these limbs became
Gaunt, wither'd, sapless, feeble, cramp'd, and lame.

"Now let me pass a cruel, cruel space,
Without one hope, without one faintest trace
Of mitigation, or redeeming bubble
Of colour'd phantasy; for I fear 'twould trouble
Thy brain to loss of reason: and next tell
How a restoring chance came down to quell
One half of the witch in me.

                     On a day,
Sitting upon a rock above the spray,
I saw grow up from the horizon's brink
A gallant vessel: soon she seem'd to sink
Away from me again, as though her course
Had been resum'd in spite of hindering force—
So vanish'd: and not long, before arose
Dark clouds, and muttering of winds morose.

Old Eolus would stifle his mad spleen,
But could not: therefore all the billows green
Toss'd up the silver spume against the clouds.
The tempest came: I saw that vessel's shrouds
In perilous bustle; while upon the deck
Stood trembling creatures. I beheld the wreck;
The final gulphing; the poor struggling souls:
I heard their cries amid loud thunder-rolls.
O they had all been sav'd but crazed eld
Annull'd my vigorous cravings: and thus quell'd
And curb'd, think on't, O Latmian! did I sit
Writhing with pity, and a cursing fit
Against that hell-born Circe. The crew had gone,
By one and one, to pale oblivion;
And I was gazing on the surges prone,
With many a scalding tear and many a groan,
When at my feet emerg'd an old man's hand,
Grasping this scroll, and this same slender wand.
I knelt with pain—reached out my hand—had grasp'd
These treasures—touch'd the knuckles—they un-
        clasp'd—
I caught a finger: but the downward weight
O'erpowered me—it sank. Then 'gan abate
The storm, and through chill aguish gloom outburst
The comfortable sun. I was athirst
To search the book, and in the warming air
Parted its dripping leaves with eager care.
Strange matters did it treat of, and drew on
My soul page after page, till well-nigh won
Into forgetfulness; when, stupefied,
I read these words, and read again, and tried
My eyes against the heavens, and read again.
O what a load of misery and pain
Each Atlas-line bore off!—a shine of hope
Came gold around me, cheering me to cope
Strenuous with hellish tyranny. Attend!
For thou hast brought their promise to an end.

"*In the wide sea there lives a forlorn wretch,*
Doom'd with enfeebled carcase to outstretch

His loath'd existence through ten centuries,
And then to die alone. Who can devise
A total opposition? No one. So
One million times ocean must ebb and flow,
And he oppressed. Yet he shall not die,
These things accomplish'd:—If he utterly
Scans all the depths of magic, and expounds
The meanings of all motions, shapes, and sounds;
If he explores all forms and substances
Straight homeward to their symbol-essences;
He shall not die. Moreover, and in chief,
He must pursue this task of joy and grief
Most piously;—all lovers tempest-tost,
And in the savage overwhelming lost,
He shall deposit side by side, until
Time's creeping shall the dreary space fulfil:
Which done, and all these labours ripened,
A youth, by heavenly power lov'd and led,
Shall stand before him; whom he shall direct
How to consummate all. The youth elect
Must do the thing, or both will be destroy'd."—

"Then," cried the young Endymion, overjoy'd,
"We are twin brothers in this destiny!
Say, I intreat thee, what achievement high
Is, in this restless world, for me reserv'd.
What! if from thee my wandering feet had swerv'd,
Had we both perish'd?"—"Look!" the sage replied,
"Dost thou not mark a gleaming through the tide,
Of divers brilliances? 'tis the edifice
I told thee of, where lovely Scylla lies;
And where I have enshrined piously
All lovers, whom fell storms have doom'd to die
Throughout my bondage." Thus discoursing, on
They went till unobscur'd the porches shone;
Which hurryingly they gain'd, and enter'd straight.
Sure never since king Neptune held his state
Was seen such wonder underneath the stars.
Turn to some level plain where haughty Mars
Has legion'd all his battle; and behold

How every soldier, with firm foot, doth hold
His even breast: see, many steeled squares,
And rigid ranks of iron—whence who dares
One step? Imagine further, line by line,
These warrior thousands on the field supine:—
So in that crystal place, in silent rows,
Poor lovers lay at rest from joys and woes.—
The stranger from the mountains, breathless, trac'd
Such thousands of shut eyes in order plac'd;
Such ranges of white feet, and patient lips
All ruddy,—for here death no blossom nips.
He mark'd their brows and foreheads; saw their hair
Put sleekly on one side with nicest care;
And each one's gentle wrists, with reverence,
Put cross-wise to its heart.

                        "Let us commence,
Whisper'd the guide, stuttering with joy, even now."
He spake, and, trembling like an aspen-bough,
Began to tear his scroll in pieces small,
Uttering the while some mumblings funeral.
He tore it into pieces small as snow
That drifts unfeather'd when bleak northerns blow;
And having done it, took his dark blue cloak
And bound it round Endymion: then struck
His wand against the empty air times nine.—
"What more there is to do, young man, is thine:
But first a little patience; first undo
This tangled thread, and wind it to a clue.
Ah, gentle! 'tis as weak as spider's skein;
And shouldst thou break it—What, is it done so clean?
A power overshadows thee! Oh, brave!
The spite of hell is tumbling to its grave.
Here is a shell; 'tis pearly blank to me,
Nor mark'd with any sign or charactery—
Canst thou read aught? O read for pity's sake!
Olympus! we are safe! Now, Carian, break
This wand against yon lyre on the pedestal."

  'Twas done: and straight with sudden swell and fall
Sweet music breath'd her soul away, and sigh'd

A lullaby to silence.—"Youth! now strew
These minced leaves on me, and passing through
Those files of dead, scatter the same around,
And thou wilt see the issue."—'Mid the sound
Of flutes and viols, ravishing his heart,
Endymion from Glaucus stood apart,
And scatter'd in his face some fragments light.
How lightning-swift the change! a youthful wight
Smiling beneath a coral diadem,
Out-sparkling, sudden like an upturn'd gem,
Appear'd, and, stepping to a beauteous corse,
Kneel'd down beside it, and with tenderest force
Press'd its cold hand, and wept—and Scylla sigh'd!
Endymion, with quick hand, the charm applied—
The nymph arose: he left them to their joy,
And onward went upon his high employ,
Showering those powerful fragments on the dead.
And, as he pass'd, each lifted up its head,
As doth a flower at Apollo's touch.
Death felt it to his inwards; 'twas too much:
Death fell a weeping in his charnel-house.
The Latmian persever'd along, and thus
All were re-animated. There arose
A noise of harmony, pulses and throes
Of gladness in the air—while many, who
Had died in mutual arms devout and true,
Sprang to each other madly; and the rest
Felt a high certainty of being blest.
They gaz'd upon Endymion. Enchantment
Grew drunken, and would have its head and bent.
Delicious symphonies, like airy flowers,
Budded, and swell'd, and, full-blown, shed full
     showers
Of light, soft, unseen leaves of sounds divine.
The two deliverers tasted a pure wine
Of happiness, from fairy-press ooz'd out.
Speechless they eyed each other, and about
The fair assembly wander'd to and fro,
Distracted with the richest overflow
Of joy that ever pour'd from heaven.

——"Away!"
Shouted the new-born god; "Follow, and pay
Our piety to Neptunus supreme!"—
Then Scylla, blushing sweetly from her dream,
They led on first, bent to her meek surprise,
Through portal columns of a giant size,
Into the vaulted, boundless emerald.
Joyous all follow'd, as the leader call'd,
Down marble steps; pouring as easily
As hour-glass sand—and fast, as you might see
Swallows obeying the south summer's call,
Or swans upon a gentle waterfall.

Thus went that beautiful multitude, nor far,
Ere from among some rocks of glittering spar,
Just within ken, they saw descending thick
Another multitude. Whereat more quick
Moved either host. On a wide sand they met,
And of those numbers every eye was wet;
For each their old love found. A murmuring rose,
Like what was never heard in all the throes
Of wind and waters: 'tis past human wit
To tell; 'tis dizziness to think of it.

This mighty consummation made, the host
Mov'd on for many a league; and gain'd, and lost
Huge sea-marks; vanward swelling in array,
And from the rear diminishing away,—
Till a faint dawn surpris'd them. Glaucus cried,
"Behold! behold, the palace of his pride!
God Neptune's palaces!" With noise increas'd,
They shoulder'd on towards that brightening east.
At every onward step proud domes arose
In prospect,—diamond gleams, and golden glows
Of amber 'gainst their faces levelling.
Joyous, and many as the leaves in spring,
Still onward; still the splendour gradual swell'd.
Rich opal domes were seen, on high upheld
By jasper pillars, letting through their shafts
A blush of coral. Copious wonder-draughts

Each gazer drank; and deeper drank more near:
For what poor mortals fragment up, as mere
As marble was there lavish, to the vast
Of one fair palace, that far far surpass'd,
Even for common bulk, those olden three,
Memphis, and Babylon, and Nineveh.

As large, as bright, as colour'd as the bow
Of Iris, when unfading it doth shew
Beyond a silvery shower, was the arch
Through which this Paphian army took its march,
Into the outer courts of Neptune's state:
Whence could be seen, direct, a golden gate,
To which the leaders sped; but not half raught
Ere it burst open swift as fairy thought,
And made those dazzled thousands veil their eyes
Like callow eagles at the first sunrise.
Soon with an eagle nativeness their gaze
Ripe from hue-golden swoons took all the blaze,
And then, behold! large Neptune on his throne
Of emerald deep: yet not exalt alone;
At his right hand stood winged Love, and on
His left sat smiling Beauty's paragon.

Far as the mariner on highest mast
Can see all round upon the calmed vast,
So wide was Neptune's hall: and as the blue
Doth vault the waters, so the waters drew
Their doming curtains, high, magnificent,
Aw'd from the throne aloof;—and when storm-rent
Disclos'd the thunder-gloomings in Jove's air;
But sooth'd as now, flash'd sudden everywhere,
Noiseless, sub-marine cloudlets, glittering
Death to a human eye: for there did spring
From natural west, and east, and south, and north,
A light as of four sunsets, blazing forth
A gold-green zenith 'bove the Sea-God's head.
Of lucid depth the floor, and far outspread
As breezeless lake, on which the slim canoe
Of feather'd Indian darts about, as through

The delicatest air: air verily,
But for the portraiture of clouds and sky:
This palace floor breath-air,—but for the amaze
Of deep-seen wonders motionless,—and blaze
Of the dome pomp, reflected in extremes,
Globing a golden sphere.

                                They stood in dreams
Till Triton blew his horn. The palace rang;
The Nereids danc'd; the Syrens faintly sang;
And the great Sea-King bow'd his dripping head.
Then Love took wing, and from his pinions shed
On all the multitude a nectarous dew.
The ooze-born Goddess beckoned and drew
Fair Scylla and her guides to conference;
And when they reach'd the throned eminence
She kist the sea-nymph's cheek,—who sat her down
A toying with the doves. Then,—"Mighty crown
And sceptre of this kingdom!" Venus said,
"Thy vows were on a time to Nais paid:
Behold!"—Two copious tear-drops instant fell
From the God's large eyes; he smil'd delectable,
And over Glaucus held his blessing hands.—
"Endymion! Ah! still wandering in the bands
Of love? Now this is cruel. Since the hour
I met thee in earth's bosom, all my power
Have I put forth to serve thee. What, not yet
Escap'd from dull mortality's harsh net?
A little patience, youth! 'twill not be long,
Or I am skilless quite: an idle tongue,
A humid eye, and steps luxurious,
Where these are new and strange, are ominous.
Aye, I have seen these signs in one of heaven,
When others were all blind; and were I given
To utter secrets, haply I might say
Some pleasant words:—but Love will have his day.
So wait awhile expectant. Pr'ythee soon,
Even in the passing of thine honey-moon,
Visit my Cytherea: thou wilt find
Cupid well-natured, my Adonis kind;

130

And pray persuade with thee—Ah, I have done,
All blisses be upon thee, my sweet son!"—
Thus the fair goddess: while Endymion
Knelt to receive those accents halcyon.

Meantime a glorious revelry began
Before the Water-Monarch. Nectar ran
In courteous fountains to all cups outreach'd;
And plunder'd vines, teeming exhaustless, pleach'd
New growth about each shell and pendent lyre;
The which, in disentangling for their fire,
Pull'd down fresh foliage and coverture
For dainty toying. Cupid, empire-sure,
Flutter'd and laugh'd, and oft-times through the
      throng
Made a delighted way. Then dance, and song,
And garlanding grew wild; and pleasure reign'd.
In harmless tendril they each other chain'd,
And strove who should be smother'd deepest in
Fresh crush of leaves.

                    O 'tis a very sin
For one so weak to venture his poor verse
In such a place as this. O do not curse,
High Muses! let him hurry to the ending.

All suddenly were silent. A soft blending
Of dulcet instruments came charmingly;
And then a hymn.

                    "KING of the stormy sea!
Brother of Jove, and co-inheritor
Of elements! Eternally before
Thee the waves awful bow. Fast, stubborn rock,
At thy fear'd trident shrinking, doth unlock
Its deep foundations, hissing into foam.
All mountain-rivers lost, in the wide home
Of thy capacious bosom ever flow.
Thou frownest, and old Eolus thy foe
Skulks to his cavern, 'mid the gruff complaint

Of all his rebel tempests. Dark clouds faint
When, from thy diadem, a silver gleam
Slants over blue dominion. Thy bright team
Gulphs in the morning light, and scuds along
To bring thee nearer to that golden song
Apollo singeth, while his chariot
Waits at the doors of heaven. Thou art not
For scenes like this; an empire stern hast thou:
And it hath furrow'd that large front: yet now,
As newly come of heaven, dost thou sit
To blend and interknit
Subdued majesty with this glad time.
O shell-borne King sublime!
We lay our hearts before thee evermore—
We sing, and we adore!

   "Breathe softly, flutes;
Be tender of your strings, ye soothing lutes;
Nor be the trumpet heard! O vain, O vain;
Not flowers budding in an April rain,
Nor breath of sleeping dove, nor river's flow,—
No, nor the Eolian twang of Love's own bow,
Can mingle music fit for the soft ear
Of goddess Cytherea!
Yet deign, white Queen of Beauty, thy fair eyes
On our souls' sacrifice.

   "Bright-winged Child!
Who has another care when thou hast smil'd?
Unfortunates on earth, we see at last
All death-shadows, and glooms that overcast
Our spirits, fann'd away by thy light pinions.
O sweetest essence! sweetest of all minions!
God of warm pulses, and dishevell'd hair,
And panting bosoms bare!
Dear unseen light in darkness! eclipser
Of light in light! delicious poisoner!
Thy venom'd goblet will we quaff until
We fill—we fill!
And by thy Mother's lips——"

                                        Was heard no more
For clamour, when the golden palace door
Opened again, and from without, in shone
A new magnificence. On oozy throne
Smooth-moving came Oceanus the old,
To take a latest glimpse at his sheep-fold,
Before he went into his quiet cave
To muse for ever—Then a lucid wave,
Scoop'd from its trembling sisters of mid-sea,
Afloat, and pillowing up the majesty
Of Doris, and the Egean seer, her spouse—
Next, on a dolphin, clad in laurel boughs,
Theban Amphion leaning on his lute:
His fingers went across it—All were mute
To gaze on Amphitrite, queen of pearls,
And Thetis pearly too.—

                                        The palace whirls
Around giddy Endymion; seeing he
Was there far strayed from mortality.
He could not bear it—shut his eyes in vain;
Imagination gave a dizzier pain.
"O I shall die! sweet Venus, be my stay!
Where is my lovely mistress? Well-away!
I die—I hear her voice—I feel my wing—"
At Neptune's feet he sank. A sudden ring
Of Nereids were about him, in kind strife
To usher back his spirit into life:
But still he slept. At last they interwove
Their cradling arms, and purpos'd to convey
Towards a crystal bower far away.

Lo! while slow carried through the pitying crowd,
To his inward senses these words spake aloud;
Written in star-light on the dark above:
Dearest Endymion! my entire love!
How have I dwelt in fear of fate: 'tis done—
Immortal bliss for me too hast thou won.
Arise then! for the hen-dove shall not hatch
Her ready eggs, before I'll kissing snatch
Thee into endless heaven. Awake! awake!

The youth at once arose: a placid lake
Came quiet to his eyes; and forest green,
Cooler than all the wonders he had seen,
Lull'd with its simple song his fluttering breast.
How happy once again in grassy nest!

ENDYMION.

BOOK IV.

MUSE of my native land! loftiest Muse!
O first-born on the mountains! by the hues
Of heaven on the spiritual air begot:
Long didst thou sit alone in northern grot,
While yet our England was a wolfish den;
Before our forests heard the talk of men;
Before the first of Druids was a child;—
Long didst thou sit amid our regions wild
Rapt in a deep prophetic solitude.
There came an eastern voice of solemn mood:—
Yet wast thou patient. Then sang forth the Nine,
Apollo's garland:—yet didst thou divine
Such home-bred glory, that they cry'd in vain,
"Come hither, Sister of the Island!" Plain
Spake fair Ausonia; and once more she spake
A higher summons:—still didst thou betake
Thee to thy native hopes. O thou hast won
A full accomplishment! The thing is done,
Which undone, these our latter days had risen
On barren souls. Great Muse, thou know'st what prison
Of flesh and bone, curbs, and confines, and frets
Our spirit's wings: despondency besets
Our pillows; and the fresh to-morrow morn
Seems to give forth its light in very scorn
Of our dull, uninspired, snail-paced lives.
Long have I said, how happy he who shrives
To thee! But then I thought on poets gone,
And could not pray:—nor can I now—so on
I move to the end in lowliness of heart.——

"Ah, woe is me! that I should fondly part
From my dear native land! Ah, foolish maid!
Glad was the hour, when, with thee, myriads bade
Adieu to Ganges and their pleasant fields!
To one so friendless the clear freshet yields
A bitter coolness; the ripe grape is sour:
Yet I would have, great gods! but one short hour
Of native air—let me but die at home."

Endymion to heaven's airy dome
Was offering up a hecatomb of vows,
When these words reach'd him. Whereupon he bows
His head through thorny-green entanglement
Of underwood, and to the sound is bent,
Anxious as hind towards her hidden fawn.

"Is no one near to help me? No fair dawn
Of life from charitable voice? No sweet saying
To set my dull and sadden'd spirit playing?
No hand to toy with mine? No lips so sweet
That I may worship them? No eyelids meet
To twinkle on my bosom? No one dies
Before me, till from these enslaving eyes
Redemption sparkles!—I am sad and lost."

Thou, Carian lord, hadst better have been tost
Into a whirlpool. Vanish into air,
Warm mountaineer! for canst thou only bear
A woman's sigh alone and in distress?
See not her charms! Is Phœbe passionless?
Phœbe is fairer far—O gaze no more:—
Yet if thou wilt behold all beauty's store,
Behold her panting in the forest grass!
Do not those curls of glossy jet surpass
For tenderness the arms so idly lain
Amongst them? Feelest not a kindred pain,
To see such lovely eyes in swimming search
After some warm delight, that seems to perch
Dovelike in the dim cell lying beyond
Their upper lids?—Hist!

135

"O for Hermes' wand,
To touch this flower into human shape!
That woodland Hyacinthus could escape
From his green prison, and here kneeling down
Call me his queen, his second life's fair crown!
Ah me, how I could love!—My soul doth melt
For the unhappy youth—Love! I have felt
So faint a kindness, such a meek surrender
To what my own full thoughts had made too tender,
That but for tears my life had fled away!—
Ye deaf and senseless minutes of the day,
And thou, old forest, hold ye this for true,
There is no lightning, no authentic dew
But in the eye of love: there's not a sound,
Melodious howsoever, can confound
The heavens and earth in one to such a death
As doth the voice of love: there's not a breath
Will mingle kindly with the meadow air,
Till it has panted round, and stolen a share
Of passion from the heart!"—

                              Upon a bough
He leant, wretched. He surely cannot now
Thirst for another love: O impious,
That he can even dream upon it thus!—
Thought he, "Why am I not as are the dead,
Since to a woe like this I have been led
Through the dark earth, and through the wondrous
      sea?
Goddess! I love thee not the less: from thee
By Juno's smile I turn not—no, no, no—
While the great waters are at ebb and flow.—
I have a triple soul! O fond pretence—
For both, for both my love is so immense,
I feel my heart is cut in twain for them."

And so he groan'd, as one by beauty slain.
The lady's heart beat quick, and he could see
Her gentle bosom heave tumultuously.
He sprang from his green covert: there she lay,

Sweet as a muskrose upon new-made hay;
With all her limbs on tremble, and her eyes
Shut softly up alive. To speak he tries.
"Fair damsel, pity me! forgive that I
Thus violate thy bower's sanctity!
O pardon me, for I am full of grief—
Grief born of thee, young angel! fairest thief!
Who stolen hast away the wings wherewith
I was to top the heavens. Dear maid, sith
Thou art my executioner, and I feel
Loving and hatred, misery and weal,
Will in a few short hours be nothing to me,
And all my story that much passion slew me;
Do smile upon the evening of my days:
And, for my tortur'd brain begins to craze,
Be thou my nurse; and let me understand
How dying I shall kiss that lily hand.—
Dost weep for me? Then should I be content.
Scowl on, ye fates! until the firmament
Outblackens Erebus, and the full-cavern'd earth
Crumbles into itself. By the cloud girth
Of Jove, those tears have given me a thirst
To meet oblivion."—As her heart would burst
The maiden sobb'd awhile, and then replied:
"Why must such desolation betide
As that thou speakest of? Are not these green nooks
Empty of all misfortune? Do the brooks
Utter a gorgon voice? Does yonder thrush,
Schooling its half-fledg'd little ones to brush
About the dewy forest, whisper tales?—
Speak not of grief, young stranger, or cold snails
Will slime the rose to night. Though if thou wilt,
Methinks 'twould be a guilt—a very guilt—
Not to companion thee, and sigh away
The light—the dusk—the dark—till break of day!"
"Dear lady," said Endymion, "'tis past:
I love thee! and my days can never last.
That I may pass in patience still speak:
Let me have music dying, and I seek
No more delight—I bid adieu to all.

Didst thou not after other climates call,
And murmur about Indian streams?"—Then she,
Sitting beneath the midmost forest tree,
For pity sang this roundelay——

"O Sorrow,
Why dost borrow
The natural hue of health, from vermeil lips?—
To give maiden blushes
To the white rose bushes?
Or is it thy dewy hand the daisy tips?

"O Sorrow,
Why dost borrow
The lustrous passion from a falcon-eye?—
To give the glow-worm light?
Or, on a moonless night,
To tinge, on syren shores, the salt sea-spry?

"O Sorrow,
Why dost borrow
The mellow ditties from a mourning tongue?—
To give at evening pale
Unto the nightingale,
That thou mayst listen the cold dews among?

"O Sorrow,
Why dost borrow
Heart's lightness from the merriment of May?—
A lover would not tread
A cowslip on the head,
Though he should dance from eve till peep of day—
Nor any drooping flower
Held sacred for thy bower,
Wherever he may sport himself and play.

"To Sorrow,
I bade good-morrow,
And thought to leave her far away behind;

But cheerly, cheerly,
She loves me dearly;
She is so constant to me, and so kind:
I would deceive her
And so leave her,
But ah! she is so constant and so kind.

"Beneath my palm trees, by the river side,
I sat a weeping: in the whole world wide
There was no one to ask me why I wept,—
And so I kept
Brimming the water-lily cups with tears
Cold as my fears.

"Beneath my palm trees, by the river side,
I sat a weeping: what enamour'd bride,
Cheated by shadowy wooer from the clouds,
But hides and shrouds
Beneath dark palm trees by a river side?

"And as I sat, over the light blue hills
There came a noise of revellers: the rills
Into the wide stream came of purple hue—
'Twas Bacchus and his crew!
The earnest trumpet spake, and silver thrills
From kissing cymbals made a merry din—
'Twas Bacchus and his kin!
Like to a moving vintage down they came,
Crown'd with green leaves, and faces all on flame;
All madly dancing through the pleasant valley,
To scare thee, Melancholy!
O then, O then, thou wast a simple name!
And I forgot thee, as the berried holly
By shepherds is forgotten, when, in June,
Tall chestnuts keep away the sun and moon:—
I rush'd into the folly!

"Within his car, aloft, young Bacchus stood,
Trifling his ivy-deart, in dancing mood,
With sidelong laughing;

And little rills of crimson wine imbrued
His plump white arms, and shoulders, enough white
      For Venus' pearly bite;
And near him rode Silenus on his ass,
Pelted with flowers as he on did pass
        Tipsily quaffing.

"Whence came ye, merry Damsels! whence came ye!
So many, and so many, and such glee?
Why have ye left your bowers desolate,
      Your lutes, and gentler fate?—
'We follow Bacchus! Bacchus on the wing,
      A conquering!
Bacchus, young Bacchus! good or ill betide,
We dance before him thorough kingdoms wide:—
Come hither, lady fair, and joined be
      To our wild minstrelsy!'

"Whence came ye, jolly Satyrs! whence came ye!
So many, and so many, and such glee?
Why have ye left your forest haunts, why left
      Your nuts in oak-tree cleft?—
'For wine, for wine we left our kernel tree;
For wine we left our heath, and yellow brooms,
      And cold mushrooms;
For wine we follow Bacchus through the earth;
Great God of breathless cups and chirping mirth!—
Come hither, lady fair, and joined be
To our mad minstrelsy!'

"Over wide streams and mountains great we went,
And, save when Bacchus kept his ivy tent,
Onward the tiger and the leopard pants,
      With Asian elephants:
Onward these myriads—with song and dance,
With zebras striped, and sleek Arabians' prance,
Web-footed alligators, crocodiles,
Bearing upon their scaly backs, in files,
Plump infant laughers mimicking the coil
Of seamen, and stout galley-rowers' toil:

With toying oars and silken sails they glide,
  Nor care for wind and tide.

"Mounted on panthers' furs and lions' manes,
From rear to van they scour about the plains;
A three days' journey in a moment done:
And always, at the rising of the sun,
About the wilds they hunt with spear and horn,
  On spleenful unicorn.

"I saw Osirian Egypt kneel adown
    Before the vine-wreath crown!
I saw parch'd Abyssinia rouse and sing
    To the silver cymbals' ring!
I saw the whelming vintage hotly pierce
    Old Tartary the fierce!
The kings of Inde their jewel-sceptres vail,
And from their treasures scatter pearled hail;
Great Brahma from his mystic heaven groans,
    And all his priesthood moans;
Before young Bacchus' eye-wink turning pale.—
Into these regions came I following him,
Sick hearted, weary—so I took a whim
To stray away into these forests drear
    Alone, without a peer:
And I have told thee all thou mayest hear.

    "Young stranger!
    I've been a ranger
In search of pleasure throughout every clime:
    Alas! 'tis not for me!
    Bewitch'd I sure must be,
To lose in grieving all my maiden prime.

    "Come then, Sorrow!
    Sweetest Sorrow!
Like an own babe I nurse thee on my breast:
    I thought to leave thee
    And deceive thee,
But now of all the world I love thee best.

141

"There is not one,
No, no, not one
But thee to comfort a poor lonely maid;
Thou art her mother,
And her brother,
Her playmate, and her wooer in the shade."

O what a sigh she gave in finishing,
And look, quite dead to every worldly thing!
Endymion could not speak, but gazed on her;
And listened to the wind that now did stir
About the crisped oaks full drearily,
Yet with as sweet a softness as might be
Remember'd from its velvet summer song.
At last he said: "Poor lady, how thus long
Have I been able to endure that voice?
Fair Melody! kind Syren! I've no choice;
I must be thy sad servant evermore:
I cannot choose but kneel here and adore.
Alas, I must not think—by Phœbe, no!
Let me not think, soft Angel! shall it be so?
Say, beautifullest, shall I never think?
O thou could'st foster me beyond the brink
Of recollection! make my watchful care
Close up its bloodshot eyes, nor see despair!
Do gently murder half my soul, and I
Shall feel the other half so utterly!—
I'm giddy at that cheek so fair and smooth;
O let it blush so ever! let it soothe
My madness! let it mantle rosy-warm
With the tinge of love, panting in safe alarm.—
This cannot be thy hand, and yet it is;
And this is sure thine other softling—this
Thine own fair bosom, and I am so near!
Wilt fall asleep? O let me sip that tear!
And whisper one sweet word that I may know
This is this world—sweet dewy blossom!"—*Woe!
Woe! Woe to that Endymion! Where is he?*—
Even these words went echoing dismally
Through the wide forest—a most fearful tone,

Like one repenting in his latest moan;
And while it died away a shade pass'd by,
As of a thunder cloud. When arrows fly
Through the thick branches, poor ring-doves sleek forth
Their timid necks and tremble; so these both
Leant to each other trembling, and sat so
Waiting for some destruction—when lo,
Foot-feather'd Mercury appear'd sublime
Beyond the tall tree tops; and in less time
Than shoots the slanted hail-storm, down he dropt
Towards the ground; but rested not, nor stopt
One moment from his home: only the sward
He with his wand light touch'd, and heavenward
Swifter than sight was gone—even before
The teeming earth a sudden witness bore
Of his swift magic. Diving swans appear
Above the crystal circlings white and clear;
And catch the cheated eye in wild surprise,
How they can dive in sight and unseen rise—
So from the turf outsprang two steeds jet-black,
Each with large dark blue wings upon his back.
The youth of Caria plac'd the lovely dame
On one, and felt himself in spleen to tame
The other's fierceness. Through the air they flew,
High as the eagles. Like two drops of dew
Exhal'd to Phœbus' lips, away they are gone,
Far from the earth away—unseen, alone,
Among cool clouds and winds, but that the free,
The buoyant life of song can floating be
Above their heads, and follow them untir'd.—
Muse of my native land, am I inspir'd?
This is the giddy air, and I must spread
Wide pinions to keep here; nor do I dread
Or height, or depth, or width, or any chance
Precipitous: I have beneath my glance
Those towering horses and their mournful freight.
Could I thus sail, and see, and thus await
Fearless for power of thought, without thine aid?—
There is a sleepy dusk, an odorous shade
From some approaching wonder, and behold

Those winged steeds, with snorting nostrils bold
Snuff at its faint extreme, and seem to tire,
Dying to embers from their native fire!

There curl'd a purple mist around them; soon,
It seem'd as when around the pale new moon
Sad Zephyr droops the clouds like weeping willow:
'Twas Sleep slow journeying with head on pillow.
For the first time, since he came nigh dead born
From the old womb of night, his cave forlorn
Had he left more forlorn; for the first time,
He felt aloof the day and morning's prime—
Because into his depth Cimmerian
There came a dream, shewing how a young man,
Ere a lean bat could plump its wintery skin,
Would at high Jove's empyreal footstool win
An immortality, and how espouse
Jove's daughter, and be reckon'd of his house.
Now was he slumbering towards heaven's gate,
That he might at the threshold one hour wait
To hear the marriage melodies, and then
Sink downward to his dusky cave again.
His litter of smooth semilucent mist,
Diversely ting'd with rose and amethyst,
Puzzled those eyes that for the centre sought;
And scarcely for one moment could be caught
His sluggish form reposing motionless.
Those two on winged steeds, with all the stress
Of vision search'd for him, as one would look
Athwart the sallows of a river nook
To catch a glance at silver throated eels,—
Or from old Skiddaw's top, when fog conceals
His rugged forehead in a mantle pale,
With an eye-guess towards some pleasant vale
Descry a favourite hamlet faint and far.

These raven horses, though they foster'd are
Of earth's splenetic fire, dully drop
Their full-veined ears, nostrils blood wide, and stop;
Upon the spiritless mist have they outspread

Their ample feathers, are in slumber dead,—
And on those pinions, level in mid air,
Endymion sleepeth and the lady fair.
Slowly they sail, slowly as icy isle
Upon a calm sea drifting: and meanwhile
The mournful wanderer dreams. Behold! he walks
On heaven's pavement; brotherly he talks
To divine powers: from his hand full fain
Juno's proud birds are pecking pearly grain:
He tries the nerve of Phœbus' golden bow,
And asketh where the golden apples grow:
Upon his arm he braces Pallas' shield,
And strives in vain to unsettle and wield
A Jovian thunderbolt: arch Hebe brings
A full-brimm'd goblet, dances lightly, sings
And tantalizes long; at last he drinks,
And lost in pleasure at her feet he sinks,
Touching with dazzled lips her starlight hand.
He blows a bugle,—an ethereal band
Are visible above: the Seasons four.—
Green-kyrtled Spring, flush Summer, golden store
In Autumn's sickle, Winter frosty hoar,
Join dance with shadowy Hours; while still the blast,
In swells unmitigated, still doth last
To sway their floating morris. "Whose is this?
Whose bugle?" he inquires: they smile—" O Dis!
Why is this mortal here? Dost thou not know
Its mistress' lips? Not thou?—'Tis Dian's: lo!
She rises crescented!" He looks, 'tis she,
His very goddess: good-bye earth, and sea,
And air, and pains, and care, and suffering;
Good-bye to all but love! Then doth he spring
Towards her, and awakes—and, strange, o'erhead,
Of those same fragrant exhalations bred,
Beheld awake his very dream: the gods
Stood smiling; merry Hebe laughs and nods;
And Phœbe bends towards him crescented.
O state perplexing! On the pinion bed,
Too well awake, he feels the panting side
Of his delicious lady. He who died

For soaring too audacious in the sun,
Where that same treacherous wax began to run,
Felt not more tongue-tied than Endymion.
His heart leapt up as to its rightful throne,
To that fair shadow'd passion puls'd its way—
Ah, what perplexity! Ah, well a day!
So fond, so beauteous was his bed-fellow,
He could not help but kiss her: then he grew
Awhile forgetful of all beauty save
Young Phœbe's, golden hair'd; and so 'gan crave
Forgiveness: yet he turn'd once more to look
At the sweet sleeper,—all his soul was shook,—
She press'd his hand in slumber; so once more
He could not help but kiss her and adore.
At this the shadow wept, melting away.
The Latmian started up: "Bright goddess, stay!
Search my most hidden breast! By truth's own tongue,
I have no dædale heart: why is it wrung
To desperation? Is there nought for me,
Upon the bourne of bliss, but misery?"

These words awoke the stranger of dark tresses:
Her dawning love-look rapt Endymion blesses
With 'haviour soft. Sleep yawned from underneath.
"Thou swan of Ganges, let us no more breathe
This murky phantasm! thou contented seem'st
Pillow'd in lovely idleness, nor dream'st
What horrors may discomfort thee and me.
Ah, shouldst thou die from my heart-treachery!—
Yet did she merely weep—her gentle soul
Hath no revenge in it: as it is whole
In tenderness, would I were whole in love!
Can I prize thee, fair maid, all price above,
Even when I feel as true as innocence?
I do, I do.—What is this soul then? Whence
Came it? It does not seem my own, and I
Have no self-passion or identity.
Some fearful end must be: where, where is it?
By Nemesis, I see my spirit flit
Alone about the dark—Forgive me, sweet:

Shall we away?" He rous'd the steeds: they beat
Their wings chivalrous into the clear air,
Leaving old Sleep within his vapoury lair.

The good-night blush of eve was waning slow,
And Vesper, risen star, began to throe
In the dusk heavens silvery, when they
Thus sprang direct towards the Galaxy.
Nor did speed hinder converse soft and strange—
Eternal oaths and vows they interchange,
In such wise, in such temper, so aloof
Up in the winds, beneath a starry roof,
So witless of their doom, that verily
'Tis well nigh past man's search their hearts to see;
Whether they wept, or laugh'd, or griev'd, or toy'd—
Most like with joy gone mad, with sorrow cloy'd.

Full facing their swift flight, from ebon streak,
The moon put forth a little diamond peak,
No bigger than an unobserved star,
Or tiny point of fairy scymetar;
Bright signal that she only stoop'd to tie
Her silver sandals, ere deliciously
She bow'd into the heavens her timid head.
Slowly she rose, as though she would have fled,
While to his lady meek the Carian turn'd,
To mark if her dark eyes had yet discern'd
This beauty in its birth—Despair! despair!
He saw her body fading gaunt and spare
In the cold moonshine. Straight he seiz'd her wrist;
It melted from his grasp: her hand he kiss'd,
And, horror! kiss'd his own—he was alone.
Her steed a little higher soar'd, and then
Dropt hawkwise to the earth.

                                There lies a den,
Beyond the seeming confines of the space
Made for the soul to wander in and trace
Its own existence, of remotest glooms.
Dark regions are around it, where the tombs

Of buried griefs the spirit sees, but scarce
One hour doth linger weeping, for the pierce
Of new-born woe it feels more inly smart:
And in these regions many a venom'd dart
At random flies; they are the proper home
Of every ill: the man is yet to come
Who hath not journeyed in this native hell.
But few have ever felt how calm and well
Sleep may be had in that deep den of all.
There anguish does not sting; nor pleasure pall:
Woe-hurricanes beat ever at the gate,
Yet all is still within and desolate.
Beset with painful gusts, within ye hear
No sound so loud as when on curtain'd bier
The death-watch tick is stifled. Enter none
Who strive therefore: on the sudden it is won.
Just when the sufferer begins to burn,
Then it is free to him; and from an urn,
Still fed by melting ice, he takes a draught—
Young Semele such richness never quaft
In her maternal longing. Happy gloom!
Dark Paradise! where pale becomes the bloom
Of health by due; where silence dreariest
Is most articulate; where hopes infest;
Where those eyes are the brightest far that keep
Their lids shut longest in a dreamless sleep.
O happy spirit-home! O wondrous soul!
Pregnant with such a den to save the whole
In thine own depth. Hail, gentle Carian!
For, never since thy griefs and woes began,
Hast thou felt so content: a grievous feud
Hath let thee to this Cave of Quietude.
Aye, his lull'd soul was there, although upborne
With dangerous speed: and so he did not mourn
Because he knew not whither he was going.
So happy was he, not the aerial blowing
Of trumpets at clear parley from the east
Could rouse from that fine relish, that high feast.
They stung the feather'd horse: with fierce alarm
He flapp'd towards the sound. Alas, no charm

Could lift Endymion's head, or he had view'd
A skye mask, a pinion'd multitude,—
And silvery was its passing: voices sweet
Warbling the while as if to lull and greet
The wanderer in his path. Thus warbled they,
While past the vision went in bright array.

"Who, who from Dian's feast would be away?
For all the golden bowers of the day
Are empty left? Who, who away would be
From Cynthia's wedding and festivity?
Not Hesperus: lo! upon his silver wings
He leans away for highest heaven and sings,
Snapping his lucid fingers merrily!—
Ah, Zephyrus! art here, and Flora too!
Ye tender bibbers of the rain and dew,
Young playmates of the rose and daffodil,
Be careful, ere ye enter in, to fill
          Your baskets high
With fennel green, and balm, and golden pines,
Savory, latter-mint, and columbines,
Cool parsley, basil sweet, and sunny thyme;
Yea, every flower and leaf of every clime,
All gather'd in the dewy morning: hie
          Away! fly, fly!—
Crystalline brother of the belt of heaven,
Aquarius! to whom king Jove has given
Two liquid pulse streams 'stead of feather'd wings,
Two fan-like fountains,—thine illuminings
          For Dian play:
Dissolve the frozen purity of air;
Let thy white shoulders silvery and bare
Shew cold through watery pinions; make more bright
The Star-Queen's crescent on her marriage night:
          Haste, haste away!—
Castor has tamed the planet Lion, see!
And of the Bear has Pollux mastery:
A thrid is in the race! who is the third,
Speeding away swift as the eagle bird?
          The ramping Centaur!

The Lion's mane's on end: the Bear how fierce!
The Centaur's arrow ready seems to pierce
Some enemy: far forth his bow is bent
Into the blue of heaven. He'll be shent,
          Pale unrelentor,
When he shall hear the wedding lutes a playing.—
Andromeda! sweet woman! why delaying
So timidly among the stars: come hither!
Join this bright throng, and nimbly follow whither
          They all are going.
Danae's Son, before Jove newly bow'd,
Has wept for thee, calling to Jove aloud.
Thee, gentle lady, did he disenthral:
Ye shall for ever live and love, for all
          Thy tears are flowing.—
By Daphne's fright, behold Apollo!—"

                                        More
Endymion heard not: down his steed him bore,
Prone to the green head of a misty hill.

    His first touch of the earth went nigh to kill.
"Alas!" said he, "were I but always borne
Through dangerous winds, had but my footsteps worn
A path in hell, for ever would I bless
Horrors which nourish an uneasiness
For my own sullen conquering: to him
Who lives beyond earth's boundary, grief is dim,
Sorrow is but a shadow: now I see
The grass; I feel the solid ground—Ah, me!
It is thy voice—divinest! Where?—who? who
Left thee so quiet on this bed of dew?
Behold upon this happy earth we are;
Let us ay love each other; let us fare
On forest-fruits, and never, never go
Among the abodes of mortals here below,
Or be by phantoms duped. O destiny!
Into a labyrinth now my soul would fly,
But with thy beauty will I deaden it.
Where didst thou melt too? By thee will I sit

For ever: let our fate stop here—a kid
I on this spot will offer: Pan will bid
Us live in peace, in love and peace among
His forest wildernesses. I have clung
To nothing, lov'd a nothing, nothing seen
Or felt but a great dream! O I have been
Presumptuous against love, against the sky,
Against all elements, against the tie
Of mortals each to each, against the blooms
Of flowers rush of rivers, and the tombs
Of heroes gone! Against his proper glory
Has my own soul conspired: so my story
Will I to children utter, and repent.
There never liv'd a mortal man, who bent
His appetite beyond his natural sphere,
But starv'd and died. My sweetest Indian, here,
Here will I kneel, for thou redeemed hast
My life from too thin breathing: gone and past
Are cloudy phantasms. Caverns lone, farewell!
And air of visions, and the monstrous swell
Of visionary seas! No, never more
Shall airy voices cheat me to the shore
Of tangled wonder, breathless and aghast.
Adieu, my daintiest Dream! although so vast
My love is still for thee. The hour may come
When we shall meet in pure elysium.
On earth I may not love thee; and therefore
Doves will I offer up, and sweetest store
All through the teeming year: so thou wilt shine
On me, and on this damsel fair of mine,
And bless our simple lives. My Indian bliss!
My river-lily bud! one human kiss!
One sigh of real breath—one gentle squeeze,
Warm as a dove's nest among summer tress,
And warm with dew at ooze from living blood!
Whither didst melt? Ah, what of that!—all good
We'll talk about—no more of dreaming.—Now,
Where shall our dwelling be? Under the brow
Of some steep mossy hill, where ivy dun
Would hide us up, although spring leaves were none;

And where dark yew trees, as we rustle through,
Will drop their scarlet berry cups of dew?
O thou wouldst joy to live in such a place;
Dusk for our loves, yet light enough to grace
Those gentle limbs on mossy bed reclin'd:
For by one step the blue sky shouldst thou find,
And by another, in deep dell below,
See, through the trees, a little river go
All in its mid-day gold and glimmering.
Honey from out the gnarled hive I'll bring,
And apples, wan with sweetness, gather thee,—
Cresses that grow where no man may them see,
And sorrel untorn by the dew-claw'd stag:
Pipes will I fashion of the syrinx flag,
That thou mayst always know whither I roam,
When it shall please thee in our quiet home
To listen and think of love. Still let me speak;
Still let me dive into the joy I seek,—
For yet the past doth prison me. The rill
Thou haply mayst delight in, will I fill
With fairy fishes from the mountain tarn,
And thou shalt feed them from the squirrel's barn.
Its bottom will I strew with amber shells,
And pebbles blue from deep enchanted wells.
Its sides I'll plant with dew-sweet eglantine,
And honeysuckles full of clear bee-wine.
I will entice this crystal rill to trace
Love's silver name upon the meadow's face.
I'll kneel to Vesta, for a flame of fire;
And to god Phœbus, for a golden lyre;
To Empress Dian, for a hunting spear;
To Vesper, for a taper silver-clear,
That I may see thy beauty through the night;
To Flora, and a nightingale shall light
Tame on thy finger; to the River-gods,
And they shall bring thee taper fishing-rods
Of gold, and lines of Naiads' long bright tress.
Heaven shield thee for thine utter loveliness!
Thy mossy footstool shall the altar be
'Fore which I'll bend, bending, dear love, to thee:

Those lips shall be my Delphos, and shall speak
Laws to my footsteps, colour to my cheek,
Trembling or stedfastness to this same voice,
And of three sweetest pleasurings the choice:
And that affectionate light, those diamond things,
Those eyes, those passions, those supreme pearl springs,
Shall be my grief or twinkle me to pleasure.
Say, is not bliss within our perfect seisure?
O that I could not doubt?"

                    The mountaineer
Thus strove by fancies vain and crude to clear
His briar'd path to some tranquillity.
It gave bright gladness to his lady's eye,
And yet the tears she wept were tears of sorrow;
Answering thus, just as the golden morrow
Beam'd upward from the vallies of the east:
"O that the flutter of this heart had ceas'd,
Or the sweet name of love had pass'd away.
Young feather'd tyrant! by a swift decay
Wilt thou devote this body to the earth:
And I do think that at my very birth
I lisp'd thy blooming titles inwardly;
For at the first, first dawn and thought of thee,
With uplift hands I blest the stars of heaven.
Art thou not cruel? Ever have I striven
To think thee kind, but ah, it will not do!
When yet a child, I heard that kisses drew
Favour from thee, and so I kisses gave
To the void air, bidding them find out love:
But when I came to feel how far above
All fancy, pride, and fickle maidenhood,
All earthly pleasure, all imagin'd good,
Was the warm tremble of a devout kiss,—
Even then, that moment, at the thought of this,
Fainting I fell into a bed of flowers,
And languish'd there three days. Ye milder powers,
Am I not cruelly wrong'd? Believe, believe
Me, dear Endymion, were I to weave
With my own fancies garlands of sweet life,

Thou shouldst be one of all. Ah, bitter strife!
I may not be thy love: I am forbidden—
Indeed I am—thwarted, affrighted, chidden,
By things I trembled at, and gorgon wrath.
Twice hast thou ask'd whither I went: henceforth
Ask me no more! I may not utter it,
Nor may I be thy love. We might commit
Ourselves at once to vengeance; we might die;
We might embrace and die: voluptuous thought!
Enlarge not to my hunger, or I'm caught
In trammels of perverse deliciousness.
No, no, that shall not be: thee will I bless,
And bid a long adieu."

The Carian
No word return'd: both lovelorn, silent, wan,
Into the valleys green together went.
Far wandering, they were perforce content
To sit beneath a fair lone beechen tree;
Nor at each other gaz'd, but heavily
Por'd on its hazel cirque of shedded leaves.

Endymion! unhappy! it nigh grieves
Me to behold thee thus in last extreme:
Ensky'd ere this, but truly that I deem
Truth the best music in a first-born song.
Thy lute-voic'd brother will I sing ere long,
And thou shalt aid—hast thou not aided me?
Yes, moonlight Emperor! felicity
Has been thy meed for many thousand years;
Yet often have I, on the brink of tears,
Mourn'd as if yet thou wert a forester;—
Forgetting the old tale.

He did not stir
His eyes from the dead leaves, or one small pulse
Of joy he might have felt. The spirit culls
Unfaded amaranth, when wild it strays
Through the old garden-ground of boyish days.
A little onward ran the very stream

By which he took his first soft poppy dream;
And on the very bark 'gainst which he leant
A crescent he had carv'd, and round it spent
His skill in little stars. The teeming tree
Had swollen and green'd the pious charactery,
But not ta'en out. Why, there was not a slope
Up which he had not feard' the antelope;
And not a tree, beneath whose rooty shade
He had not with his tamed leopards play'd.
Nor could an arrow light, or javelin,
Fly in the air where his had never been—
And yet he knew it not.

     O treachery!
Why does his lady smile, pleasing her eye
With all his sorrowing? He sees her not.
But who so stares on him? His sister sure!
Peona of the woods!—Can she endure—
Impossible—how dearly they embrace!
His lady smiles; delight is in her face;
It is no treachery.

    "Dear brother mine!
Endymion, weep not so! Why shouldst thou pine
When all great Latmos so exalt wilt be?
Thank the great gods, and look not bitterly;
And speak not one pale word, and sigh no more.
Sure I will not believe thou hast such store
Of grief, to last thee to my kiss again.
Thou surely canst not bear a mind in pain,
Come hand in hand with one so beautiful.
Be happy both of you! for I will pull
The flowers of autumn for your coronals.
Pan's holy priest for young Endymion calls;
And when he is restor'd, thou, fairest dame,
Shalt be our queen. Now, is it not a shame
To see ye thus,—not very, very sad?
Perhaps ye are too happy to be glad:
O feel as if it were a common day;
Free-voic'd as one who never was away.

No tongue shall ask, whence come ye? but ye shall
Be gods of your own rest imperial.
Not even I, for one whole month, will pry
Into the hours that have pass'd us by,
Since in my arbour I did sing to thee.
O Hermes! on this very night will be
A hymning up to Cynthia, queen of light;
For the soothsayers old saw yesternight
Good visions in the air,—whence will befal,
As say these sages, health perpetual
To shepherds and their flocks; and furthermore,
In Dian's face they read the gentle lore:
Therefore for her these vesper-carols are.
Our friends will all be there from nigh and far.
Many upon thy death have ditties made;
And many, even now, their foreheads shade
With cypress, on a day of sacrifice.
New singing for our maids shalt thou devise,
And pluck the sorrow from our huntsmen's brows.
Tell me, my lady-queen, how to espouse
This wayward brother to his rightful joys!
His eyes are on thee bent, as thou didst poise
His fate most goddess-like. Help me, I pray,
To lure—Endymion, dear brother, say
What ails thee?" He could bear no more, and so
Bent his soul fiercely like a spiritual bow,
And twang'd it inwardly, and calmly said:
"I would have thee my only friend, sweet maid!
My only visitor! not ignorant though,
That those deceptions which for pleasure go
'Mong men, are pleasures real as real may be:
But there are higher ones I may not see,
If impiously an earthly realm I take.
Since I saw thee, I have been wide awake
Night after night, and day by day, until
Of the empyrean I have drunk my fill.
Let it content thee, Sister, seeing me
More happy than betides mortality.
A hermit young, I'll live in mossy cave,
Where thou alone shalt come to me, and lave

Thy spirit in the wonders I shall tell.
Through me the shepherd realm shall prosper well;
For to thy tongue will I all health confide.
And, for my sake, let this young maid abide
With thee as a dear sister. Thou alone,
Peona, mayst return to me. I own
This may sound strangely: but when, dearest girl,
Thou seest it for my happiness, no pearl
Will trespass down those cheeks. Companion fair!
Wilt be content to dwell with her, to share
This sister's love with me?" Like one resign'd
And bent by circumstance, and thereby blind
In self-commitment, thus that meek unknown:
"Aye, but a buzzing by my ears has flown,
Of jubilee to Dian:—truth I heard!
Well then, I see there is no little bird,
Tender soever, but is Jove's own care.
Long have I sought for rest, and, unaware,
Behold I find it! so exalted too!
So after my own heart! I knew, I knew
There was a place untenanted in it:
In that same void white Chastity shall sit,
And monitor me nightly to lone slumber.
With sanest lips I vow me to the number
Of Dian's sisterhood; and, kind lady,
With thy good help, this very night shall see
My future days to her fane consecrate."

    As feels a dreamer what doth most create
His own particular fright, so these three felt:
Or like one who, in after ages, knelt
To Lucifer or Baal, when he'd pine
After a little sleep: or when in mine
Far under-ground, a sleeper meets his friends
Who know him not. Each diligently bends
Towards common thoughts and things for very fear;
Striving their ghastly malady to cheer,
By thinking it a thing of yes and no,
That housewives talk of. But the spirit-blow
Was struck, and all were dreamers. At the last

Endymion said: "Are not our fates all cast?
Why stand we here? Adieu, ye tender pair!
Adieu!" Whereat those maidens, with wild stare,
Walk'd dizzily away. Pained and hot
His eyes went after them, until they got
Near to a cypress grove, whose deadly maw,
In one swift moment, would what then he saw
Engulph for ever. "Stay!" he cried, "ah, stay!
Turn, damsels! hist! one word I have to say.
Sweet Indian, I would see thee once again.
It is a thing I dote on: so I'd fain,
Peona, ye should hand in hand repair
Into those holy groves, that silent are
Behind great Dian's temple. I'll be yon,
At vesper's earliest twinkle—they are gone—
But once, once, once again—" At this he press'd
His hands against his face, and then did rest
His head upon a mossy hillock green,
And so remain'd as he a corpse had been
All the long day; save when he scantly lifted
His eyes abroad, to see how shadows shifted
With the slow move of time,—sluggish and weary
Until the poplar tops, in journey dreary,
Had reach'd the river's brim. Then up he rose,
And, slowly as that very river flows,
Walk'd towards the temple grove with this lament:
"Why such a golden eve? The breeze is sent
Careful and soft, that not a leaf may fall
Before the serene father of them all
Bows down his summer head below the west.
Now am I of breath, speech, and speed possest,
But at the setting I must bid adieu
To her for the last time. Night will strew
On the damp grass myriads of lingering leaves,
And with them shall I die; nor much it grieves
To die, when summer dies on the cold sward.
Why, I have been a butterfly, a lord
Of flowers, garlands, love-knots, silly posies,
Groves, meadows, melodies, and arbour roses;
My kingdom's at its death, and just it is

That I should die with it: so in all this
We miscall grief, bale, sorrow, heartbreak, woe,
What is there to plain of? By Titan's foe
I am but rightly serv'd." So saying, he
Tripp'd lightly on, in sort of deathful glee;
Laughing at the clear stream and setting sun,
As though they jests had been: nor had he done
His laugh at nature's holy countenance,
Until that grove appear'd, as if perchance,
And then his tongue with sober seemlihead
Gave utterance as he entered: "Ha!" I said,
"King of the butterflies; but by this gloom,
And by old Rhadamanthus' tongue of doom,
This dusk religion, pomp of solitude,
And the Promethean clay by thief endued,
By old Saturnus' forelock, by his head
Shook with eternal palsy, I did wed
Myself to things of light from infancy;
And thus to be cast out, thus lorn to die,
Is sure enough to make a mortal man
Grow impious." So he inwardly began
On things for which no wording can be found;
Deeper and deeper sinking, until drown'd
Beyond the reach of music: for the choir
Of Cynthia he heard not, though rough briar
Nor muffling thicket interpos'd to dull.
The vesper hymn, far swollen, soft and full,
Through the dark pillars of those sylvan aisles.
He saw not the two maidens, nor their smiles,
Wan as primroses gather'd at midnight
By chilly finger'd spring. "Unhappy wight!
Endymion!" said Peona, "we are here!
What wouldst thou ere we all are laid on bier?"
Then he embrac'd her, and his lady's hand
Press'd, saying: "Sister, I would have command,
If it were heaven's will, on our sad fate."
At which that dark-eyed stranger stood elate
And said, in a new voice, but sweet as love,
To Endymion's amaze: "By Cupid's dove,
And so thou shalt! and by the lily truth

Of my own breast thou shalt, beloved youth!"
And as she spake, into her face there came
Light, as reflected from a silver flame:
Her long black hair swell'd ampler, in display
Full golden; in her eyes a brighter day
Dawn'd blue and full of love. Aye, he beheld
Phœbe, his passion! joyous she upheld
Her lucid bow, continuing thus; "Drear, drear
Has our delaying been; but foolish fear
Withheld me first; and then decrees of fate;
And then 'twas fit that from this mortal state
Thou shouldst, my love, by some unlook'd for change
Be spiritualiz'd. Peona, we shall range
These forests, and to thee they safe shall be
As was thy cradle; hither shalt thou flee
To meet us many a time." Next Cynthia bright
Peona kiss'd, and bless'd with fair good night:
Her brother kiss'd her too, and knelt adown
Before his goddess, in a blissful swoon.
She gave her fair hands to him, and behold,
Before three swiftest kisses he had told,
They vanish'd dar away!—Peona went
Home through the gloomy wood in wonderment.

THE END

LAMIA,
ISABELLA,
THE EVE OF ST. AGNES,
AND
OTHER POEMS

ADVERTISEMENT.

If any apology be thought necessary for the appearance of the unfinished poem of Hyperion, the publishers beg to state that they alone are responsible, as it was printed at their particular request, and contrary to the wish of the author. The poem was intended to have been of equal length with Endymion, but the reception given to that work discouraged the author from proceeding.

Fleet-Street, June 26, 1820.

LAMIA.

PART I.

Upon a time, before the faery broods
Drove Nymph and Satyr from the prosperous woods,
Before King Oberon's bright diadem,
Sceptre, and mantle, clasp'd with dewy gem,
Frighted away the Dryads and the Fauns
From rushes green, and brakes, and cowslip'd lawns,
The ever-smitten Hermes empty left
His golden throne, bent warm on amorous theft:
From high Olympus had he stolen light,
On this side of Jove's clouds, to escape the sight
Of his great summoner, and made retreat
Into a forest on the shores of Crete.
For somewhere in that sacred island dwelt
A nymph, to whom all hoofed Satyrs knelt;
At whose white feet the languid Tritons poured
Pearls, while on land they wither'd and adored.
Fast by the springs where she to bathe was wont,
And in those meads where sometime she might haunt,
Were strewn rich gifts, unknown to any Muse,
Though Fancy's casket were unlock'd to choose.
Ah, what a world of love was at her feet!
So Hermes thought, and a celestial heat
Burnt from his winged heels to either ear,
That from a whiteness, as the lily clear,
Blush'd into roses 'mid his golden hair,
Fallen in jealous curls about his shoulders bare.
From vale to vale, from wood to wood, he flew,
Breathing upon the flowers his passion new,
And wound with many a river to its head,
To find where this sweet nymph prepar'd her secret bed:
In vain; the sweet nymph might nowhere be found,
And so he rested, on the lonely ground,

Pensive, and full of painful jealousies
Of the Wood-Gods, and even the very trees.
There as he stood, he heard a mournful voice,
Such as once heard, in gentle heart, destroys
All pain but pity: thus the lone voice spake:
"When from this wreathed tomb shall I awake!
"When move in a sweet body fit for life,
"And love, and pleasure, and the ruddy strife
"Of hearts and lips! Ah, miserable me!"
The God, dove-footed, glided silently
Round bush and tree, soft-brushing, in his speed,
The taller grasses and full-flowering weed,
Until he found a palpitating snake,
Bright, and cirque-couchant in a dusky brake.

She was a gordian shape of dazzling hue,
Vermilion-spotted, golden, green, and blue;
Striped like a zebra, freckled like a pard,
Eyed like a peacock, and all crimson barr'd;
And full of silver moons, that, as she breathed,
Dissolv'd, or brighter shone, or interwreathed
Their lustres with the gloomier tapestries—
So rainbow-sided, touch'd with miseries,
She seem'd, at once, some penanced lady elf,
Some demon's mistress, or the demon's self.
Upon her crest she wore a wannish fire
Sprinkled with stars, like Ariadne's tiar:
Her head was serpent, but ah, bitter-sweet!
She had a woman's mouth with all its pearls complete:
And for her eyes: what could such eyes do there
But weep, and weep, that they were born so fair?
As Proserpine still weeps for her Sicilian air.
Her throat was serpent, but the words she spake
Came, as through bubbling honey, for Love's sake,
And thus; while Hermes on his pinions lay,
Like a stoop'd falcon ere he takes his prey.

"Fair Hermes, crown'd with feathers, fluttering light"
"I had a splendid dream of thee last night:
"I saw thee sitting, on a throne of gold,

"Among the Gods, upon Olympus old,
"The only sad one; for thou didst not hear
"The soft, lute-finger'd Muses chaunting clear,
"Nor even Apollo when he sang alone,
"Deaf to his throbbing throat's long, long melodious
    moan.
"I dreamt I saw thee, robed in purple flakes,
"Break amorous through the clouds, as morning breaks,
"And, swiftly as a bright Phœbean dart,
"Strike for the Cretan isle; and here thou art!
"Too gentle Hermes, hast thou found the maid?"
Whereat the star of Lethe not delay'd
His rosy eloquence, and thus inquired:
"Thou smooth-lipp'd serpent, surely high inspired!
"Thou beauteous wreath, with melancholy eyes,
"Possess whatever bliss thou canst devise,
"Telling me only where my nymph is fled,—
"Where she doth breathe!" "Bright planet, thou hast
    said,"
Return'd the snake, "but seal with oaths, fair God!"
"I swear," said Hermes, "by my serpent rod,
"And by thine eyes, and by thy starry crown!"
Light flew his earnest words, among the blossoms
    blown.
Then thus again the brilliance feminine:
"Too frail of heart! for this lost nymph of thine,
"Free as the air, invisibly, she strays
"About these thornless wilds; her pleasant days
"She tastes unseen; unseen her nimble feet
"Leave traces in the grass and flowers sweet;
"From weary tendrils, and bow'd branches green,
"She plucks the fruit unseen, she bathes unseen:
"And by my power is her beauty veil'd
"To keep it unaffronted, unassail'd
"By the love-glances of unlovely eyes,
"Of Satyrs, Fauns, and blear'd Silenus' sighs.
"Pale grew her immortality, for woe
"Of all these lovers, and she grieved so
"I took compassion on her, bade her steep
"Her hair in weird syrops, that would keep

"Her loveliness invisible, yet free
"To wander as she loves, in liberty.
"Thou shalt behold her, Hermes, thou alone,
"If thou wilt, as thou swearest, grant my boon!"
Then, once again, the charmed God began
An oath, and through the serpent's ears it ran
Warm, tremulous, devout, psalterian.
Ravish'd, she lifted her Circean head,
Blush'd a live damask, and swift-lisping said,
"I was a woman, let me have once more
"A woman's shape, and charming as before.
"I love a youth of Corinth—O the bliss!
"Give me my woman's form, and place me where
 he is.
"Stoop, Hermes, let me breathe upon thy brow,
"And thou shalt see thy sweet nymph even now."
The God on half-shut feathers sank serene,
She breath'd upon his eyes, and swift was seen
Of both the guarded nymph near-smiling on the
 green.
It was no dream; or say a dream it was,
Real are the dreams of Gods, and smoothly pass
Their pleasures in a long immortal dream.
One warm, flush'd moment, hovering, it might seem
Dash'd by the wood-nymph's beauty, so he burn'd;
Then, lighting on the printless verdure, turn'd
To the swoon'd serpent, and with languid arm,
Delicate, put to proof the lythe Caducean charm.
So done, upon the nymph his eyes he bent,
Full of adoring tears and blandishment,
And towards her stept: she, like a moon in wane,
Faded before him, cower'd, nor could restrain
Her fearful sobs, self-folding like a flower
That faints into itself at evening hour:
But the God fostering her chilled hand,
She felt the warmth, her eyelids open'd bland,
And, like new flowers at morning song of bees,
Bloom'd, and gave up her honey to the lees.
Into the green-recessed woods they flew;
Nor grew they pale, as mortal lovers do.

Left to herself, the serpent now began
To change; her elfin blood in madness ran,
Her mouth foam'd, and the grass, therewith besprent,
Wither'd at dew so sweet and virulent;
Her eyes in torture fix'd, and anguish drear,
Hot, glaz'd, and wide, with lid-lashes all sear,
Flash'd phosphor and sharp sparks, without one cool-
        ing tear.
The colours all inflam'd throughout her train,
She writh'd about, convuls'd with scarlet pain:
A deep volcanian yellow took the place
Of all her milder-mooned body's grace;
And, as the lava ravishes the mead,
Spoilt all her silver mail, and golden brede;
Made gloom of all her frecklings, streaks and bars,
Eclips'd her crescents, and lick'd up her stars:
So that, in moments few, she was undrest
Of all her sapphires, greens, and amethyst,
And rubious-argent: of all these bereft,
Nothing but pain and ugliness were left.
Still shone her crown; that vanish'd, also she
Melted and disappear'd as suddenly;
And in the air, her new voice luting soft,
Cried, "Lycius! gentle Lycius!"—Borne aloft
With the bright mists about the mountains hoar
These words dissolv'd: Crete's forests heard no
        more.

Whither fled Lamia, now a lady bright,
A full-born beauty new and exquisite?
She fled into that valley they pass o'er
Who go to Corinth from Cenchreas' shore;
And rested at the foot of those wild hills,
The rugged founts of the Peræan rills,
And of that other ridge whose barren back
Stretches, with all its mist and cloudy rack,
South-westward to Cleone. There she stood
About a young bird's flutter from a wood,
Fair, on a sloping green of mossy tread,
By a clear pool, wherein she passioned

To see herself escap'd from so sore ills,
While her robes flaunted with the daffodils.

Ah, happy Lycius!—for she was a maid
More beautiful than ever twisted braid,
Or sigh'd, or blush'd, or on spring-flowered lea
Spread a green kirtle to the minstrelsy:
A virgin purest lipp'd, yet in the lore
Of love deep learned to the red heart's core:
Not one hour old, yet of sciential brain
To unperplex bliss from its neighbour pain;
Define their pettish limits, and estrange
Their points of contact, and swift counterchange;
Intrigue with the specious chaos, and dispart
Its most ambiguous atoms with sure art;
As though in Cupid's college she had spent
Sweet days a lovely graduate, still unshent,
And kept his rosy terms in idle languishment.

Why this fair creature chose so fairily
By the wayside to linger, we shall see;
But first 'tis fit to tell how she could muse
And dream, when in the serpent prison-house,
Of all she list, strange or magnificent:
How, ever, where she will'd, her spirit went;
Whether to faint Elysium, or where
Down through tress-lifting waves the Nereids fair
Wind into Thetis' bower by many a pearly stair;
Or where God Bacchus drains his cups divine,
Stretch'd out, at ease, beneath a glutinous pine;
Or where in Pluto's gardens palatine
Mulciber's columns gleam in far piazzian line.
And sometimes into cities she would send
Her dream, with feast and rioting to blend;
And once, while among mortals dreaming thus,
She saw the young Corinthian Lycius
Charioting foremost in the envious race,
Like a young Jove with calm uneager face,
And fell into a swooning love of him.
Now on the moth-time of that evening dim

He would return that way, as well she knew,
To Corinth from the shore; for freshly blew
The eastern soft wind, and his galley now
Grated the quaystones with her brazen prow
In port Cenchreas, from Egina isle
Fresh anchor'd; whither he had been awhile
To sacrifice to Jove, whose temple there
Waits with high marble doors for blood and incense
    rare.
Jove heard his vows, and better'd his desire;
For by some freakful chance he made retire
From his companions, and set forth to walk,
Perhaps grown wearied of their Corinth talk:
Over the solitary hills he fared,
Thoughtless at first, but ere eve's star appeared
His phantasy was lost, where reason fades,
In the calm'd twilight of Platonic shades.
Lamia beheld him coming, near, more near—
Close to her passing, in indifference drear,
His silent sandals swept the mossy green;
So neighbour'd to him, and yet so unseen
She stood: he pass'd, shut up in mysteries,
His mind wrapp'd like his mantle, while her eyes
Follow'd his steps, and her neck regal white
Turn'd—syllabling thus, "Ah, Lycius bright,
"And will you leave me on the hills alone?
"Lycius, look back! and be some pity shown."
He did; not with cold wonder fearingly,
But Orpheus-like at an Eurydice;
For so delicious were the words she sung,
It seem'd he had lov'd them a whole summer long:
And soon his eyes had drunk her beauty up,
Leaving no drop in the bewildering cup,
And still the cup was full,—while he, afraid
Lest she should vanish ere his lip had paid
Due adoration, thus began to adore;
Her soft look growing coy, she saw his chain so sure:
"Leave thee alone! Look back! Ah, Goddess, see
"Whether my eyes can ever turn from thee!
"For pity do not this sad heart belie—

"Even as thou vanishest so I shall die.
"Stay! though a Naiad of the rivers, stay!
"To thy far wishes will thy streams obey:
"Stay! though the greenest woods be thy domain,
"Alone they can drink up the morning rain;
"Though a descended Pleiad, will not one
"Of thine harmonious sisters keep in tune
"Thy spheres, and as thy silver proxy shine?
"So sweetly to these ravish'd ears of mine
"Came thy sweet greeting, that if thou shouldst fade
"Thy memory will waste me to a shade:—
"For pity do not melt!"—"If I should stay,"
Said Lamia, "here, upon this floor of clay,
"And pain my steps upon these flowers too rough,
"What canst thou say or do of charm enough
"To dull the nice remembrance of my home?
"Thou canst not ask me with thee here to roam
"Over these hills and vales, where no joy is,—
"Empty of immortality and bliss!
"Thou art a scholar, Lycius, and must know
"That finer spirits cannot breathe below
"In human climes, and live: Alas! poor youth,
"What taste of purer air hast thou to soothe
"My essence? What serener palaces,
"Where I may all my many senses please,
"And by mysterious sleights a hundred thirsts appease?
"It cannot be—Adieu!" So said, she rose
Tiptoe with white arms spread. He, sick to lose
The amorous promise of her lone complain,
Swoon'd murmuring of love, and pale with pain.
The cruel lady, without any show
Of sorrow for her tender favourite's woe,
But rather, if her eyes could brighter be,
With brighter eyes and slow amenity,
Put her new lips to his, and gave afresh
The life she had so tangled in her mesh:
And as he from one trance was wakening
Into another, she began to sing,
Happy in beauty, life, and love, and every thing,

A song of love, too sweet for earthly lyres,
While, like held breath, the stars drew in their panting
            fires.
And then she whisper'd in such trembling tone,
As those who, safe together met alone
For the first time through many anguish'd days,
Use other speech than looks; bidding him raise
His drooping head, and clear his soul of doubt,
For that she was a woman, and without
Any more subtle fluid in her veins
Than throbbing blood, and that the self-same pains
Inhabited her frail-strung heart as his.
And next she wonder'd how his eyes could miss
Her face so long in Corinth, where, she said,
She dwelt but half retir'd, and there had led
Days happy as the gold coin could invent
Without the aid of love; yet in content
Till she saw him, as once she pass'd him by,
Where 'gainst a column he leant thoughtfully
At Venus' temple porch, 'mid baskets heap'd
Of amorous herbs and flowers, newly reap'd
Late on that eve, as 'twas the night before
The Adonian feast; whereof she saw no more,
But wept alone those days, for why should she adore?
Lycius from death awoke into amaze,
To see her still, and singing so sweet lays;
Then from amaze into delight he fell
To hear her whisper woman's lore so well;
And every word she spake entic'd him on
To unperplex'd delight and pleasure known.
Let the mad poets say whate'er they please
Of the sweets of Fairies, Peris, Goddesses,
There is not such a treat among them all,
Haunters of cavern, lake, and waterfall,
As a real woman, lineal indeed
From Pyrrha's pebbles or old Adam's seed.
Thus gentle Lamia judg'd, and judg'd aright,
That Lycius could not love in half a fright,
So threw the goddess off, and won his heart
More pleasantly by playing woman's part,

With no more awe than what her beauty gave,
That, while it smote, still guaranteed to save.
Lycius to all made eloquent reply,
Marrying to every word a twinborn sigh;
And last, pointing to Corinth, ask'd her sweet,
If 'twas too far that night for her soft feet.
The way was short, for Lamia's eagerness
Made, by a spell, the triple league decrease
To a few paces; not at all surmised
By blinded Lycius, so in her comprized.
They pass'd the city gates, he knew not how,
So noiseless, and he never thought to know.

As men talk in a dream, so Corinth all,
Throughout her palaces imperial,
And all her populous streets and temples lewd,
Mutter'd, like tempest in the distance brew'd,
To the wide-spreaded night above her towers.
Men, women, rich and poor, in the cool hours,
Shuffled their sandals o'er the pavement white,
Companion'd or alone; while many a light
Flared, here and there, from wealthy festivals,
And threw their moving shadows on the walls,
Or found them cluster'd in the corniced shade
Of some arch'd temple door, or dusky colonnade.

Muffling his face, of greeting friends in fear,
Her fingers he press'd hard, as one came near
With curl'd gray beard, sharp eyes, and smooth bald
     crown,
Slow-stepp'd, and robed in philosophic gown:
Lycius shrank closer, as they met and past,
Into his mantle, adding wings to haste,
While hurried Lamia trembled: "Ah," said he,
"Why do you shudder, love, so ruefully?
"Why does your tender palm dissolve in dew?"—
"I'm wearied," said fair Lamia: "tell me who
"Is that old man? I cannot bring to mind
"His features:—Lycius! wherefore did you blind
"Yourself from his quick eyes?" Lycius replied,

172

"'Tis Apollonius sage, my trusty guide
"And good instructor; but to-night he seems
"The ghost of folly haunting my sweet dreams.

While yet he spake they had arrived before
A pillar'd porch, with lofty portal door,
Where hung a silver lamp, whose phosphor glow
Reflected in the slabbed steps below,
Mild as a star in water; for so new,
And so unsullied was the marble hue,
So through the crystal polish, liquid fine,
Ran the dark veins, that none but feet divine
Could e'er have touch'd there. Sounds Æolian
Breath'd from the hinges, as the ample span
Of the wide doors disclos'd a place unknown
Some time to any, but those two alone,
And a few Persian mutes, who that same year
Were seen about the markets: none knew where
They could inhabit; the most curious
Were foil'd, who watch'd to trace them to their house:
And but the flitter-winged verse must tell,
For truth's sake, what woe afterwards befel,
'Twould humour many a heart to leave them thus,
Shut from the busy world of more incredulous.

LAMIA.

PART II.

Love in a hut, with water and a crust,
Is—Love, forgive us!—cinders, ashes, dust;
Love in a palace is perhaps at last
More grievous torment than a hermit's fast:—
That is a doubtful tale from faery land,
Hard for the non-elect to understand.
Had Lycius liv'd to hand his story down,
He might have given the moral a fresh frown,
Or clench'd it quite: but too short was their bliss
To breed distrust and hate, that make the soft voice
    hiss.

Besides, there, nightly, with terrific glare,
Love, jealous grown of so complete a pair,
Hover'd and buzz'd his wings, with fearful roar,
Above the lintel of their chamber door,
And down the passage cast a glow upon the floor.

For all this came a ruin: side by side
They were enthroned, in the even tide,
Upon a couch, near to a curtaining
Whose airy texture, from a golden string,
Floated into the room, and let appear
Unveil'd the summer heaven, blue and clear,
Betwixt two marble shafts:—there they reposed,
Where use had made it sweet, with eyelids closed,
Saving a tythe which love still open kept,
That they might see each other while they almost slept;
When from the slope side of a suburb hill,
Deafening the swallow's twitter, came a thrill
Of trumpets—Lycius started—the sounds fled,
But left a thought, a buzzing in his head.
For the first time, since first he harbour'd in
That purple-lined palace of sweet sin,
His spirit pass'd beyond its golden bourn
Into the noisy world almost forsworn.
The lady, ever watchful, penetrant,
Saw this with pain, so arguing a want
Of something more, more than her empery
Of joys; and she began to moan and sigh
Because he mused beyond her, knowing well
That but a moment's thought is passion's passing bell.
"Why do you sigh, fair creature?" whisper'd he:
"Why do you think?" return'd she tenderly:
"You have deserted me;—where am I now?
"Not in your heart while care weighs on your brow:
"No, no, you have dismiss'd me; and I go
"From your breast houseless: ay, it must be so."
He answer'd, bending to her open eyes,
Where he was mirror'd small in paradise,
"My silver planet, both of eve and morn!
"Why will you plead yourself so sad forlorn,

"While I am striving how to fill my heart
"With deeper crimson, and a double smart?
"How to entangle, trammel up and snare
"Your soul in mine, and labyrinth you there
"Like the hid scent in an unbudded rose?
"Ay, a sweet kiss—you see your mighty woes.
"My thoughts! shall I unveil them? Listen then!
"What mortal hath a prize, that other men
"May be confounded and abash'd withal,
"But lets it sometimes pace abroad majestical,
"And triumph, as in thee I should rejoice
"Amid the hoarse alarm of Corinth's voice.
"Let my foes choke, and my friends shout afar,
"While through the thronged streets your bridal car
"Wheels round its dazzling spokes."—The lady's cheek
Trembled; she nothing said, but, pale and meek,
Arose and knelt before him, wept a rain
Of sorrows at his words; at last with pain
Beseeching him, the while his hand she wrung,
To change his purpose. He thereat was stung,
Perverse, with stronger fancy to reclaim
Her wild and timid nature to his aim;
Besides, for all his love, in self despite,
Against his better self, he took delight
Luxurious in her sorrows, soft and new.
His passion, cruel grown, took on a hue
Fierce and sanguineous as 'twas possible
In one whose brow had no dark veins to swell.
Fine was the mitigated fury, like
Apollo's presence when in act to strike
The serpent—Ha, the serpent! certes, she
Was none. She burnt, she lov'd the tyranny,
And, all subdued, consented to the hour
When to the bridal he should lead his paramour.
Whispering in midnight silence, said the youth,
"Sure some sweet name thou hast, though, by my truth,
"I have not ask'd it, ever thinking thee
"Not mortal, but of heavenly progeny,
"As still I do. Hast any mortal name,
"Fit appellation for this dazzling frame?

"Or friends or kinsfolk on the citied earth,
"To share our marriage feast and nuptial mirth?"
"I have no friends," said Lamia, "no, not one;
"My presence in wide Corinth hardly known:
"My parents' bones are in their dusty urns
"Sepulchred, where no kindled incense burns,
"Seeing all their luckless race are dead, save me,
"And I neglect the holy rite for thee.
"Even as you list invite your many guests;
"But if, as now it seems, your vision rests
"With any pleasure on me, do not bid
"Old Apollonius—from him keep me hid."
Lycius, perplex'd at words so blind and blank,
Made close inquiry; from whose touch she shrank,
Feigning a sleep; and he to the dull shade
Of deep sleep in a moment was betray'd.

It was the custom then to bring away
The bride from home at blushing shut of day,
Veil'd, in a chariot, heralded along
By strewn flowers, torches, and a mariage song,
With other pageants: but this fair unknown
Had not a friend. So being left alone,
(Lycius was gone to summon all his kin)
And knowing surely she could never win
His foolish heart from its mad pompousness,
She set herself, high-thoughted, how to dress
The misery in fit magnificence.
She did so, but 'tis doubtful how and whence
Came, and who were her subtle servitors.
About the halls, and to and from the doors,
There was a noise of wings, till in short space
The glowing banquet-room shone with wide-arched
        grace.
A haunting music, sole perhaps and lone
Supportress of the faery-roof, made moan
Throughout, as fearful the whole charm might fade.
Fresh carved cedar, mimicking a glade
Of palm and plantain, met from either side,
High in the midst, in honour of the bride:

Two palms and then two plantains, and so on,
From either side their stems branch'd one to one
All down the aisled place; and beneath all
There ran a stream of lamps straight on from wall to
    wall.
So canopied, lay an untasted feast
Teeming with odours. Lamia, regal drest,
Silently paced about, and as she went,
In pale contented sort of discontent,
Mission'd her viewless servants to enrich
The fretted splendour of each nook and niche.
Between the tree-stems, marbled plain at first,
Came jasper pannels; then, anon, there burst
Forth creeping imagery of slighter trees,
And with the larger wove in small intricacies.
Approving all, she faded at self-will,
And shut the chamber up, close, hush'd and still,
Complete and ready for the revels rude,
When dreadful guests would come to spoil her solitude.

The day appear'd, and all the gossip rout.
O senseless Lycius! Madman! wherefore flout
The silent-blessing fate, warm cloister'd hours,
And show to common eyes these secret bowers?
The herd approach'd; each guest, with busy brain,
Arriving at the portal, gaz'd amain,
And enter'd marveling: for they knew the street,
Remember'd it from childhood all complete
Without a gap, yet ne'er before had seen
That royal porch, that high-built fair demesne;
So in they hurried all, maz'd, curious and keen:
Save one, who look'd thereon with eye severe,
And with calm-planted steps walk'd in austere;
'Twas Apollonius: something too he laugh'd,
As though some knotty problem, that had daft
His patient thought, had now begun to thaw,
And solve and melt:—'twas just as he foresaw.

He met within the murmurous vestibule
His young disciple. "'Tis no common rule,

"Lycius," said he, "for uninvited guest
"To force himself upon you, and infest
"With an unbidden presence the bright throng
"Of younger friends; yet must I do this wrong,
"And you forgive me." Lycius blush'd, and led
The old man through the inner doors broad-
	spread;
With reconciling words and courteous mien
Turning into sweet milk the sophist's spleen.

Of wealthy lustre was the banquet-room,
Fill'd with pervading brilliance and perfume:
Before each lucid pannel fuming stood
A censer fed with myrrh and spiced wood,
Each by a sacred tripod held aloft,
Whose slender feet wide-swerv'd upon the soft
Wool-woofed carpets: fifty wreaths of smoke
From fifty censers their light voyage took
To the high roof, still mimick'd as they rose
Along the mirror'd walls by twin-clouds odorous.
Twelve sphered tables, by silk seats insphered,
High as the level of a man's breast rear'd
On libbard's paws, upheld the heavy gold
Of cups and goblets, and the store thrice told
Of Ceres' horn, and, in huge vessels, wine
Came from the gloomy tun with merry shine.
Thus loaded with a feast the tables stood,
Each shrining in the midst the image of a God.

When in an antichamber every guest
Had felt the cold full sponge to pleasure press'd,
By minist'ring slaves, upon his hands and feet,
And fragrant oils with ceremony meet
Pour'd on his hair, they all mov'd to the feast
In white robes, and themselves in order placed
Around the silken couches, wondering
Whence all this mighty cost and blaze of wealth could
	spring.

Soft went the music the soft air along,
While fluent Greek a vowel'd undersong
Kept up among the guests, discoursing low
At first, for scarcely was the wine at flow;
But when the happy vintage touch'd their brains,
Louder they talk, and louder come the strains
Of powerful instruments:—the gorgeous dyes,
The space, the splendour of the draperies,
The roof of awful richness, nectarous cheer,
Beautiful slaves, and Lamia's self, appear,
Now, when the wine has done its rosy deed,
And every soul from human trammels freed,
No more so strange; for merry wine, sweet wine,
Will make Elysian shades not too fair, too divine.
Soon was God Bacchus at meridian height;
Flush'd were their cheeks, and bright eyes double
        bright:
Garlands of every green, and every scent
From vales deflower'd, or forest-trees branch-rent,
In baskets of bright osier'd gold were brought
High as the handles heap'd, to suit the thought
Of every guest; that each, as he did please,
Might fancy-fit his brows, silk-pillow'd at his ease.

    What wreath for Lamia? What for Lycius?
What for the sage, old Apollonius?
Upon her aching forehead be there hung
The leaves of willow and of adder's tongue;
And for the youth, quick, let us strip for him
The thyrsus, that his watching eyes may swim
Into forgetfulness; and, for the sage,
Let spear-grass and the spiteful thistle wage
War on his temples. Do not all charms fly
At the mere touch of cold philosophy?
There was an awful rainbow once in heaven:
We know her woof, her texture; she is given
In the dull catalogue of common things.
Philosophy will clip an Angel's wings,
Conquer all mysteries by rule and line,
Empty the haunted air, and gnomed mine—

Unweave a rainbow, as it erewhile made
The tender-person'd Lamia melt into a shade.

By her glad Lycius sitting, in chief place,
Scarce saw in all the room another face,
Till, checking his love trance, a cup he took
Full brimm'd, and opposite sent forth a look
'Cross the broad table, to beseech a glance
From his old teacher's wrinkled countenance,
And pledge him. The bald-head philosopher
Had fix'd his eye, without a twinkle or stir
Full on the alarmed beauty of the bride,
Brow-beating her fair form, and troubling her sweet
     pride.
Lycius then press'd her hand, with devout touch,
As pale it lay upon the rosy couch:
'Twas icy, and the cold ran through his veins;
Then sudden it grew hot, and all the pains
Of an unnatural heat shot to his heart.
"Lamia, what means this? Wherefore dost thou
     start?
"Know'st thou that man?" Poor Lamia answer'd
     not.
He gaz'd into her eyes, and not a jot
Own'd they the lovelorn piteous appeal:
More, more he gaz'd: his human senses reel:
Some hungry spell that loveliness absorbs;
There was no recognition in those orbs.
"Lamia!" he cried—and no soft-toned reply.
The many heard, and the loud revelry
Grew hush; the stately music no more breathes;
The myrtle sicken'd in a thousand wreaths.
By faint degrees, voice, lute, and pleasure ceased;
A deadly silence step by step increased,
Until it seem'd a horrid presence there,
And not a man but felt the terror in his hair.
"Lamia!" he shriek'd; and nothing but the shriek
With its sad echo did the silence break.
"Begone, foul dream!" he cried, gazing again
In the bride's face, where now no azure vein

Wander'd on fair-spaced temples; no soft bloom
Misted the cheek; no passion to illume
The deep-recessed vision:—all was blight;
Lamia, no longer fair, there sat a deadly white.
"Shut, shut those juggling eyes, thou ruthless
    man!
"Turn them aside, wretch! or the righteous ban
"Of all the Gods, whose dreadful images
"Here represent their shadowy presences,
"May pierce them on the sudden with the thorn
"Of painful blindness; leaving thee forlorn,
"In trembling dotage to the feeblest fright
"Of conscience, for their long offended might,
"For all thine impious proud-heart sophistries,
"Unlawful magic, and enticing lies.
"Corinthians! look upon that gray-beard wretch!
"Mark how, possess'd, his lashless eyelids stretch
"Around his demon eyes! Corinthians, see!
"My sweet bride withers at their potency."
"Fool!" said the sophist, in an under-tone
Gruff with contempt; which a death-nighing moan
From Lycius answer'd, as heart-struck and lost,
He sank supine beside the aching ghost.
"Fool! Fool!" repeated he, while his eyes still
Relented not, nor mov'd; "from every ill
"Of life have I preserv'd thee to this day,
"And shall I see thee made a serpent's prey?
Then Lamia breath'd death breath; the sophist's
    eye,
Like a sharp spear, went through her utterly,
Keen, cruel, perceant, stinging: she, as well
As her weak hand could any meaning tell,
Motion'd him to be silent; vainly so,
He look'd and look'd again a level—No!
"A Serpent!" echoed he; no sooner said,
Than with a frightful scream she vanished:
And Lycius' arms were empty of delight,
As were his limbs of life, from that same night.
On the high couch he lay!—his friends came
    round—

Supported him—no pulse, or breath they found,
And, in its marriage robe, the heavy body wound.*

ISABELLA;
OR,
THE POT OF BASIL.
A STORY FROM BOCCACCIO.

I.

Fair Isabel, poor simple Isabel!
Lorenzo, a young palmer in Love's eye!
They could not in the self-same mansion dwell
  Without some stir of heart, some malady;
They could not sit at meals but feel how well
  It soothed each to be the other by;
They could not, sure, beneath the same roof sleep
But to each other dream, and nightly weep.

II.

With every morn their love grew tenderer,
  With every eve deeper and tenderer still;

---

* "Philostratus, in his fourth book *De Vita Apollinii*, hath a memorable instance in this kind, which I may not omit, of one Menippus Lycius, a young man twenty-five years of age, that going betwixt. Cenchreas and Corinth, met such a phantasm in the habit of a fair gentlewoman, which taking him by the hand, carried him home to her house, in the suburbs of Corinth, and told him she was a Phœnician by birth, and if he would tarry with her, he should hear sing and play and drink such wine as never any drank, and no man should molest him; but she, being fair and lovely, would live and die with him, that was fair and lovely to behold. The young man, a philosopher, otherwise staid and discreet, able to moderate his passions, though not this of love, tarried with her a while to his great content, and at last married her, to whose wedding, amongst other guests, came Apollonius; who, by some probable conjectures, found her out to be a serpent, a lamia; and that all her furniture was, like Tantalus' gold, described by Homer, no substance but mere illusions. When she saw herself descried, she wept, and desired Apollonius to be silent, but he would not be moved, and thereupon she, plate, house, and all that was in it, vanished in an instant: many thousand took notice of his fact, for it was done in the midst of Greece."

Burton's 'Anatomy of Melancholy.' *Part 3. Sect. 2. Memb. 1. Subs. 1.*

He might not in house, field, or garden stir,
　But her full shape would all his seeing fill;
And his continual voice was pleasanter
　To her, than noise of trees or hidden rill;
Her lute-string gave an echo of his name,
She spoilt her half-done broidery with the same.

III.

He knew whose gentle hand was at the latch,
　Before the door had given her to his eyes;
And from her chamber-window he would catch
　Her beauty farther than the falcon spies;
And constant as her vespers would he watch,
　Because her face was turn'd to the same skies;
And with sick longing all the night outwear,
To hear her morning-step upon the stair.

IV.

A whole long month of May in this sad plight
　Made their cheeks paler by the break of June:
"To-morrow will I bow to my delight,
　"To-morrow will I ask my lady's boon."—
"O may I never see another night,
　"Lorenzo, if thy lips breathe not love's tune."—
So spake they to their pillows; but, alas,
Honeyless days and days did he let pass;

V.

Until sweet Isabella's untouch'd cheek
　Fell sick within the rose's just domain,
Fell thin as a young mother's, who doth seek
　By every lull to cool her infant's pain:
"How ill she is," said he, "I may not speak,
　"And yet I will, and tell my love all plain:
"If looks speak love-laws, I will drink her tears,
"And at the least 'twill startle off her cares."

VI.

So said he one fair morning, and all day
　His heart beat awfully against his side;

And to his heart he inwardly did pray
    For power to speak; but still the ruddy tide
Stifled his voice, and puls'd resolve away—
    Fever'd his high conceit of such a bride,
Yet brought him to the meekness of a child:
Alas! when passion is both meek and wild!

VII.

So once more he had wak'd and anguished
    A dreary night of love and misery,
If Isabel's quick eye had not been wed
    To every symbol on his forehead high;
She saw it waxing very pale and dead,
    And straight all flush'd; so, lisped tenderly,
"Lorenzo!"—here she ceas'd her timid quest,
But in her tone and look he read the rest.

VIII.

"O Isabella, I can half perceive
    "That I may speak my grief into thine ear;
"If thou didst ever any thing believe,
    "Believe how I love thee, believe how near
"My soul is to its doom: I would not grieve
    "Thy hand by unwelcome pressing, would not fear
"Thine eyes by gazing; but I cannot live
"Another night, and not my passion shrive.

IX.

"Love! thou art leading me from wintry cold,
    "Lady! thou leadest me to summer clime,
"And I must taste the blossoms that unfold
    "In its ripe warmth this gracious morning time."
So said, his erewhile timid lips grew bold,
    And poesied with hers in dewy rhyme:
Great bliss was with them, and great happiness
Grew, like a lusty flower in June's caress.

X.

Parting they seem'd to tread upon the air,
    Twin roses by the zephyr blown apart

Only to meet again more close, and share
　　The inward fragrance of each other's heart.
She, to her chamber gone, a ditty fair
　　Sang, of delicious love and honey'd dart;
He with light steps went up a western hill,
And bade the sun farewell, and joy'd his fill.

XI.

All close they met again, before the dusk
　　Had taken from the stars its pleasant veil,
All close they met, all eves, before the dusk
　　Had taken from the stars its pleasant veil,
Close in a bower of hyacinth and musk,
　　Unknown of any, free from whispering tale.
Ah! better had it been for ever so,
Than idle ears should pleasure in their woe.

XII.

Were they unhappy then?—It cannot be—
　　Too many tears for lovers have been shed,
Too many sighs give we to them in fee,
　　Too much of pity after they are dead,
Too many doleful stories do we see,
　　Whose matter in bright gold were best be read;
Except in such a page where Theseus' spouse
Over the pathless waves towards him bows.

XIII.

But, for the general award of love,
　　The little sweet doth kill much bitterness;
Though Dido silent is in under-grove,
　　And Isabella's was a great distress,
Though young Lorenzo in warm Indian clove
　　Was not embalm'd, this truth is not the less—
Even bees, the little almsmen of spring-bowers,
Know there is richest juice in poison-flowers.

XIV.

With her two brothers this fair lady dwelt,
　　Enriched from ancestral merchandize,

And for them many a weary hand did swelt
  In torched mines and noisy factories,
And many once proud-quiver'd loins did melt
  In blood from stinging whip;—with hollow eyes
Many all day in dazzling river stood,
To take the rich-ored driftings of the flood.

XV.

For them the Ceylon diver held his breath,
  And went all naked to the hungry shark;
For them his ears gush'd blood; for them in death
  The seal on the cold ice with piteous bark
Lay full of darts; for them alone did seethe
A thousand men in troubles wide and dark:
Half-ignorant, they turn'd an easy wheel,
That set sharp racks at work, to pinch and peel.

XVI.

Why were they proud? Because their marble founts
  Gush'd with more pride than do a wretch's tears?—
Why were they proud? Because fair orange-mounts
  Were of more soft ascent than lazar stairs?—
Why were they proud? Because red-lin'd accounts
  Were richer than the songs of Grecian years?—
Why were they proud? again we ask aloud,
Why in the name of Glory were they proud?

XVII.

Yet were these Florentine as self-retired
  In hungry pride and gainful cowardice,
As two close Hebrews in that land inspired,
  Paled in and vineyarded from beggar-spies;
The hawks of ship-mast forests—the untired
  And pannier'd mules for ducats and old lies—
Quick cat's-paws on the generous stray-away,—
Great wits in Spanish, Tuscan, and Malay.

XVIII.

How was it these same ledger-men could spy
  Fair Isabella in her downy nest?

How could they find out in Lorenzo's eye
　　A straying from his toil? Hot Egypt's pest
Into their vision covetous and sly!
　　How could these money-bags see east and west?—
Yet so they did—and every dealer fair
Must see behind, as doth the hunted hare.

XIX.

O eloquent and famed Boccaccio!
　　Of thee we now should ask forgiving boon,
And of thy spicy myrtles as they blow,
　　And of thy roses amorous of the moon,
And of thy lilies, that do paler grow
　　Now they can no more hear thy ghittern's tune,
For venturing syllables that ill beseem
The quiet glooms of such a piteous theme.

XX.

Grant thou a pardon here, and then the tale
　　Shall move on soberly, as it is meet;
There is no other crime, no mad assail
　　To make old prose in modern rhyme more sweet:
But it is done—succeed the verse or fail—
　　To honour thee, and thy gone spirit greet;
To stead thee as a verse in English tongue,
An echo of thee in the north-wind sung.

XXI.

These brethren having found by many signs
　　What love Lorenzo for their sister had,
And how she lov'd him too, each unconfines
　　His bitter thoughts to other, well nigh mad
That he, the servant of their trade designs,
　　Should in their sister's love be blithe and glad
When 'twas their plan to coax her by degrees
To some high noble and his olive-trees.

XXII.

And many a jealous conference had they,
　　And many times they bit their lips alone,

Before they fix'd upon a surest way
　　To make the youngster for his crime atone;
And at the last, these men of cruel clay
　　Cut Mercy with a sharp knife to the bone;
For thy resolved in some forest dim
To kill Lorenzo, and there bury him.

XXIII.

So on a pleasant morning, as he leant
　　Into the sun-rise, o'er the balustrade
Of the garden-terrace, towards him they bent
　　Their footing through the dews; and to him said,
"You seem there in the quiet of content,
　　"Lorenzo, and we are most loth to invade
"Calm speculation; but if you are wise,
"Bestride your steed while cold is in the skies.

XXIV.

"To-day we purpose, ay, this hour we mount
　　"To spur three leagues towards the Apennine;
"Come down, we pray thee, ere the hot sun count
　　"His dewy rosary on the eglantine."
Lorenzo, courteously as he was wont,
　　Bow'd a fair greeting to these serpents' whine;
And went in haste, to get in readiness,
With belt, and spur, and bracing huntsman's dress.

XXV.

And as he to the court-yard pass'd along,
　　Each third step did he pause, and listen'd oft
If he could hear his lady's matin-song,
　　Or the light whisper of her footstep soft;
And as he thus over his passion hung,
　　He heard a laugh full musical aloft;
When, looking up, he saw her features bright
Smile through an in-door lattice, all delight.

XXVI.

"Love, Isabel!" said he, "I was in pain
　　"Lest I should miss to bid thee a good morrow:

"Ah! what if I should lose thee, when so fain
   "I am to stifle all the heavy sorrow
"Of a poor three hour's absence? but we'll gain
   "Out of the amorous dark what day doth borrow.
"Good bye! I'll soon be back."—"Good bye!" said
   she:—
And as he went she chanted merrily.

XXVII.

So the two brothers and their murder'd man
   Rode past fair Florence, to where Arno's stream
Gurgles through straiten'd banks, and still doth fan
   Itself with dancing bulrush, and the bream
Keeps head against the freshets. Sick and wan
   The brothers' faces in the ford did seem,
Lorenzo's flush with love.—They pass'd the water
Into a forest quiet for the slaughter.

XXVIII.

There was Lorenzo slain and buried in,
   There in that forest did his great love cease;
Ah! when a soul doth thus its freedom win,
   It aches in loneliness—is ill at peace
As the break-covert blood-hounds of such sin:
   They dipp'd their swords in the water, and did tease
Their horses homeward, with convulsed spur,
Each richer by his being a murderer.

XXIX.

They told their sister how, with sudden speed,
   Lorenzo had ta'en ship for foreign lands,
Because of some great urgency and need
   In their affairs, requiring trusty hands.
Poor Girl! put on thy stifling widow's weed,
   And 'scape at once from Hope's accursed bands;
To-day thou wilt not see him, nor to-morrow,
And the next day will be a day of sorrow.

XXX.

She weeps alone for pleasures not to be;
   Sorely she wept until the night came on,

And then, instead of love, O misery!
  She brooded o'er the luxury alone:
His image in the dusk she seem'd to see,
  And to the silence made a gentle moan,
Spreading her perfect arms upon the air,
And on her couch low murmuring, "Where? O where?"

XXXI.

But Selfishness, Love's cousin, held not long
  Its fiery vigil in her single breast;
She fretted for the golden hour, and hung
  Upon the time with feverish unrest—
Not long—for soon into her heart a throng
  Of higher occupants, a richer zest,
Came tragic; passion not to be subdued,
And sorrow for her love in travels rude.

XXXII.

In the mid days of autumn, on their eves
  The breath of Winter comes from far away,
And the sick west continually bereaves
  Of some gold tinge, and plays a roundelay
Of death among the bushes and the leaves,
  To make all bare before he dares to stray
From his north cavern. So sweet Isabel
By gradual decay from beauty fell,

XXXIII.

Because Lorenzo came not. Oftentimes
  She ask'd her brothers, with an eye all pale,
Striving to be itself, what dungeon climes
  Could keep him off so long? They spake a tale
Time after time, to quiet her. Their crimes
  Came on them, like a smoke from Hinnom's vale;
And every night in dreams they groan'd aloud,
To see their sister in her snowy shroud.

XXXIV.

And she had died in drowsy ignorance,
  But for a thing more deadly dark than all;

It came like a fierce potion, drunk by chance,
　Which saves a sick man from the feather'd pall
For some few gasping moments; like a lance,
　Waking an Indian from his cloudy hall
With cruel pierce, and bringing him again
Sense of the gnawing fire at heart and brain.

XXXV.

It was a vision.—In the drowsy gloom,
　The dull of midnight, at her couch's foot
Lorenzo stood, and wept: the forest tomb
　Had marr'd his glossy hair which once could shoot
Lustre into the sun, and put cold doom
　Upon his lips, and taken the soft lute
From his lorn voice, and past his loamed ears
Had made a miry channel for his tears.

XXXVI.

Strange sound it was, when the pale shadow spake;
　For there was striving, in its piteous tongue,
To speak as when on earth it was awake,
　And Isabella on its music hung:
Languor there was in it, and tremulous shake,
　As in a palsied Druid's harp unstrung;
And through it moan'd a ghostly under-song,
Like hoarse night-gusts sepulchral briars among.

XXXVII.

Its eyes, though wild, were still all dewy bright
　With love, and kept all phantom fear aloof
From the poor girl by magic of their light,
　The while it did unthread the horrid woof
Of the late darken'd time,—the murderous spite
　Of pride and avarice,—the dark pine roof
In the forest,—and the sodden turfed dell,
Where, without any word, from stabs he fell.

XXXVIII.

Saying moreover, "Isabel, my sweet!
　"Red whortle-berries droop above my head,

"And a large flint-stone weighs upon my feet;
  "Around me beeches and high chestnuts shed
"Their leaves and prickly nuts; a sheep-fold bleat
  "Comes from beyond the river to my bed:
"Go, shed one tear upon my heather-bloom,
"And it shall comfort me within the tomb.

XXXIX.

"I am a shadow now, alas! alas!
  "Upon the skirts of human-nature dwelling
"Alone: I chant alone the holy mass,
  "While little sounds of life are round me knelling,
"And glossy bees at noon do fieldward pass,
  "And many a chapel bell the hour is telling,
"Paining me through: those sounds grow strange to me,
"And thou art distant in Humanity.

XL.

"I know what was, I feel full well what is,
  "And I should rage, if spirits could go mad;
"Though I forget the taste of earthly bliss,
  "That paleness warms my grave, as though I had
"A Seraph chosen from the bright abyss
  "To be my spouse: thy paleness makes me glad;
"Thy beauty grows upon me, and I feel
"A greater love through all my essence steal."

XLI.

The Spirit mourn'd "Adieu!"—dissolv'd, and left
  The atom darkness in a slow turmoil;
As when of healthful midnight sleep bereft,
  Thinking on rugged hours and fruitless toil,
We put our eyes into a pillowy cleft,
  And see the spangly gloom froth up and boil:
It made sad Isabella's eyelids ache,
And in the dawn she started up awake;

XLII.

"Ha! ha!" said she, "I knew not this hard life,
  "I thought the worst was simple misery;

"I thought some Fate with pleasure or with strife
　"Portion'd us—happy days, or else to die;
"But there is crime—a brother's bloody knife!
　"Sweet Spirit, thou hast school'd my infancy:
"I'll visit thee for this, and kiss thine eyes,
"And greet thee morn and even in the skies."

XLIII.

When the full morning came, she had devised
　How she might secret to the forest hie;
How she might find the clay, so dearly prized,
　And sing to it one latest lullaby;
How her short absence might be unsurmised,
　While she the inmost of the dream would try.
Resolv'd, she took with her an aged nurse,
And went into that dismal forest-hearse.

XLIV.

See, as they creep along the river side,
　How she doth whisper to that aged Dame,
And, after looking round the champaign wide,
　Shows her a knife.—"What feverous hectic flame
"Burns in thee, child?—What good can thee betide,
　"That thou should'st smile again?"—The evening
　　came,
And they had found Lorenzo's earthy bed;
The flint was there, the berries at his head.

XLV.

Who hath not loiter'd in a green church-yard,
　And let his spirit, like a demon-mole,
Work through the clayey soil and gravel hard,
　To see skull, coffin'd bones, and funeral stole;
Pitying each form that hungry Death hath marr'd,
　And filling it once more with human soul?
Ah! this is holiday to what was felt
When Isabella by Lorenzo knelt.

XLVI.

She gaz'd into the fresh-thrown mould, as though
　One glance did fully all its secrets tell;

Clearly she saw, as other eyes would know
    Pale limbs at bottom of a crystal well;
Upon the murderous spot she seem'd to grow,
    Like to a native lily of the dell:
Then with her knife, all sudden, she began
To dig more fervently than misers can.

XLVII.

Soon she turn'd up a soiled glove, whereon
    Her silk had play'd in purple phantasies,
She kiss'd it with a lip more chill than stone,
    And put it in her bosom, where it dries
And freezes utterly unto the bone
    Those dainties made to still an infant's cries:
Then 'gan she work again; nor stay'd her care,
But to throw back at times her veiling hair.

XLVIII.

That old nurse stood beside her wondering,
    Until her heart felt pity to the core
At sight of such a dismal labouring,
    And so she kneeled, with her locks all hoar,
And put her lean hands to the horrid thing:
    Three hours they labour'd at this travail sore;
At last they felt the kernel of the grave,
And Isabella did not stamp and rave.

XLIX.

Ah! wherefore all this wormy circumstance?
    Why linger at the yawning tomb so long?
O for the gentleness of old Romance,
    The simple plaining of a minstrel's song!
Fair reader, at the old tale take a glance,
    For here, in truth, it doth not well belong
To speak:—O turn thee to the very tale,
And taste the music of that vision pale.

L.

With duller steel than the Perséan sword
    They cut away no formless monster's head,

But one, whose gentleness did well accord
  With death, as life. The ancient harps have said,
Love never dies, but lives, immortal Lord:
  If Love impersonate was ever dead,
Pale Isabella kiss'd it, and low moan'd.
'Twas love; cold,—dead indeed, but not dethroned.

LI.

In anxious secrecy they took it home,
  And then the prize was all for Isabel:
She calm'd its wild hair with a golden comb,
  And all around each eye's sepulchral cell
Pointed each fringed lash; the smeared loam
  With tears, as chilly as a dripping well,
She drench'd away:—and still she comb'd, and kept
Sighing all day—and still she kiss'd, and wept.

LII.

Then in a silken scarf,—sweet with the dews
  Of precious flowers pluck'd in Araby,
And divine liquids come with odorous ooze
  Through the cold serpent pipe refreshfully,—
She wrapp'd it up; and for its tomb did choose
  A garden-pot, wherein she laid it by,
And cover'd it with mould, and o'er it set
Sweet Basil, which her tears kept ever wet.

LIII.

And she forgot the stars, the moon, and sun,
  And she forgot the blue above the trees,
And she forgot the dells where waters run,
  And she forgot the chilly autumn breeze;
She had no knowledge when the day was done,
  And the new morn she saw not: but in peace
Hung over her sweet Basil evermore,
And moisten'd it with tears unto the core.

LIV.

And so she ever fed it with thin tears,
  Whence thick, and green, and beautiful it grew,

So that it smelt more balmy than its peers
   Of Basil-tufts in Florence; for it drew
Nurture besides, and life, from human fears,
   From the fast mouldering head there shut from view:
So that the jewel, safely casketed,
Came forth and in perfumed leaflets spread.

LV.

O Melancholy, linger here awhile!
   O Music, Music, breathe despondingly!
O Echo, Echo, from some sombre isle,
   Unknown, Lethean, sigh to us—O sigh!
Spirits in grief, lift up your heads, and smile;
   Lift up your heads, sweet Spirits, heavily,
And make a pale light in your cypress glooms,
Tinting with silver wan your marble tombs.

LVI.

Moan hither, all ye syllables of woe,
   From the deep throat of sad Melpomene!
Through bronzed lyre in tragic order go,
   And touch the strings into a mystery;
Sound mournfully upon the winds and low;
   For simple Isabel is soon to be
Among the dead: She withers, like a palm
Cut by an Indian for its juicy balm.

LVII.

O leave the palm to wither by itself;
   Let not quick Winter chill its dying hour!—
It may not be—those Baälites of pelf,
   Her brethren, noted the continual shower
From her dead eyes; and many a curious elf,
   Among her kindred, wonder'd that such dower
Of youth and beauty should be thrown aside
By one mark'd out to be a Noble's bride.

LVIII.

And, furthermore, her brethren wonder'd much
   Why she sat drooping by the Basil green,

And why it flourish'd, as by magic touch;
 Greatly they wonder'd what the thing might mean:
They could not surely give belief, that such
 A very nothing would have power to wean
Her from her own fair youth, and pleasures gay,
And even remembrance of her love's delay.

LIX.

Therefore they watch'd a time when they might sift
 This hidden whim; and long they watch'd in vain;
For seldom did she go to chapel-shrift,
 And seldom felt she any hunger-pain;
And when she left, she hurried back, as swift
 As bird on wing to breast its eggs again;
And, patient as a hen-bird, sat her there
Beside her Basil, weeping through her hair.

LX.

Yet they contriv'd to steal the Basil-pot,
 And to examine it in secret place:
The thing was vile with green and livid spot,
 And yet they knew it was Lorenzo's face:
The guerdon of their murder they had got,
 And so left Florence in a moment's space,
Never to turn again.—Away they went,
With blood upon their heads, to banishment.

LXI.

O Melancholy, turn thine eyes away!
 O Music, Music, breathe despondingly!
O Echo, Echo, on some other day,
 From isles Lethean, sigh to us—O sigh!
Spirits of grief, sing not your "Well-a-way!"
 For Isabel, sweet Isabel, will die;
Will die a death too lone and incomplete,
Now they have ta'en away her Basil sweet.

LXII.

Piteous she look'd on dead and senseless things,
 Asking for her lost Basil amorously:

And with melodious chuckle in the strings
  Of her lorn voice, she oftentimes would cry
After the Pilgrim in his wanderings,
  To ask him where her Basil was; and why
'Twas hid from her: "For cruel 'tis," said she,
"To steal my Basil-pot away from me."

LXIII.

And so she pined, and so she died forlorn,
  Imploring for her Basil to the last.
No heart was there in Florence but did mourn
  In pity of her love, so overcast.
And a sad ditty of this story born
  From mouth to mouth through all the cuntry pass'd:
Still is the burthen sung—"O cruelty,
  "To steal my Basil-pot away from me!"

THE
EVE OF ST. AGNES.

I.

St. Agnes' Eve—Ah, bitter chill it was!
The owl, for all his feathers, was a-cold;
The hare limp'd trembling through the frozen grass
And silent was the flock in woolly fold:
Numb were the Beadsman's fingers, while he told
His rosary, and while his frosted breath,
Like pious incense from a censer old,
Seem'd taking flight for heaven, without a death,
Past the sweet Virgin's picture, while his prayer he
  saith.

II.

His prayer he saith, this patient, holy man;
Then takes his lamp, and riseth from his knees,
And back returneth, meagre, barefoot, wan,
Along the chapel aisle by slow degrees:
The sculptur'd dead, on each side, seem to freeze,

Emprison'd in black, purgatorial rails:
Knights, ladies, praying in dumb orat'ries,
He passeth by; and his weak spirit fails
To think how they may ache in icy hoods and mails.

III.

Northward he turneth through a little door,
And scarce three steps, ere Music's golden tongue
Flatter'd to tears this aged man and poor;
But no—alreday had his deathbell rung;
The joys of all his life were said and sung:
His was harsh penance on St. Agnes' Eve:
Another way he went, and soon among
Rough ashes sat he for his soul's reprieve,
And all night kept awake, for sinners' sake to grieve.

IV.

That ancient Beadsman heard the prelude soft;
And so it chanc'd, for many a door was wide,
From hurry to and fro. Soon, up aloft,
The silver, snarling trumpets 'gan to chide:
The level chambers, ready with their pride,
Were glowing to receive a thousand guests:
The carved angels, ever eager-eyed,
Star'd, where upon their heads the cornice rests,
With hair blown back, and wings put cross-wise on
        their breasts.

V.

At length burst in the argent revelry,
With plume, tiara, and all rich array,
Numerous as shadows haunting fairily
The brain, new stuff'd, in youth, with triumphs gay
Of old romance. These let us wish away,
And turn, sole-thoughted, to one Lady there,
Whose heart had brooded, all that wintry day,
On love, and wing'd St. Agnes' saintly care,
As she had heard old dames full many times declare.

VI.

They told her how, upon St. Agnes' Eve,
  Young virgins might have visions of delight,
  And soft adorings from their loves receive
  Upon the honey'd middle of the night,
  If ceremonies due they did aright;
  As, supperless to bed they must retire,
  And couch supine their beauties, lily white;
  Nor look behind, nor sideways, but require
Of Heaven with upward eyes for all that they desire.

VII.

Full of this whim was thoughtful Madeline:
  The music, yearning like a God in pain,
  She scarcely heard: her maiden eyes divine,
  Fix'd on the floor, saw many a sweeping train
  Pass by—she heeded not at all: in vain
  Came many a tiptoe, amorous cavalier,
  And back retir'd; not cool'd by high disdain,
  But she saw not: her heart was otherwhere:
She sigh'd for Agnes' dreams, the sweetest of the year.

VIII.

She danc'd along with vague, regardless eyes,
  Anxious her lips, her breathing quick and short:
  The hallow'd hour was near at hand: she sighs
  Amid the timbrels, and the throng'd resort
  Of whisperers in anger, or in sport;
  'Mid looks of love, defiance, hate, and scorn,
  Hoodwink'd with faery fancy; all amort,
  Save to St. Agnes and her lambs unshorn,
And all the bliss to be before to-morrow morn.

IX.

So, purposing each moment to retire,
  She linger'd till. Meantime, across the moors,
  Had come young Porphyro, with heart on fire
  For Madeline. Beside the portal doors,
  Buttress'd from moonlight, stands he, and implores
  All saints to give him sight of Madeline,

But for one moment in the tedious hours,
That he might gaze and worship all unseen;
Perchance speak, kneel, touch, kiss—in sooth such
    things have been.

X.

He ventures in: let no buzz'd whisper tell:
All eyes be muffled, or a hundred swords
Will storm his heart, Love's fev'rous citadel:
For him, those chambers held barbarian hordes,
Hyena foemen, and hot-blooded lords,
    Whose very dogs would execrations howl
    Against his lineage: not one breast affords
    Him any mercy, in that mansion foul,
Save one old beldame, weak in body and in soul.

XI.

Ah, happy chance! the aged creature came,
Shuffling along with ivory-headed wand,
To where he stood, hid from the torch's flame,
Behind a broad hall-pillar, far beyond
The sound of merriment and chorus bland:
He startled her; but soon she knew his face,
And grasp'd his fingers in her palsied hand,
    Saying, "Mercy, Porphyro! hie thee from this place;
"They are all here to-night, the whole blood-thirsty
    race!

XII.

"Get hence! get hence! there's dwarfish Hildebrand;
"He had a fever late, and in the fit
"He cursed thee and thine, both house and land:
"Then there's that old Lord Maurice, not a whit
"More tame for his gray hairs—Alas me! flit!
"Flit like a ghost away."—"Ah, Gossip dear,
"We're safe enough; here in this arm-chair sit,
"And tell me how"—"Good Saints! not here, not
    here;
"Follow me, child, or else these stones will be thy
    bier."

XIII.

He follow'd through a lowly arched way,
Brushing the cobwebs with his lofty plume;
And as she mutter'd "Well-a—well-a-day!"
He found him in a little moonlight room,
Pale, lattic'd, chill, and silent as a tomb.
"Now tell me where is Madeline," said he,
"O tell me, Angela, by the holy loom
"Which none but secret sisterhood may see,
"When they St. Agnes' wool are weaving piously."

XIV.

"St. Agnes! Ah! it is St. Agnes' Eve—
"Yet men will murder upon holy days:
"Thou must hold water in a witch's sieve,
"And be liege-lord of all the Elves and Fays,
"To venture so: it fills me with amaze
"To see thee, Porphyro!—St. Agnes' Eve!
"God's help! my lady fair the conjuror plays
"This very night: good angels her deceive!
"But let me laugh awhile, I've mickle time to grieve."

XV.

Feebly she laugheth in the languid moon,
While Porphyro upon her face doth look,
Like puzzled urchin on an aged crone
Who keepeth clos'd a wond'rous riddle-book,
As spectacled she sits in chimney nook.
But soon his eyes grew brilliant when she told
His lady's purpose; and he scarce could brook
Tears, at the thought of those enchantments cold,
And Madeline asleep in lap of legends old.

XVI.

Sudden a thought came like a full-blown rose,
Flushing his brow, and in his pained heart
Made purple riot: then doth he propose
A stratagem, that makes the beldame start:
"A cruel man and impious thou art:
"Sweet lady, let her pray, and sleep, and dream

"Alone with her good angels, far apart
"From wicked men like thee. Go, go!—I deem
"Thou canst not surely be the same that thou didst
    seem.

XVII.

"I will not harm her, by all saints I swear,"
Quoth Porphyro: "O may I ne'er find grace
"When my weak voice shall whisper its last prayer,
"If one of her soft ringlets I displace,
"Or look with ruffian passion in her face:
"Good Angela, believe me by these tears;
"Or I will, even in a moment's space,
"Awake, with horrid shout, my foemen's ears,
"And beard them, though they be more fang'd than
    wolves and bears."

XVIII.

"Ah! why wilt thou affright a feeble soul?
"A poor, weak, palsy-stricken, churchyard thing,
"Whose passing-bell may ere the midnight toll;
"Whose prayers for thee, each morn and evening,
"Were never miss'd."—Thus plaining, doth she
    bring
A gentler speech from burning Porphyro;
So woful, and of such deep sorrowing,
That Angela gives promise she will do
Whatever he shall wish, betide her weal or woe.

XIX.

Which was, to lead him, in close secrecy,
Even to Madeline's chamber, and there hide
Him in a closet, of such privacy
That he might see her beauty unespied,
And win perhaps that night a peerless bride,
While legion'd fairies pac'd the coverlet,
And pale enchantment held her sleepy-eyed.
Never on such a night have lovers met,
Since Merlin paid his Demon all the monstrous debt.

XX.

"It shall be as thou wishest," said the Dame:
"All cates and dainties shall be stored there
"Quickly on this feast-night: by the tambour frame
"Her own lute thou wilt see: no time to spare,
"For I am slow and feeble, and scarce dare
"On such a catering trust my dizzy head.
"Wait here, my child, with patience; kneel in prayer
"The while: Ah! thou must needs the lady wed,
"Or may I never leave my grave among the dead."

XXI.

So saying, she hobbled off with busy fear.
The lover's endless minutes slowly pass'd;
The dame return'd, and whisper'd in his ear
To follow her; with aged eyes aghast
From fright of dim espial. Safe at last,
Through many a dusky gallery, they gain
The maiden's chamber, silken, hush'd, and chaste;
Where Porphyro took covert, pleas'd amain.
His poor guide hurried back with agues in her brain.

XXII.

Her falt'ring hand upon the balustrade,
Old Angela was feeling for the stair,
When Madeline, St. Agnes' charmed maid,
Rose, like a mission'd spirit, unaware:
With silver taper's light, and pious care,
She turn'd, and down the aged gossip led
To a safe level matting. Now prepare,
Young Porphyro, for gazing on that bed;
She comes, she comes again, like ring-dove fray'd and
    fled.

XXIII.

Out went the taper as she hurried in;
Its little smoke, in pallid moonshine, died:
She clos'd the door, she panted, all akin
To spirits of the air, and visions wide:
No uttered syllable, or, woe betide!

But to her heart, her heart was voluble,
Paining with eloquence her balmy side;
As though a tongueless nightingale should swell
Her throat in vain, and die, heart-stifled, in her
dell.

XXIV.

A casement high and triple-arch'd there was,
All garlanded with carven imag'ries
Of fruits, and flowers, and bunches of knot-grass,
And diamonded with panes and quaint device
Innumerable of stains and splendid dyes,
As are the tiger-moth's deep-damask'd wings;
And in the midst, 'mong thousand heraldries,
And twilight saints, and dim emblazonings,
A shielded scutcheon blush'd with blood of queens and
kings.

XXV.

Full on this casement shone the wintry moon,
And threw warm gules on Madeline's fair breast,
As down she knelt for heaven's grace and boon;
Rose-bloom fell on her hands, together prest,
And on her silver cross soft amethyst,
And on her hair a glory, like a saint:
She seem'd a splendid angel, newly drest,
Save wings, for heaven:—Porphyro grew faint:
She knelt, so pure a thing, so free from mortal
taint.

XXVI.

Anon his heart revives: her vespers done,
Of all its wreathed pearls her hair she frees;
Unclasps her warmed jewels one by one;
Loosens her fragrant boddice; by degrees
Her rich attire creeps rustling to her knees:
Half-hidden, like a mermaid in sea-weed,
Pensive awhile she dreams awake, and sees,
In fancy, fair St. Agnes in her bed,
But dares not look behind, or all the charm is fled.

XXVII.

Soon, trembling in her soft and chilly nest,
In sort of wakeful swoon, perplex'd she lay,
Until the poppied warmth of sleep oppress'd
Her soothed limbs, and soul fatigued away;
Flown, like a thought, until the morrow-day;
Blissfully haven'd both from joy and pain;
Clasp'd like a missal where swart Paynims pray;
Blinded alike from sunshine and from rain,
As though a rose should shut, and be a bud again.

XXVIII.

Stol'n to this paradise, and so entranced,
Porphyro gazed upon her empty dress,
And listen'd to her breathing, if it chanced
To wake into a slumberous tenderness;
Which when he heard, that minute did he bless,
And breath'd himself: then from the closet crept,
Noiseless as fear in a wide wilderness,
And over the hush'd carpet, silent, stept,
And 'tween the curtains peep'd, where, lo!—how fast
    she slept.

XXIX.

Then by the bed-side, where the faded moon
Made a dim, silver twilight, soft he set
A table, and half anguish'd, threw thereon
A cloth of woven crimson, gold, and jet:—
O for some drowsy Morphean amulet!
The boisterous, midnight, festive clarion,
The kettle-drum, and far-heard clarionet,
Affray his ears, though but in dying tone:—
The hall door shuts again, and all the noise is gone.

XXX.

And still she slept an azure-lidded sleep,
In blanched linen, smooth, and lavender'd,
While he from forth the closet brought a heap
Of candied apple, quince, and plum, and gourd;
With jellies soother than the creamy curd,

And lucent syrops, tinct with cinnamon;
Manna and dates, in argosy transferr'd
From Fez; and spiced dainties, every one,
From silken Samarcand to cedar'd Lebanon.

XXXI.

These delicates he heap'd with glowing hand
On golden dishes and in baskets bright
　Of wreathed silver: sumptuous they stand
　In the retired quiet of the night,
　Filling the chilly room with perfume light.—
"And now, my love, my seraph fair, awake!
"Thou art my heaven, and I thine eremite:
"Open thine eyes, for meek St. Agnes' sake,
"Or I shall drowse beside thee, so my soul doth
　　ache."

XXXII.

Thus whispering, his warm, unnerved arm
Sank in her pillow. Shaded was her dream
　By the dusk curtains:—'twas a midnight charm
　Impossible to melt as iced stream:
　The lustrous salvers in the moonlight gleam;
Broad golden fringe upon the carpet lies:
It seem'd he never, never could redeem
From such a stedfast spell his lady's eyes;
So mus'd awhile, entoil'd in woofed phantasies.

XXXIII.

Awakening up, he took her hollow lute,—
Tumultuous,—and, in chords that tenderest be,
　He play'd an ancient ditty, long since mute,
　In Provence call'd, "La belle dame sans mercy:"
　Close to her ear touching the melody;—
Wherewith disturb'd, she utter'd a soft moan:
He ceased—she panted quick—and suddenly
Her blue affrayed eyes wide open shone:
Upon his knees he sank, pale as smooth-sculptured
　　stone.

XXXIV.

Her eyes were open, but she still beheld,
Now wide awake, the vision of her sleep:
There was a painful change, that nigh expell'd
The blisses of her dream so pure and deep
At which fair Madeline began to weep,
And moan forth witless words with many a sigh;
While still her gaze on Porphyro would keep;
Who knelt, with joined hands and piteous eye,
Fearing to move or speak, she look'd so dreamingly.

XXXV.

"Ah, Porphyro!" said she, "but even now
"Thy voice was at sweet tremble in mine ear,
"Made tuneable with every sweetest vow;
"And those sad eyes were spiritual and clear:
"How chang'd thou art! how pallid, chill, and drear!
"Give me that voice again, my Porphyro,
"Those looks immortal, those complainings dear!
"Oh leave me not in this eternal woe,
"For if thou diest, my Love, I know not where to go."

XXXVI.

Beyond a mortal man impassion'd far
At these voluptuous accents, he arose,
Ethereal, flush'd, and like a throbbing star
Seen mid the sapphire heaven's deep repose;
Into her dream he melted, as the rose
Blendeth its odour with the violet,—
Solution sweet: meantime the frost-wind blows
Like Love's alarum pattering the sharp sleet
Against the window-panes; St. Agnes' moon hath set.

XXXVII.

'Tis dark: quick pattereth the flaw-blown sleet:
"This is no dream, my bride, my Madeline!"
'Tis dark: the iced gusts still rave and beat:
"No dream, alas! alas! and woe is mine!
"Porphyro will leave me here to fade and pine.—
"Cruel! what traitor could thee hither bring?

"I curse, for my heart is lost in thine,
"Though thou forsakest a deceived thing;—
"A dove forlorn and lost with sick unpruned wing."

XXXVIII.

"My Madeline! sweet dreamer! lovely bride!
"Say, may I be for aye thy vassal blest?
"Thy beauty's shield, heart-shap'd and vermeil
    dyed?
"Ah, silver shrine, here will I take my rest
"After so many hours of toil and quest,
"A famish'd pilgrim,—saved by miracle.
"Though I have found, I will not rob thy nest
"Saving of thy sweet self; if thou think'st well
"To trust, fair Madeline, to no rude infidel."

XXXIX.

"Hark! 'tis an elfin-storm from faery land,
"Of haggard seeming, but a boon indeed:
"Arise—arise! the morning is at hand;—
"The bloated wassaillers will never heed:—
"Let us away, my love, with happy speed;
"There are no ears to hear, or eyes to see,—
"Drown'd all in Rhenish and the sleepy mead:
"Awake! arise! my love, and fearless be,
"For o'er the southern moors I have a home for thee."

XL.

She hurried at his words, beset with fears,
For there were sleeping dragons all around,
At glaring watch, perhaps, with ready spears—
Down the wide stairs a darkling way they found.—
In all the house was heard no human sound.
A chain-droop'd lamp was flickering by each door;
The arras, rich with horseman, hawk, and hound,
Flutter'd in the besieging wind's uproar;
And the long carpets rose along the gusty floor.

XLI.

They glide, like phantoms, into the wide hall;
Like phantoms, to the iron porch, they glide;

Where lay the Porter, in uneasy sprawl,
With a huge empty flaggon by his side:
The wakeful bloodhound rose, and shook his hide,
But his sagacious eye an inmate owns:
By one, and one, the bolts full easy slide:—
The chains lie silent on the footworn stones;—
The key turns, and the door upon its hinges groans.

XLII.

And they are gone: ay, ages long ago
These lovers fled away into the storm.
That night the Baron dreamt of many a woe,
And all his warrior-guests, with shade and form
Of witch, and demon, and large coffin-worm,
Were long be-nightmar'd. Angela the old
Died palsy-twitch'd, with meagre face deform;
The Beadsman, after thousand aves told,
For aye unsought for slept among his ashes cold.

ODE TO A NIGHTINGALE.
POEMS.
I.

My heart aches, and a drowsy numbness pains
  My sense, as though of hemlock I had drunk,
Or emptied some dull opiate to the drains
  One minute past, and Lethe-wards had sunk:
'Tis not through envy of thy happy lot,
  But being too happy in thine happiness,—
    That thou, light-winged Dryad of the trees,
      In some melodious plot
  Of beechen green, and shadows numberless,
    Singest of summer in full-throated ease.

2.

O, for a draught of vintage! that hath been
  Cool'd a long age in the deep-delved earth,
Tasting of Flora and the country green,
  Dance, and Provençal song, and sunburnt mirth!

O for a beaker full of the warm South,
  Full of the true, the blushful Hippocrene,
    With beaded bubbles winking at the brim,
      And purple-stained mouth;
  That I might drink, and leave the world unseen,
  And with thee fade away into the forest dim:

3.

Fade far away, dissolve, and quite forget
  What thou among the leaves hast never known,
The weariness, the fever, and the fret
  Here, where men sit and hear each other groan;
Where palsy shakes a few, sad, last gray hairs,
  Where youth grows pale, and spectre-thin, and dies;
    Where but to think is to be full of sorrow
      And leaden-eyed despairs,
  Where Beauty cannot keep her lustrous eyes,
    Or new Love pine at them beyond to-morrow.

4.

Away! away! for I will fly to thee,
  Not charioted by Bacchus and his pards,
But on the viewless wings of Poesy,
  Though the dull brain perplexes and retards:
Already with thee! tender is the night,
  And haply the Queen-Moon is on her throne,
    Cluster'd around by all her starry Fays;
      But here there is no light,
  Save what from heaven is with the breezes blown
    Through verdurous glooms and winding mossy
      ways.

5.

I cannot see what flowers are at my feet,
  Nor what soft incense hangs upon the boughs,
But, in embalmed darkness, guess each sweet
  Wherewith the seasonable month endows
The grass, the thicket, and the fruit-tree wild;
  White hawthorn, and the pastoral eglantine;
    Fast fading violets cover'd up in leaves;
      And mid-May's eldest child,

The coming musk-rose, full of dewy wine,
　　The murmurous haunt of flies on summer eves.

6.

Darkling I listen; and, for many a time
　　I have been half in love with easeful Death,
Call'd him soft names in many a mused rhyme,
　　To take into the air my quiet breath;
Now more than ever seems it rich to die,
　　To cease upon the midnight with no pain,
　　　　While thou art pouring forth thy soul abroad
　　　　　　In such an ecstasy!
　　Still wouldst thou sing, and I have ears in vain—
　　　　To thy high requiem become a sod.

7.

Thou wast not born for death, immortal Bird!
　　No hungry generations tread thee down;
The voice I hear this passing night was heard
　　In ancient days by emperor and clown:
Perhaps the self-same song that found a path
　　Through the sad heart of Ruth, when, sick for home,
　　　　She stood in tears amid the alien corn;
　　　　　　The same that oft-times hath
　　Charm'd magic casements, opening on the foam
　　Of perilous seas, in faery lands forlorn.

8.

Forlorn! the very word is like a bell
　　To toll me back from thee to my sole self!
Adieu! the fancy cannot cheat so well
　　As she is fam'd to do, deceiving elf.
Adieu! adieu! thy plaintive anthem fades
　　Past the near meadows, over the still stream,
　　　　Up the hill-side; and now 'tis buried deep
　　　　　　In the next valley-glades:
　　Was it a vision, or a waking dream?
　　Fled is that music:—Do I wake or sleep?

ODE ON A GRECIAN URN.

1.

Thou still unravish'd bride of quietness,
  Thou foster-child of silence and slow time,
Sylvan historian, who canst thus express
  A flowery tale more sweetly than our rhyme:
What leaf-fring'd legend haunts about thy shape
  Of deities or mortals, or of both,
    In Tempe or the dales of Arcady?
  What men or gods are these? What maidens loth?
What mad pursuit? What struggle to escape?
    What pipes and timbrels? What wild ecstasy?

2.

Heard melodies are sweet, but those unheard
  Are sweeter; therefore, ye soft pipes, play on;
Not to the sensual ear, but, more endear'd,
  Pipe to the spirit ditties of no tone:
Fair youth, beneath the trees, thou canst not leave
  Thy song, nor ever can those trees be bare;
    Bold Lover, never, never canst thou kiss,
Though winning near the goal—yet, do not grieve;
  She cannot fade, though thou hast not thy bliss,
    For ever wilt thou love, and she be fair!

3.

Ah, happy, happy boughs! that cannot shed
  Your leaves, nor ever bid the Spring adieu;
And, happy melodist, unwearied,
  For ever piping songs for ever new;
More happy love! more happy, happy love!
  For ever warm and still to be enjoy'd,
    For ever panting, and for ever young;
All breathing human passion far above,
  That leaves a heart high-sorrowful and cloy'd,
    A burning forehead, and a parching tongue.

4.

Who are these coming to the sacrifice?
  To what green altar, O mysterious priest,
Lead'st thou that heifer lowing at the skies,
  And all her silken flanks with garlands drest?
What little town by river or sea shore,
  Or mountain-built with peaceful citadel,
    Is emptied of this folk, this pious morn?
And, little town, thy streets for evermore
  Will silent be; and not a soul to tell
    Why thou art desolate can e'er return.

5.

O Attic shape! Fair attitude! with brede
  Of marble men and maidens overwrought,
With forest branches and the trodden weed;
  Thou, silent form, dost tease us out of thought
As doth eternity: Cold Pastoral!
  When old age shall this generation waste,
    Thou shalt remain, in midst of other woe
Than ours, a friend to man, to whom thou say'st,
  "Beauty is truth, truth beauty,"—that is all
    Ye know on earth, and all ye need to know.

ODE TO PSYCHE.

O Goddess! hear these tuneless numbers, wrung
  By sweet enforcement and remembrance dear,
And pardon that thy secrets should be sung
  Even into thine own soft-conched ear:
Surely I dreamt to-day, or did I see
  The winged Psyche with awaken'd eyes?
I wander'd in a forest thoughtlessly,
  And, on the sudden, fainting with surprise,
Saw two fair creatures, couched side by side
  In deepest grass, beneath the whisp'ring roof
  Of leaves and trembled blossoms, where there ran
    A brooklet, scarce espied:

'Mid hush'd, cool-rooted flowers, fragrant-eyed,
  Blue, silver-white, and budded Tyrian,
They lay calm-breathing on the bedded grass;
  Their arms embraced, and their pinions too;
  Their lips touch'd not, but had not bade adieu,
As if disjoined by soft-handed slumber,
And ready still past kisses to outnumber
  At tender eye-dawn of aurorean love:
      The winged boy I knew;
  But who wast thou, O happy, happy dove?
      His Psyche true!

O latest born and loveliest vision far
  Of all Olympus' faded hierarchy!
Fairer than Phœbe's saphire-region'd star,
  Or Vesper, amorous glow-worm of the sky;
Fairer than these, though temple thou hast none,
      Nor altar heap'd with flowers;
Nor virgin-choir to make delicious moan
      Upon the midnight hours;
No voice, no lute, no pipe, no incense sweet
  From chain-swung censer teeming;
No shrine, no grove, no oracle, no heat
  Of pale-mouth'd prophet dreaming.

O brightest! though too late for antique vows,
  Too, too late for the fond believing lyre,
When holy were the haunted forest boughs,
  Holy the air, the water, and the fire;
Yet even in these days so far retir'd
  From happy pieties, thy lucent fans,
  Fluttering among the faint Olympians,
I see, and sing, by my own eyes inspired.
So let me be thy choir, and make a moan
      Upon the midnight hours;
Thy voice, thy lute, thy pipe, thy incense sweet
  From swinged censer teeming;
Thy shrine, thy grove, thy oracle, thy heat
  Of pale-mouth'd prophet dreaming.

Yes, I will be thy priest, and build a fane
　In some untrodden region of my mind,
Where branched thoughts, new grown with pleasant
　　pain,
　Instead of pines shall murmur in the wind:
Far, far around shall those dark-cluster'd trees
　Fledge the wild-ridged mountains steep by steep;
And there by zephyrs, streams, and birds, and bees,
　The moss-lain Dryads shall be lull'd to sleep;
And in the midst of this wide quiteness
A rosy sanctuary will I dress
With the wreath'd trellis of a working brain,
　With buds, and bells, and stars without a name,
With all the gardener Fancy e'er could feign,
　Who breeding flowers, will never breed the same:
And there shall be for thee all soft delight
　That shadowy thought can win,
A bright torch, and a casement ope at night,
　To let the warm Love in!

FANCY.

Ever let the Fancy roam,
Pleasure never is at home:
At a touch sweet Pleasure melteth,
Like to bubbles when rain pelteth;
Then let winged Fancy wander
Through the thought still spread beyond her:
Open wide the mind's cage-door,
She'll dart forth, and cloudward soar.
O sweet Fancy! let her loose;
Summer's joys are spoilt by use,
And the enjoying of the Spring
Fades as does its blossoming;
Autumn's red-lipp'd fruitage too,
Blushing through the mist and dew,
Cloys with tasting: What do then?
Sit thee by the ingle, when

The sear faggot blazes bright,
Spirit of a winter's night;
When the soundless earth is muffled,
And the caked snow is shuffled
From the ploughboy's heavy shoon;
When the Night doth meet the Noon
In a dark conspiracy
To banish Even from her sky.
Sit thee there, and send abroad,
With a mind self-overaw'd,
Fancy, high-commission'd:—send her!
She has vassals to attend her:
She will bring, in spite of frost,
Beauties that the earth hath lost;
She will bring thee, all together,
All delights of summer weather;
All the buds and bells of May,
From dewy sward or thorny spray;
All the heaped Autumn's wealth,
With a still, mysterious stealth:
She will mix these pleasures up
Like three fit wines in a cup,
And thou shalt quaff it:—thou shalt hear
Distant harvest-carols clear;
Rustle of the reaped corn;
Sweet birds antheming the morn:
And, in the same moment—hark!
'Tis the early April lark,
Or the rooks, with busy caw,
Foraging for sticks and straw.
Thou shalt, at one glance, behold
The daisy and the marigold;
White-plum'd lilies, and the first
Hedge-grown primrose that hath burst;
Shaded hyacinth, alway
Sapphire queen of the mid-May;
And every leaf, and every flower
Pearled with the self-same shower.
Thou shalt see the field-mouse peep
Meagre from its celled sleep;

And the snake all winter-thin
Cast on sunny bank its skin;
Freckled nest-eggs thou shalt see
Hatching in the hawthorn-tree,
When the hen-bird's wing doth rest
Quiet on her mossy nest;
Then the hurry and alarm
When the bee-hive casts its swarm;
Acorns ripe down-pattering,
While the autumn breezes sing.

Oh, sweet Fancy! let her loose;
Every thing is spoilt by use:
Where's the cheek that doth not fade,
Too much gaz'd at? Where's the maid
Whose lip mature is ever new?
Where's the eye, however bule,
Doth not weary? Where's the face
One would meet in every place?
Where's the voice, however soft,
One would hear so very oft?
At a touch sweet Pleasure melteth
Like to bubbles when rain pelteth.
Let, then, winged Fancy find
Thee a mistress to thy mind;
Dulcet-eyed as Ceres' daughter,
Ere the God of Torment taught her
How to frown and how to chide;
With a waist and with a side
White as Hebe's, when her zone
Slipt its golden clasp, and down
Fell her kirtle to her feet,
While she held the goblet sweet,
And Jove grew languid.—Break the mesh
Of the Fancy's silken leash;
Quickly break her prison-string
And such joys as these she'll bring.—
Let the winged Fancy roam,
Pleasure never is at home.

ODE.

BARDS of Passion and of Mirth,
Ye have left your souls on earth!
Have ye souls in heaven too,
Double-lived in regions new?
Yes, and those of heaven commune
With the spheres of sun and moon;
With the noise of fountains wond'rous,
And the parle of voices thund'rous;
With the whisper of heaven's trees
And one another, in soft ease
Seated on Elysian lawns
Brows'd by none but Dian's fawns;
Underneath large blue-bells tented,
Where the daisies are rose-scented,
And the rose herself has got
Perfume which on earth is not;
Where the nightingale doth sing
Not a senseless, tranced thing,
But divine melodious truth;
Philosophic numbers smooth;
Tales and golden histories
Of heaven and its mysteries.

Thus ye live on high, and then
On the earth ye live again;
And the souls ye left behind you
Teach us, here, the way to find you,
Where your other souls are joying,
Never slumber'd, never cloying.
Here, your earth-born souls still speak
To mortals, of their little week;
Of their sorrows and delights;
Of their passions and their spites;
Of their glory and their shame;
What doth strengthen and what maim.
Thus ye teach us, every day,
Wisdom, though fled far away.

Bards of Passion and of Mirth,
Ye have left your souls on earth!
Ye have souls in heaven too,
Double-lived in regions new!

LINES
ON
THE MERMAID TAVERN.

Souls of Poets dead and gone,
What Elysium have ye known,
Happy field or mossy cavern,
Choicer than the Mermaid Tavern?
Have ye tippled drink more fine
Than mine host's Canary wine?

Or are fruits of Paradise
Sweeter than those dainty pies
Of venison? O generous food!
Drest as though bold Robin Hood
Would, with his maid Marian,
Sup and bowse from horn and can.

I have heard that on a day
Mine host's sign-board flew away,
Nobody knew whither, till
An astrologer's old quill
To a sheepskin gave the story,
Said he saw you in your glory,
Underneath a new old-sign
Sipping beverage divine,
And pledging with contented smack
The Mermaid in the Zodiac.

Souls of Poets dead and gone,
What Elysium have ye known,
Happy field or mossy cavern,
Choicer than the Mermaid Tavern?

ROBIN HOOD.
TO A FRIEND

No! those days are gone away,
And their hours are old and gray,
And their minutes buried all
Under the down-trodden pall
Of the leaves of many years:
Many times have winter's shears,
Frozen North, and chilling East,
Sounded tempests to the feast
Of the forest's whispering fleeces,
Since men knew nor rent nor leases.

No, the bugle sounds no more,
And the twanging bow no more;
Silent is the ivory shrill
Past the heath and up the hill;
There is no mid-forest laugh,
Where lone Echo gives the half
To some wight, amaz'd to hear
Jesting, deep in forest drear.

On the fairest time of June
You may go, with sun or moon,
Or the seven stars to light you,
Or the polar ray to right you;
But you never may behold
Little John, or Robin bold;
Never one, of all the clan,
Thrumming on an empty can
Some old hunting ditty, while
He doth his green way beguile
To fair hostess Merriment,
Down beside he pasture Trent;
For he left the merry tale
Messenger for spicy ale.

Gone, the merry morris din;
Gone, the song of Gamelyn;

Gone, the tough-belted outlaw
Idling in the "grenè shawe;"
All are gone away and past!
And if Robin should be cast
Sudden from his turfed grave,
And if Marian should have
Once again her forest days,
She would weep, and he would craze:
He would swear, for all his oaks,
Fall'n beneath the dockyard strokes,
Have rotted on the briny seas;
She would weep that her wild bees
Sang not to her—strange! that honey
Can't be got without hard money!

So it is: yet let us sing,
Honour to the old bow-string!
Honour to the bugle-horn!
Honour to the woods unshorn!
Honour to the Lincoln green!
Honour to the archer keen!
Honour to tight Little John,
And the horse he rode upon!
Honour to bold Robin Hood,
Sleeping in the underwood!
Honour to Maid Marian,
And to all the Sherwood-clan!
Though their days have hurried by,
Let us two a burden try.

TO AUTUMN.

1.

SEASON of mists and mellow fruitfulness,
  Close bosom-friend of the maturing sun;
Conspiring with him how to load and bless
  With fruit the vines that round the thatch-eves run;
To bend with apples the moss'd cottage-trees,

And fill all fruit with ripeness to the core;
  To swell the gourd, and plump the hazel shells
With a sweet kernel; to set budding more,
  And still more, later flowers for the bees,
  Until they think warm days will never cease,
    For Summer has o'er-brimm'd their clammy cells.

2.

Who hath not seen thee oft amid thy store?
  Sometimes whoever seeks abroad may find
Thee sitting careless on a granary floor,
  Thy hair soft-lifted by the winnowing wind;
Or on a half-reap'd furrow sound asleep,
  Drows'd with the fume of poppies, while thy hook
    Spares the next swath and all its twined flowers:
And sometimes like a gleaner thou dost keep
  Steady thy laden head across a brook;
  Or by a cyder-press, with patient look,
    Thou watchest the last oozings hours by hours.

3.

Where are the songs of Spring? Ay, where are they?
  Think not of them, thou hast thy music too,—
While barred clouds bloom the soft-dying day,
  And touch the stubble-plains with rosy hue;
Then in a wailful choir the small gnats mourn
  Among the river sallows, borne aloft
  Or sinking as the light wind lives or dies;
And full-grown lambs loud bleat from hilly bourn;
  Hedge-crickets sing; and now with treble soft
  The red-breast whistles from a garden-croft;
    And gathering swallows twitter in the skies.

ODE ON MELANCHOLY.

1.

No, no, go not to Lethe, neither twist
  Wolf's-bane, tight-rooted, for its poisonous wine;

Nor suffer thy pale forehead to be kiss'd
　　By nightshade, ruby grape of Proserpine;
Make not your rosary of yew-berries,
　　Nor let the beetle, nor the death-moth be
　　　　Your mournful Psyche, nor the downy owl
A partner in your sorrow's mysteries;
　　For shade to shade will come too drowsily,
　　　　And drown the wakeful anguish of the soul.

2.

But when the melancholy fit shall fall
　　Sudden from heaven like a weeping cloud,
That fosters the droop-headed flowers all,
　　And hides the green hill in an April shroud;
Then glut thy sorrow on a morning rose,
　　Or on the rainbow of the salt sand-wave,
　　　　Or on the wealth of globed peonies;
Or if thy mistress some rich anger shows,
　　Emprison her soft hand, and let her rave,
　　　　And feed deep, deep upon her peerless eyes.

3.

She dwells with Beauty—Beauty that must die;
　　And Joy, whose hand is ever at his lips
Bidding adieu; and aching Pleasure nigh,
　　Turning to poison while the bee-mouth sips:
Ay, in the very temple of Delight
　　Veil'd Melancholy has her sovran shrine,
　　　　Though seen of none save him whose strenous
　　　　　　tongue
Can burst Joy's grape against his palate fine;
　　His soul shall taste the sadness of her might,
　　　　And be among her cloudy trophies hung.

HYPERION.

A FRAGMENT

BOOK I.

DEEP in the shady sadness of a vale
Far sunken from the healthy breath of morn,
Far from the fiery noon, and eve's one star,
Sat gray-hair'd Saturn, quiet as a stone,
Still as the silence round about his lair;
Forest on forest hung about his head
Like cloud on cloud. No stir of air was there,
Not so much life as on a summer's day
Robs not one light seed from the feather'd grass,
But where the dead leaf fell, there did it rest.
A stream went voiceless by, still deadened more
By reason of his fallen divinity
Spreading a shade: the Naiad 'mid her reeds
Press'd her cold finger closer to her lips.

Along the margin-sand large foot-marks went,
No further than to where his feet had stray'd,
And slept there since. Upon the sodden ground
His old right hand lay nerveless, listless, dead,
Unsceptred; and his realmless eyes were closed;
While his bow'd head seem'd list'ning to the Earth,
His ancient mother, for some comfort yet.

It seem'd no force could wake him from his place;
But there came one, who with a kindred hand
Touch'd his wide shoulders, after bending low
With reverence, though to one who knew it not.
She was a Goddess of the infant world;
By her in stature the tall Amazon
Had stood a pigmy's height: she would have ta'en
Achilles by the hair and bent his neck;
Or with a finger stay'd Ixion's wheel.
Her face was large as that of Memphian sphinx,

Pedestal'd haply in a palace court,
When sages look'd to Egypt for their lore.
But oh! how unlike marble was that face:
How beautiful, if sorrow had not made
Sorrow more beautiful than Beauty's self.
There was a listening fear in her regard,
As if calamity had but begun;
As if the vanward clouds of evil days
Had spent their malice, and the sullen rear
Was with its stored thunder labouring up.
One hand she press'd upon that aching spot
Where beats the human heart, as if just there,
Though an immortal, she felt cruel pain:
The other upon Saturn's bended neck
She laid, and to the level of his ear
Leaning with parted lips, some words she spake
In solemn tenour and deep organ tone:
Some mourning words, which in our feeble tongue
Would come in these like accents; O how frail
To that large utterance of the early Gods!
"Saturn, look up!—though wherefore, poor old King?
"I have no comfort for thee, no not one:
"I cannot say. 'O wherefore sleepest thou?'
"For heaven is parted from thee, and the earth
"Knows thee not, thus afflicted, for a God;
"And ocean too, with all its solemn noise,
"Has from thy sceptre pass'd; and all the air
"Is emptied of thine hoary majesty.
"Thy thunder, conscious of the new command,
"Rumbles reluctant o'er our fallen house;
"And thy sharp lightning in unpractised hands
"Scorches and burns our once serene domain.
"O aching time! O moments big as years!
"All as ye pass swell out the monstrous truth,
"And press it so upon our weary griefs
"That unbelief has not a space to breathe.
"Saturn, sleep on:—O thoughtless, why did I
"Thus violate thy slumbrous solitude?
"Why should I ope thy melancholy eyes?
"Saturn, sleep on! while at thy feet I weep."

As when, upon a tranced summer-night,
Those green-rob'd senators of mighty woods,
Tall oaks, branch-charmed by the earnest stars,
Dream, and so dream all night without a stir,
Save from one gradual solitary gust
Which comes upon the silence, and dies off,
As if the ebbing air had but one wave;
So came these words and went; the while in tears
She touch'd her fair large forehead to the ground,
Just where her falling hair might be outspread
A soft and silken mat for Saturn's feet.
One moon, with alteration slow, had shed
Her silver seasons four upon the night,
And still these two were postured motionless,
Like natural sculpture in cathedral cavern;
The frozen God still couchant on the earth,
And the sad Goddess weeping at his feet:
Until at length old Saturn lifted up
His faded eyes, and saw his kingdom gone,
And all the gloom and sorrow of the place,
And that fair kneeling Goddess; and then spake,
As with a palsied tongue, and while his beard
Shook horrid with such aspen-malady:
"O tender spouse of gold Hyperion,
"Thea, I feel thee ere I see thy face;
"Look up, and let me see our doom in it;
"Look up, and tell me if this feeble shape
"Is Saturn's; tell me, if tou hear'st the voice
"Of Saturn; tell me, if this wrinkling brow,
"Naked and bare of its great diadem,
"Peers like the front of Saturn. Who had power
"To make me desolate? whence came the strength?
"How was it nurtur'd to such bursting forth,
"While Fate seem'd strangled in my nervous grasp?
"But it is so; and I am smother'd up,
"And buried from all godlike exercise
"Of influence benign on planets pale,
"Of admonitions to the winds and seas,
"Of peaceful sway above man's harvesting,
"And all those acts which Deity supreme

"Doth ease its heart of love in.—I am gone
"Away from my own bosom: I have left
"My strong identity, my real self,
"Somewhere between the throne, and where I sit
"Here on this spot of earth. Search, Thea, search!
"Open thine eyes eterne, and sphere them round
"Upon all space: space starr'd, and lorn of light;
"Space region'd with life-air; and barren void;
"Spaces of fire, and all the yawn of hell.—
"Search, Thea, search! and tell me, if thou seest
"A certain shape or shadow, making way
"With wings or chariot fierce to repossess
"A heaven he lost erewhile: it must—it must
"Be of ripe progress—Saturn must be King.
"Yes, there must be a golden victory;
"There must be Gods thrown down, and trumpets
        blown
"Of triumph calm, and hymns of festival
"Upon the gold clouds metropolitan,
"Voices of soft proclaim, and silver stir
"Of strings in hollow shells; and there shall be
"Beautiful things made new, for the surprise
"Of the sky-children; I will give command:
"Thea! Thea! Thea! where is Saturn?"

    This passion lifted him upon his feet,
And made his hands to struggle in the air,
His Druid locks to shake and ooze with sweat,
His eyes to fever out, his voice to cease.
He stood, and heard not Thea's sobbing deep;
A little time, and then again he snatch'd
Utterance thus.—"But cannot I create?
"Cannot I form? Cannot I fashion forth
"Another world, another universe,
"To overbear and crumble this to nought?
"Where is another chaos? Where?"—That word
Found way unto Olympus, and made quake
The rebel three.—Thea was startled up,
And in her bearing was a sort of hope,
As thus she quick-voic'd spake, yet full of awe.

"This cheers our fallen house: come to our friends,
"O Saturn! come away, and give them heart:
"I know the covert, for thence came I hither."
Thus brief; then with beseeching eyes she went
With backward footing through the shade a space:
He follow'd, and she turn'd to lead the way
Through aged boughs, that yielded like the mist
Which eagles cleave upmounting from their nest.

Meanwhile in other realms big tears were shed,
More sorrow like to this, and such like woe,
Too huge for mortal tongue or pen of scribe:
The Titans fierce, self-hid, or prison-bound,
Groan'd for the old allegiance once more,
And listen'd in sharp pain for Saturn's voice.
But one of the whole mammoth-brood still kept
His sov'reignty, and rule, and majesty;—
Blazing Hyperion on his orbed fire
Still sat, still snuff'd the incense, teeming up
From man to the sun's God; yet unsecure:
For as among us mortals omens drear
Fright and perplex, so also shuddered he—
Not at dog's howl, or gloom-bird's hated screech,
Or the familiar visiting of one
Upon the first toll of his passing-bell,
Or prophesyings of the midnight lamp;
But horrors, portion'd to a giant nerve,
Oft made Hyperion ache. His palace bright
Bastion'd with pyramids of glowing gold,
And touch'd with shade of bronzed obelisks,
Glar'd a blood-red through all its thousand courts,
Arches, and domes, and fiery galleries;
And all its curtains of Aurorian clouds
Flush'd angerly: while sometimes eagle's wings,
Unseen before by Gods or wondering men,
Darken'd the place; and neighing steeds were heard,
Not heard before by Gods or wondering men.
Also, when he would taste the spicy wreaths
Of incense, breath'd aloft from sacred hills,
Instead of sweets, his ample palate took

Savour of poisonous brass and metal sick:
And so, when harbour'd in the sleepy west,
After the full completion of fair day,—
For rest divine upon exalted couch
And slumber in the arms of melody,
He pac'd away the pleasant hours of ease
With stride colossal, on from hall to hall;
While far within each aisle and deep recess,
His winged minions in close clusters stood,
Amaz'd and full of fear; like anxious men
Who on wide plains gather in panting troops,
When earthquakes jar their battlements and towers.
Even now, while Saturn, rous'd from icy trance,
Went step for step with Thea through the woods,
Hyperion, leaving twilight in the rear,
Came slope upon the threshold of the west;
Then, as was wont, his palace-door flew ope
In smoothest silence, save what solemn tubes,
Blown by the serious Zephyrs, gave of sweet
And wandering sounds, slow-breathed melodies;
And like a rose in vermeil tint and shape,
In fragrance soft, and coolness to the eye.
That inlet to severe magnificence
Stood full blown, for the God to enter in.

He enter'd, but he enter'd full of wrath;
His flaming robes stream'd out beyond his heels,
And gave a roar, as if of earthly fire,
That scar'd away the meek ethereal Hours
And made their dove-wings tremble. On the flared,
From stately nave to nave, from vault to vault,
Through bowers of fragrant and enwreathed light,
And diamond-paved lustrous long arcades,
Until he reach'd the great main cupola;
There standing fierce beneath, he stampt his foot,
And from the basements deep to the high towers
Jarr'd his own golden region; and before
The quavering thunder thereupon had ceas'd,
His voice leapt out, despite of godlike curb,
To this result: "O dreams of day and night!

"O monstrous forms! O effigies of pain!
"O spectres busy in a cold, cold gloom!
"O lank-ear'd Phantoms of black-weeded pools!
"Why do I know ye? why have I seen ye? why
"Is my eternal thus distraught
"To see and to behold these horrors new?
"Saturn is fallen, am I too to fall?
"Am I to leave this haven of my rest,
"This cradle of my glory, this soft clime,
"This calm luxuriance of blissful light,
".These crystalline pavilions, and pure fanes,
"Of all my lucent empire? It is left
"Deserted, void, nor any haunt of mine.
"The blaze, the splendor, and the symmetry,
"I cannot see—but darkness, death and darkness.
"Even here, into my centre of repose,
"The shady visions come to domineer,
'Insult, and blind, and stifle up my pomp.—
"Fall!—No, by Tellus and her briny robes!
"Over the fiery frontier of my realms
"I will advance a terrible right arm
"Shall scare that infant thunderer, rebel Jove,
"And bid old Saturn take his throne again."—
He spake, and ceas'd, the while a heavier threat
Held struggle with his throat but came not forth;
For as in theatres of crowded men
Hubbub increases more they call out "Hush!"
So at Hyperion's words the Phantoms pale
Bestirr'd themselves, thrice horrible and cold;
And from the mirror'd level where he stood
A mist arose, as from a scummy marsh.
At this, through all his bulk an agony
Crept gradual, from the feet unto the crown,
Like a lithe serpent vast and muscular
Making slow way, with head and neck convuls'd
From over-strained might. Releas'd, he fled
To the eastern gates, and full six dewy hours
Before the dawn in season due should blush,
He breath'd fierce breath against the sleepy portals,
Clear'd them of heavy vapours, burst them wide

Suddenly on the ocean's chilly streams.
The planet orb of fire, whereon he rode
Each day from east to west the heavens through,
Spun round in sable curtaining of clouds;
Not therefore veiled quite, blindfold, and hid,
But ever and anon the glancing spheres,
Circles, and arcs, and broad-belting colure,
Glow'd through, and wrought upon the muffling dark
Sweet-shaped lightnings from the nadir deep
Up to the zenith,—hieroglyphics old,
Which sages and keen-eyed astrologers
Then living on the earth, with labouring thought
Won from the gaze of many centuries:
Now lost; save what we find on remnants huge
Of stone, or marble swart; their import gone,
Their wisdom long since fled.—Two wings this orb
Possess'd for glory, two fair argent wings,
Ever exalted at the God's approach:
And now, from forth the gloom their plumes immense
Rose, one by one, till all outspreaded were;
While still the dazzling globe maintain'd eclipse,
Awaiting for Hyperion's command.
Fain would he have commanded, fain took throne
And bid the day begin, if but for change.
He might not:—No, though a primeval God:
The sacred seasons might not be disturb'd.
Therefore the operations of the dawn
Stay'd in their birth, even as here 'tis told.
Those silver wings expanded sisterly,
Eager to sail their orb; the porches wide
Open'd upon the dusk demesnes of night;
And the bright Titan, phrenzied with new woes,
Unus'd to bend, by hard compulsion bent
His spirit to the sorrow of the time;
And all along a dismal rack of clouds,
Upon the boundaries of day and night,
He stretch'd himself in grief and radiance faint.
There as he lay, the Heaven with its stars
Look'd down on him with pity, and the voice
Of Coelus, from the universal space,

Thus whisper'd low and solemn in his ear.
"O brightest of my children dear, earth-born
"And sky-engendered, Son of Mysteries
"All unrevealed even to the powers
"Which met at thy creating; at whose joys
"And palpitations sweet, and pleasures soft,
"I, Cœlus, wonder, how they came and whence;
"And at the fruits thereof what shapes they be,
"Distinct. and visible; symbols divine,
"Manifestations of that beauteous life
"Diffus'd unseen throughout eternal space:
"Of these new-form'd art thou, oh brightest child!
"Of these, thy brethren and the Goddesses!
"There is sad feud among ye, and rebellion
"Of son against his sire. I saw him fall,
"I saw my first-born tumbled from his throne!
"To me his arms were spread, to me his voice
"Found way from forth the thunders round his head!
"Pale wox I, and in vapours hid my face.
"Art thou, too, near such doom? vague fear there is:
"For I have seen my sons most unlike Gods.
"Divine ye were created, and divine
"In sad demeanour, solemn, undisturb'd,
"Unruffled, like high Gods, ye liv'd and ruled:
"Now I behold in you fear, hope, and wrath;
"Actions of rage and passion; even as
"I see them, on the mortal world beneath,
"In men who die.—This is the grief, O Son!
"Sad sign of ruin, sudden dismay, and fall!
"Yet do thou strive; as thou art capable,
"As thou canst move about, an evident God;
"And canst oppose to each malignant hour
"Ethereal presence:—I am but a voice;
"My life is but the life of winds and tides,
"No more than winds and tides can I avail:—
"But thou canst.—Be thou therefore in the van
"Of circumstance; yea, seize the arrow's barb
"Before the tense string murmur.—To the earth!
"For there thou wilt find Saturn, and his woes.
"Meantime I will keep watch on thy bright sun,

"And of thy seasons be a careful nurse."—
Ere half this region-whisper had come down,
Hyperion arose, and on the stars
Lifted his curved lids, and kept them wide
Until it ceas'd; and still he kept them wide:
And still they were the same bright, patient stars.
Then with a slow incline of his broad breast,
Like to a diver in the pearly seas,
Forward he stopp'd over the airy shore,
And plung'd all noiseless into the deep night.

HYPERION.
BOOK II.

Just at the self-same beat of Time's wide wings
Hyperion slid into the rustled air,
And Saturn gain'd with Thea that sad place
Where Cybele and the bruised Titans mourn'd.
It was a den where no insulting light
Could glimmer on their tears; where their own groans
They felt, but heard not, for the solid roar
Of thunderous waterfalls and torrents hoarse,
Pouring a constant bulk, uncertain where.
Crag jutting forth to crag, and rocks that seem'd
Ever as if just rising from a sleep,
Forehead to forehead held their monstrous horns;
And thus in thousand hugest phantasies
Made a fit roofing to this nest of woe.
Instead of thrones, hard flint they sat upon,
Couches of rugged stone, and slaty ridge
Stubborn'd with iron. All were not assembled:
Some chain'd in torture, and some wandering.
Cœus, and Gyges, and Briareüs,
Typhon, and Dolor, and Porphyrion,
With many more, the brawniest in assault,
Were pent in regions of laborious breath;
Dungeon'd in opaque element, to keep
Their clenched teeth still clench'd, and all their limbs

Lock'd up like veins of metal, crampt and screw'd;
Without a motion, save of their big hearts
Heaving in pain, and horribly convuls'd
With sanguine feverous boiling gurge of pulse.
Mnemosyne was straying in the world;
Far from her moon had Phœbe wandered;
And many else were free to roam abroad,
But for the main, here found they covert drear.
Scarce images of life, one here, one there,
Lay vast and edgeways; like a dismal cirque
Of Druid stones, upon a forlorn moor,
When the chill rain begins at shut of eve,
In dull November, and their chancel vault,
The Heaven itself, is blinded throughout night.
Each one kept shroud, nor to his neighbour gave
Or word, or look, or action of despair.
Creüs was one; his ponderous iron mace
Lay by him, and a shatter'd rib of rock
Told of his rage, ere he thus sank and pined.
Iäpetus another; in his grasp,
A serpent's plashy neck; its barbed tongue
Squeez'd from the gorge, and all its uncurl'd length
Dead; and because the creature could not spit
Its poison in the eyes of conquering Jove.
Next Cottus: prone he lay, chin uppermost,
As though in pain; for still upon the flint
He ground severe his skull, with open mouth
And eyes at horrid working. Nearest him
Asia, born of most enormous Caf,
Who cost her mother Tellus keener pangs,
Though feminine, than any of her sons:
More thought than woe was in her dusky face,
For she was prophesying of her glory;
And in her wide imagination stood
Palm-shaded temples, and high rival fanes,
By Oxus or in Ganges' sacred isles.
Even as Hope upon her anchor leans,
So leant she, not so fair, upon a tush
Shed from the broadest of her elephants.
Above her, on a crag's uneasy shelve,

Upon his elbow rais'd, all prostrate else,
As grazing ox unworried in the meads;
Now tiger-passion'd, lion-thoughted, wroth,
He meditated, plotted, and even now
Was hurling mountains in that second war,
Not long delay'd, that scar'd the younger Gods
To hide themselves in forms of beast and bird.
Nor far hence Atlas; and beside him prone
Phorcus, the sire of Gorgons. Neighbour'd close
Oceanus, and Tethys, in whose lap
Sobb'd Clymene among her tangled hair.
In midst of all lay Themis, at the feet
Of Ops the queen all clouded round from sight;
No shape distinguishable, more than when
Thick night confounds the pine-tops with the clouds:
And many else whose names may not be told.
For when the Muse's wings are air-ward spread,
Who shall delay her flight? And she must chaunt
Of Saturn, and his guide, who now had climb'd
With damp and slippery footing from a depth
More horrid still. Above a sombre cliff
Their heads appear'd, and up their stature grew
Till on the level height their steps found ease:
Then Thea spread abroad her trembling arms
Upon the precincts of this nest of pain,
And sidelong fix'd her eye on Saturn's face:
There saw she direst strife; the supreme God
At war with all the frailty of grief,
Of rage, of fear, anxiety, revenge,
Remorse, spleen, hope, but most of all despair.
Against these plagues he strove in vain; for Fate
Had pour'd a mortal oil upon his head,
A disanointing poison: so that Thea,
Affrighted, kept her still, and let him pass
First onwards in, among the fallen tribe.

As with us mortal men, the laden heart
Is persecuted more, and fever'd more,
When it is nighing to the mournful house
Where other hearts are sick of the same bruise;

So Saturn, as he walk'd into the midst,
Felt faint, and would have sunk among the rest,
But that e hmet Enceladus's eye,
Whose mightiness, and awe of him, at once
Came like an inspiration; and he shouted,
"Titans, behold your God!" at which some groan'd;
Some started on their feet; some also shouted;
Some wept, some wail'd, all bow'd with reverence;
And Ops, uplifting her black folded veil,
Show'd her pale cheeks, and all her forehead wan,
Her eye-brows thin and jet, and hollow eyes.
There is a roaring in the bleak-grown pines
When Winter lifts his voice; there is a noise
Among immortals when a God gives sign,
With hushing finger, how he means to load
His tongue with the full weight of utterless thought,
With thunder, and with music, and with pomp:
Such noise is like the roar of bleak-grown pines;
Which, when it ceases in this mountain'd world,
No other sound succeeds; but ceasing here,
Among these fallen, Saturn's voice therefrom
Grew up like organ, that begins anew
Its strain, when other harmonies, stopt short,
Leave the dinn'd air vibrating silverly.
Thus grew it up—"Not in my own sad breast,
"Which is its own great judge and searcher out,
"Can I find reason why ye should be thus:
"Not in the legends of the first of days,
"Studied from that old spirit-leaved book
"Which starry Uranus with finger bright
"Sav'd from the shores of darkness, when the waves
"Low-ebb'd still hid it up in shallow gloom;—
"And the which book ye know I ever kept
"For my firm-based footstool:—Ah, infirm!
"Not there, nor in sign, symbol, or portent
"Of element, earth, water, air, and fire,—
"At war, at peace, or inter-quarrelling
"One against one, or two, or three, or all
"Each several one against the other three,
"As fire with air loud warring when rain-floods

"Drown both, and press them both against earth's face,
"Where, finding sulphur, a quadruple wrath
"Unhinges the poor world;—not in that strife,
"Wherefrom I take strange lore, and read it deep,
"Can I find reason why ye should be thus:
"No, no-where can unriddle, though I search,
"And pore on Nature's universal scroll
"Even to swooning, why ye, Divinities,
"The first-born of all shap'd and palpable Gods,
"Should cower beneath what, in comparison,
"Is untremendous might. Yet ye are here,
"O'erwhelm'd, and spurn'd, and batter'd, ye are here!
"O Titans, shall I say 'Arise!'—Ye groan:
"Shall I say 'Crouch!'—Ye groan. What can I then?
"O Heaven wide! O unseen parent dear!
"What can I? Tell me, all ye brethren Gods,
"How we can war, how engine our great wrath!
"O speak your counsel now, for Saturn's ear
"Is all a-hunger'd. Thou, Oceanus,
"Ponderest high and deep; and in thy face
"I see, astonied, that severe content
"Which comes of thought and musing: give us help!"

So ended Saturn; and the God of the Sea,
Sophist and sage, from no Athenian grove,
But cogitation in his watery shades,
Arose, with locks not oozy, and began,
In murmurs, which his first-endeavouring tongue
Caught infant-like from the far-foamed sands.
"O ye, whom wrath consumes! who, passion-stung,
"Writhe at defeat, and nurse your agonies!
"Shut up your senses, stifle up your ears,
"My voice is not a bellows unto ire.
"Yet listen, ye who will, whilst I bring proof
"How ye, perforce, must be content to stoop:
"And in the proof much comfort will I give,
"If ye will take that comfort in its truth.
"We fall by course of Nature's law, not force
"Of thunder, or of Jove. Great Saturn, thou
"Hast sifted well the atom-universe;

"But for this reason, that thou art the King,
"And only blind from sheer supremacy,
"One avenue was shaded from thine eyes,
"Through which I wandered to eternal truth.
"And first, as thou wast not he first of powers,
"So art thou not the last; it cannot be:
"Thou art not the beginning nor the end.
"From chaos and parental darkness came
"Light, the first fruits of that intestine broil,
"That sullen ferment, which for wondrous ends
"Was ripening in itself. The ripe hour came,
"And with it light, and light, engendering
"Upon its own producer, forthwith touch'd
"The whole enormous matter into life.
"Upon that very hour, our parentage,
"The Heavens and the Earth, were manifest:
"Then thou first-born, and we the giant-race,
"Found ourselves ruling new and beauteous realms.
"Now comes the pain of truth, to whom 'tis pain;
"O folly! for to bear all naked truths,
"And to envisage circumstance, all calm,
"That is the top of sovereignty. Mark well!
"As Heaven and Earth are fairer, fairer far
"Than Chaos and blank Darkness, though once chiefs;
"And as we show beyond that Heaven and Earth
"In form and shape compact and beautiful,
"In will, in action free, companionship,
"And thousand other signs of purer life;
"So on our heels a fresh perfection treads,
"A power more strong in beauty, born of us
"And fated to excel us, as we pass
"In glory that old Darkness: nor are we
"Thereby more conquer'd, than by us the rule
"Of shapeless Chaos. Say, doth the dull soil
"Quarrel with the proud forests it hath fed,
"And feedeth still, more comely than itself?
"Can it deny the chiefdom of green groves?
"Or shall the tree be envious of the dove
"Because it cooeth, and hath snowy wings
"To wander wherewithal and find its joys?

"We are such forest trees, and our fair boughs
"Have bred forth, not pale solitary doves,
"But eagles golden-feather'd, who do tower
"Above us in their beauty, and must reign
"In right thereof; for 'tis the eternal law
"That first in beauty should be first in might:
"Yea, by that law, another race may drive
"Our conquerors to mourn as we do now.
"Have ye beheld the young God of the Seas,
"My dispossessor? Have ye seen his face?
"Have ye beheld his chariot, foam'd along
"By noble winged creatures he hath made?
"I saw him on the calmed waters scud,
"With such a glow of beauty in his eyes,
"That it enforc'd me to bid sad farewell
"To all my empire: farewell sad I took,
"And hither came, to see how dolorous fate
"Had wrought upon ye; and how I might best
"Give consolation in this woe extreme.
"Receive the truth, and let it be your balm."

Whether through poz'd conviction, or disdain,
They guarded silence, when Oceanus
Left murmuring, what deepest thought can tell?
But so it was, none answer'd for a space,
Save one whom none regarded, Clymene;
And yet she answer'd not, only complain'd,
With hectic lips, and eyes up-looking mild,
Thus wording timidly among the fierce:
"O Father, I am here the simplest voice,
"And all my knowledge is that joy is gone,
"And this thing woe crept in among our hearts,
"There to remain for ever, as I fear:
"I would not bode of evil, if I thought
"So weak a creature could turn off the help
"Which by just right should come of mighty Gods;
"Yet let me tell my sorrow, let me tell
"Of what I heard, and how it made me weep,
"And know that we had parted from all hope.
"I stood upon a shore, a pleasant shore,

240

"Where a sweet clime was breathed from a land
"Of fragrance, quietness, and trees, and flowers.
"Full of calm joy it was, as I of grief;
"Too full of joy and soft delicious warmth;
"So that I felt a movement in my heart
"To chide, and to reproach that solitude
"With songs of misery, music of our woes;
"And sat me down, and took a mouthed shell
"And murmur'd into it, and made melody—
"O melody no more! for while I sang,
"And with poor skill let pass into the breeze
"The dull shell's echo, from a bowery strand
"Just opposite, an island of the sea,
"There came enchantment with the shifting wind,
"That did both drown and keep alive my ears.
"I threw my shell away upon the sand,
"And a wave fill'd it, as my sense was fill'd
"With that new blissful golden melody.
"A living death was in each gush of sounds,
"Each family of rapturous hurried notes,
"That fell, one after one, yet all at once,
"Like pearl beads dropping sudden from their string:
"And then another, then another strain,
"Each like a dove leaving its olive perch,
"With music wing'd instead of silent plumes,
"To hover round my head, and make me sick
"Of joy and grief at once. Grief overcame,
"And I was stopping up my frantic ears,
"When, past all hindrance of my trembling hands,
"A voice came sweeter, sweeter than all tune,
"And still it cried, 'Apollo! young Apollo!
"The morning-bright Apollo! young Apollo!'
"I fled, it follow'd me, and cried 'Apollo!'
"O Father, and O Brethren, had ye felt
"Those pains of mine; O Saturn, hadst thou felt,
"Ye would not call this too indulged tongue
"Presumptuous, in thus venturing to be heard."

So far her voice flow'd on, like timorous brook
That, lingering along a pebbled coast,

Doth fear to meet the sea: but sea it met,
And shudder'd; for the overwhelming voice
Of huge Enceladus swallow'd it in wrath:
The ponderous syllables, like sullen waves
In the half-glutted hollows of reef-rocks,
Came booming thus, while still upon his arm
He lean'd; not rising, from supreme contempt.
"Or shall we listen to the over-wise,
"Or to the over-foolish giant, Gods?
"Not thunderbolt on thunderbolt, till all
"That rebel Jove's whole armoury were spent,
"Not world on world upon these shoulders piled,
"Could agonize me more than baby-words
"In midst of this dethronement horrible.
"Speak! roar! shout! yell! ye sleepy Titans all.
"Do ye forget the blows, the buffets vile?
"Are ye not smitten by a youngling arm?
"Dost thou forget, sham Monarch of the Waves,
"Thy scalding in the seas? What, have I rous'd
"Your spleens with so few simple words as these?
"O joy! for now I see ye are not lost:
"O joy! for now I see a thousand eyes
"Wide glaring for revenge!"—As this he said,
He lifted up his stature vast, and stood,
Still without intermission speaking thus:
"Now ye are flames, I'll tell you how to burn,
"And purge the ether of our enemies;
"How to feed fierce the crooked stings of fire,
"And singe away the swollen clouds of Jove,
"Stifling that puny essence in its tent.
"O let him feel the evil he hath done;
"For though I scorn Oceanus's lore,
"Much' pain have I for more than loss of realms:
"The days of peace and slumberous calm are fled;
"Those days, all innocent of scathing war,
"When all the fair Existences of heaven
"Came open-eyed to guess what we would speak:—
"That was before our brows were taught to frown,
"Before our lips knew else but solemn sounds;
"That was before we knew the winged thing,

"Victory, might be lost, or might be won.
"And be ye mindful that Hyperion,
"Our brightest brother, still is undisgraced—
"Hyperion, lo! his radiance is here!"

All eyes were on Enceladus's face,
And they beheld, while still Hyperion's name
Flew from his lips up to the vaulted rocks,
A pallid gleam across his features stern:
Not savage, for he saw full many a God
Wroth as himself. He look'd upon them all,
And in each face he saw a gleam of light,
But splendider in Saturn's, whose hoar locks
Shone like the bubbling foam about a keel
When the prow sweeps into a midnight cove.
In pale and silver silence they remain'd,
Till suddenly a splendour, like the morn,
Pervaded all the beetling gloomy steeps,
All the sad spaces of oblivion,
And every gulf, and every chasm old,
And every height, and every sullen depth,
Voiceless, or hoarse with loud tormented streams:
And all the everlasting cataracts,
And all the headlong torrents far and near,
Mantled before in darkness and huge shade,
Now saw the light and made it terrible.
It was Hyperion:—a granite peak
His bright feet touch'd, and there he stay'd to view
The misery his brilliance had betray'd
To the most hateful seeing of itself.
Golden his hair of short Numidian curl,
Regal his shape majestic, a vast shade
In midst of his own brightness, like the bulk
Of Memnon's image at the set of sun
To one who travels from the dusking East:
Sighs, too, as mournful as that Memnon's harp
He utter'd, while his hands contemplative
He press'd together, and in silence stood.
Despondence seiz'd again the fallen Gods
At sight of the dejected King of Day,

And many hid their faces from the light:
But fierce Enceladus sent forth his eyes
Among the brotherhood; and, at their glare,
Uprose Iäpetus, and Creüs too,
And Phorcus, sea-born, and together strode
To where he towered on his eminence.
There those four shouted forth old Saturn's name;
Hyperion from the peak loud answered, "Saturn!"
Saturn sat near the Mother of the Gods,
In whose face was no joy, though all the Gods
Gave from their hollow throats the name of "Saturn!"

HYPERION.
BOOK III.

Thus in alternate uproar and sad peace,
Amazed were those Titans utterly.
O leave them, Muse! O leave them to their woes;
For thou art weak to sing such tumults dire:
A solitary sorrow best befits
Thy lips, and antheming a lonely grief.
Leave them, O Muse! for thou anon wilt find
Many a fallen old Divinity
Wandering in vain about bewildered shores.
Meantime touch piously the Delphic harp,
And not a wind of heaven but will breathe
In aid soft warble from the Dorian flute;
For lo! 'tis for the Father of all verse.
Flush every thing that hath a vermeil hue,
Let the rose glow intense and warm the air,
And let the clouds of even and of morn
Float in voluptuous fleeces o'er the hills;
Let the red wine within the goblet boil,
Cold as a bubbling well; let faint-lipp'd shells,
On sands, or in great deeps, vermilion turn
Through all their labyrinths; and let the maid
Blush keenly, as with some warm kiss surpris'd.
Chief isle of the embowered Cyclades,
Rejoice, O Delos, with thine olives green,

And poplars, and lawn-shading palms, and beech,
In which the Zephyr breathes the loudest song,
And hazels thick, dark-stemm'd beneath the shade:
Apollo is once more the golden theme!
Where was he, when the Giant of the Sun
Stood bright, amid the sorrow of his peers?
Together had he left his mother fair
And his twin-sister sleeping in their bower,
And in the morning twilight wandered forth
Beside the osiers of a rivulet,
Full ankle-deep in lilies of the vale.
The nightingale had ceas'd, and a few stars
Were lingering in the heavens, while the thrush
Began calm-throated. Throughout all the isle
There was no covert, no retired cave
Unhaunted by the murmurous noise of waves,
Though scarcely heard in many a green recess.
He listen'd, and he wept, and his bright tears
Went trickling down the golden bow he held.
Thus with half-shut suffused eyes he stood,
While from beneath some cumbrous boughs hard by
With solemn step an awful Goddess came,
And there was purport in her looks for him,
Which he with eager guess began to read
Perplex'd, the while melodiously he said:
"How cam'st thou over the unfooted sea?
"Or hath that antique mien and robed form
"Mov'd in these vales invisible till now?
"Sure I have heard those vestments sweeping o'er
"The fallen leaves, when I have sat alone
"In cool mid-forest. Surely I have traced
"The rustle of those ample skirts about
"These grassy solitudes, and seen the flowers
"Lift up their heads, as still the whisper pass'd.
"Goddess! I have beheld those eyes before,
"And their eternal calm, and all that face,
"Or I have dream'd."—"Yes," said the supreme shape,
"Thou hast dream'd of me; and awaking up
"Didst find a lyre all golden by thy side,
"Whose strings touch'd by thy fingers, all the vast

"Unwearied ear of the whole universe
"Listen'd in pain and pleasure at the birth
"Of such new tuneful wonder. Is't not strange
"That thou shouldst weep, so gifted? Tell me, youth,
"What sorrow thou canst feel; for I am sad
"When thou dost shed a tear: explain thy griefs
"To one who in this lonely isle hath been
"The watcher of thy sleep and hours of life,
"From the young day when first thy infant hand
"Pluck'd witless the weak flowers, till thine arm
"Could bend that bow heroic to all times.
"Show thy heart's secret to an ancient Power
"Who hath forsaken old and sacred thrones
"For prophecies of thee, and for the sake
"Of loveliness new born."—Apollo then,
With sudden scrutiny and gloomless eyes,
Thus answer'd, while his white melodious throat
Throbb'd with the syllables.—"Mnemosyne!
"Thy name is on my tongue, I know not how;
"Why should I tell thee what thou so well seest?
"Why should I strive to show what from thy lips
"Would come no mystery? For me, dark, dark,
"And painful vile oblivion seals my eyes:
"I strive to search wherefore I am so sad,
"Until a melancholy numbs my limbs;
"And then upon the grass I sit, and moan,
"Like one who once had wings.—O why should I
"Feel curs'd and thwarted, when the liegeless air
"Yields to my step aspirant? why should I
"Spurn the green turf as hateful to my feet?
"Goddess benign, point forth some unknown thing:
"Are there not other regions than this isle?
"What are the stars? There is the sun, the sun!
"And the most patient brilliance of the moon!
"And stars by thousands! Point me out the way
"To any one particular beauteous star,
"And I will flit into it with my lyre,
"And make its silvery splendour pant with bliss.
"I have heard the cloudy thunder: Where is power?
"Whose hand, whose essence, what divinity

"Makes this alarum in the elements,
"While I here idle listen on the shores
"In fearless yet in aching ignorance?
"O tell me, lonely Goddess, by thy harp,
"That waileth every morn and eventide,
"Tell me why thus I rave, about these groves!
"Mute thou remainest—Mute! yet I can read
"A wondrous lesson in thy silent face:
"Knowledge enormous makes a God of me.
"Names, deeds, gray legends, dire events, rebellions,
"Majesties, sovran voices, agonies,
"Creations and destroyings, all at once
"Pour into the wide hollows of my brain,
"And deify me, as if some blithe wine
"Or bright elixir peerless I had drunk,
"And so become immortal."—Thus the God,
While his enkindled eyes, with level glance
Beneath his white soft temples, stedfast kept
Trembling with light upon Mnemosyne.
Soon wild commotions shook him, and made flush
All the immortal fairness of his limbs;
Most like the struggle at the gate of death;
Or liker still to one who should take leave
Of pale immortal death, and with a pang
As hot as death's is chill, with fierce convulse
Die into life: so young Apollo anguish'd;
His very hair, his golden tresses famed
Kept undulation round his eager neck.
During the pain Mnemosyne upheld
Her arms as one who prophesied.—At length
Apollo shriek'd;—and lo! from all his limbs
Celestial   *   *   *   *   *   *
*   *   *   *   *   *   *   *   *

THE END

PENGUIN POPULAR CLASSICS

Published or forthcoming

Aesop	Aesop's Fables
Hans Andersen	Fairy Tales
Louisa May Alcott	Good Wives
	Little Women
Eleanor Atkinson	Greyfriars Bobby
Jane Austen	Emma
	Mansfield Park
	Northanger Abbey
	Persuasion
	Pride and Prejudice
	Sense and Sensibility
R. M. Ballantyne	The Coral Island
J. M. Barrie	Peter Pan
Frank L. Baum	The Wonderful Wizard of Oz
Anne Brontë	Agnes Grey
	The Tenant of Wildfell Hall
Charlotte Brontë	Jane Eyre
	The Professor
	Shirley
	Villette
Emily Brontë	Wuthering Heights
John Buchan	Greenmantle
	The Thirty-Nine Steps
Frances Hodgson Burnett	A Little Princess
	Little Lord Fauntleroy
	The Secret Garden
Samuel Butler	The Way of All Flesh
Lewis Carroll	Alice's Adventures in Wonderland
	Through the Looking Glass
Geoffrey Chaucer	The Canterbury Tales
G. K. Chesterton	Father Brown Stories
Erskine Childers	The Riddle of the Sands
John Cleland	Fanny Hill
Wilkie Collins	The Moonstone
	The Woman in White
Sir Arthur Conan Doyle	The Adventures of Sherlock Holmes
	His Last Bow
	The Hound of the Baskervilles

PENGUIN POPULAR CLASSICS

Published or forthcoming

PENGUIN POPULAR CLASSICS

Published or forthcoming